THE
MONTESSORI
CHILD

ALSO AVAILABLE

The Montessori Baby

The Montessori Toddler

THE
MONTESSORI
CHILD

A PARENT'S GUIDE TO RAISING CAPABLE CHILDREN
WITH CREATIVE MINDS
AND COMPASSIONATE HEARTS

SIMONE DAVIES AND **JUNNIFA UZODIKE**

WORKMAN PUBLISHING | NEW YORK

Workman
Workman Publishing
Hachette Book Group, Inc.
1290 Avenue of the Americas
New York, NY 10104
workman.com

Workman is an imprint of Workman Publishing, a division of Hachette Book Group, Inc.
The Workman name and logo are registered trademarks of Hachette Book Group, Inc.

Design by Galen Smith and Hiyoko Imai

Constructive Rhythm of Life chart (p. 24) and The Bulb chart (p. 207) © Association
Montessori Internationale (AMI)

The publisher is not responsible for websites (or their content) that are not owned
by the publisher.

Workman books may be purchased in bulk for business, educational, or promotional use.
For information, please contact your local bookseller or the Hachette Book Group
Special Markets Department at special.markets@hbgusa.com.

Library of Congress Cataloging-in-Publication Data
Names: Davies, Simone, author. | Uzodike, Junnifa, author.
Title: The Montessori child : a parent's guide to raising capable children
    with creative minds and compassionate hearts / Simone Davies and Junnifa Uzodike.
Description: New York : Workman Publishing, [2024] | Includes
    bibliographical references and index.
Identifiers: LCCN 2023039678 | ISBN 9781523512416 (paperback) | ISBN
    9781523512416 (epub)
Subjects: LCSH: Parenting. | Montessori method of education. | Home and school.
Classification: LCC HQ755.8 .D37274 2024 | DDC 649/.1--dc23/eng/20230902
LC record available at https://lccn.loc.gov/2023039678

First edition March 2024
Printed in China on responsibly sourced paper.

10 9 8 7 6 5 4 3 2 1

In memory of Onongono.
Thank you Daddy and Mummy for giving me the roots that grounded me,
for giving me wings, and encouraging me to fly.
—Junnifa

To mum and dad,
Thank you for all your support, kindness, and love.
With so much gratitude.
—Simone

ON CHILDREN

Kahlil Gibran (1883-1931)

And a woman who held a babe against her bosom said, Speak to us of Children.
And he said:
Your children are not your children.
They are the sons and daughters of Life's longing for itself.
They come through you but not from you,
And though they are with you yet they belong not to you.

You may give them your love but not your thoughts,
For they have their own thoughts.
You may house their bodies but not their souls,
For their souls dwell in the house of tomorrow, which you cannot visit,
    not even in your dreams.
You may strive to be like them, but seek not to make them like you.
For life goes not backward nor tarries with yesterday.
You are the bows from which your children as living arrows are sent forth.
The archer sees the mark upon the path of the infinite, and He bends you with
    His might that His arrows may go swift and far.
Let your bending in the archer's hand be for gladness;
For even as He loves the arrow that flies, so He loves also the bow that is stable.

CONTENTS

CHAPTER EIGHT

PREPARATION OF THE ADULT

CHAPTER NINE

WHAT'S NEXT

ONLINE RESOURCES

GO TO WORKMAN.COM/MONTESSORI FOR:

40 Ways to Build Self-Discipline and Intrinsic Motivation

A Caterpillar's Journey

The Montessori Adolescent at the Montessori Centre for Work and Study, Rydet, Sweden

How does Montessori work?

Activity starter kits

Activities listing based on interest

An introduction to the Great Lessons

How to make a booklet

Play dough recipe

What to look for in a Montessori school

What the Montessori program looks like for the 3–6 and 6–12 child at school

If they don't want to go to school and other common questions

When parents are separated

Further reading

INTRODUCTION

1

WHY WE NEED MONTESSORI AT HOME

What if there was an easier way to raise children? As parents, we are juggling demands from work and home, trying to find time to enjoy ourselves and our family, and to contribute to our community, all while fending off serious concerns about humanity, the impact of technologies, and the future of our planet.

We (Junnifa and Simone) believe that Montessori is the antidote to this juggling act. We can learn the tools to understand our children, see from their perspective, and raise them with joy. Even, and especially, for a future full of uncertainty.

The Montessori approach offers what Junnifa and Simone like to affectionately call the "triumvirate."

First, there is raising our child in the spirit of respect, love, and understanding. As parents and caregivers, we are our child's guide, not their boss or servant. We are on their side, and we are on this journey together. A journey where everything (good or bad) is an opportunity for learning and growth.

Second, there is the prepared environment. We can set up our homes intentionally (and introduce our child to the world outside our home) so that our child can be capable, feel like they belong, and become a meaningful member of our family and the community.

Third, there are activities that meet the needs of our unique child to support their development in a holistic way—cognitively, emotionally, socially, and spiritually.

Dr. Montessori developed this approach to children's development over 100 years ago. We might wonder how it is still relevant in today's world. To that we would remind the reader that the needs and characteristics of children have not changed. Children need to move, to express themselves, to connect with others, and to learn about the world around them. In Montessori, we want children to learn, not because someone is forcing them, but because there is an intrinsic desire and flame inside them that is being protected and stoked. In addition, Montessori is an approach that has worked for all types of children around the world for more than a century. It is a philosophy that allows every child to develop uniquely on their own timeline, with their own way of learning, and with their unique interests.

Our children can benefit from the Montessori approach whether or not they attend a Montessori school when we apply the Montessori principles in our homes. In fact, this makes Montessori accessible, equitable, and culturally responsive as we apply the principles for our unique family and circumstances.

Many people might say, "Well, I turned out okay without Montessori." That may be true for a handful of folks who had families who were able to offer unconditional support and opportunities or who were able to take care of themselves in spite of their circumstances. Far more often we think that we are doing okay; however, if we dig a little deeper, we may have dreams we never fulfilled; or we may have followed a path set by our parents or societal expectations; or perhaps we feel like we cannot be 100 percent ourselves; or we may hold resentment and anger toward people who think differently from us (be it politics, religion, interests, cultural background, economic status, etc.) or our own family members; or we never learned how to express our emotions, or to set kind and clear boundaries with others; or we have old wounds and unresolved trauma. So, we think we turned out okay, but we are only beginning to unpack that we also would have benefited from a Montessori upbringing.

Montessori is booming in popularity not because it's a trend but because we are looking for a way to raise our children to be creative and critical thinkers, who know how to live in society with others, and to be caretakers of the Earth.

We cannot promise you that your child will become a tech giant like the Google guys (although they do credit a lot of their creativity to attending a Montessori school). What we will do is share with you all the secrets we know about raising capable children with creative minds and compassionate hearts. Children who become self-aware adults who are kind and respectful and who care for themselves, others, and our planet. They will go into society in any role that they desire—be it a mechanic, a CEO, a parent, a scientist, a programmer, a farmer, an educator—and make their contribution to society.

We'll be referring to the child, the adult, and the environment a lot. There is a dynamic relationship among these three things. We'll learn to understand the child and how we can prepare ourselves and our environment to support them. We'll see that the principles are quite commonsense and intuitive, yet many of us have forgotten them. We'll learn how to observe, how to respond rather than react, how to understand the needs and characteristics of children as they grow, and so much more.

Let's learn more about The Montessori Child.

WHO WE ARE

Junnifa is an Association Montessori Internationale (AMI) 0–3, 3–6, and 6–12 trained teacher, a wife, and mother to four children, all raised with Montessori principles from in utero. Junnifa is the founder and head of school of Fruitful Orchard Montessori school in Abuja, Nigeria, serving children from 15 months to 12 years old; she is an AMI board member and also trained in the Resources for Infant Educarers (RIE) approach.

Junnifa feels blessed to have found Montessori education before her first child was born. It allowed her to start her parenting journey empowered with an understanding of her children's needs and the tools she needed as a parent. She has continued to learn with her children as they have passed through the planes of development. Parenting her children, leading the school, guiding the elementary classroom, and supporting the families in her community and around the world continue to reinforce her trust in Montessori principles. She believes them to be a foundation for building a good life and a cohesive society founded on respect and stewardship with everyone learning to care for and support themselves, others, the environment (both tangible and intangible), and the society as a whole.

As a Montessori educator and parent, Junnifa sees the gift in every child she works with. At home, she trusts her children, guides them, and fosters a strong sense of independence while building a tight-knit family unit and community. She applies Montessori principles in a culturally relevant way and has participated in Montessori trainings in the United States, Italy, India, and South Africa.

Simone is an Association Montessori Internationale (AMI) 0–3 teacher, holds 3–6 and 6–12 AMI assistant certificates, and is a Positive Discipline educator. She's been working in Montessori classrooms since 2004 and running her own parent-child classes at Jacaranda Tree Montessori in the Netherlands since 2008.

Simone raised her two children (now young adults) applying Montessori principles. Disillusioned with the traditional educational system, she sent her children to a Montessori playgroup and preschool in Castlecrag, Australia, and then to a public Montessori school in the Netherlands until they were 12 years old. Even after they entered regular high school and then university, Simone continued to use Montessori principles at home.

She has seen how the Montessori principles lay the foundation for empathetic, kind, curious children. She has had a respectful relationship with her children: She hasn't needed to threaten them to get cooperation; they helped prepare meals and learned to be great bakers; they each played a sport, taught themselves the keyboard, spent time with friends, and enjoyed hours stretched out on the living room floor making comic books and signs for secret clubs inspired by their favorite books. Living in a Montessori way extended to family vacations spent running around a farm, creating a dam at a beach, or exploring museums in different cities. Simone is the first to acknowledge that there was a lot of privilege in having been able to offer all this to her children. And she assures you that Montessori does not mean raising perfect children—her children also experienced their difficulties and struggles during these years, and she will share how such situations were navigated as we go further in the book.

We have found so much peace, joy, and connection with our children from applying the Montessori principles in our home, and we hope you do too.

ABOUT THIS BOOK

After Simone wrote *The Montessori Toddler* and Junnifa and Simone wrote *The Montessori Baby* together, people kept requesting a book for the later years. This book is the result. We have collected wisdom from Dr. Montessori, our Montessori training, our experience with our own children and many families, a lot of research, professional education, training courses, podcasts, workshops, and many other Montessori educators who have contributed to this book and compiled it into a guide for Montessori families with children from 3 to 12 years old.

The goal of this book is not to set up our homes as a Montessori classroom. In fact, we would advise against it. And this is not a book about Montessori homeschooling. It's about how you can apply the Montessori principles at home whether your child goes to a Montessori school or not.

You can read this book from cover to cover or open it to any page to find some wisdom you can put into practice today. Our hope is that you can use this book as a scaffold. You can absorb the principles, and over time, they will become second nature. Then you can remove the scaffold and stand on your own (and revisit the book when you need a refresher or when difficult situations arise).

Whether you are reading about Montessori for the first time or you've been practicing Montessori since before your children were born, we hope you will walk away with confidence, a deeper understanding of your children, and a stronger connection with your family. If you have never practiced Montessori before in your home, we like to say it's never too early to start with Montessori, and it's never too late. It might feel at first like a huge shift to observe, prepare your home and yourselves, and support your child's development in a new way, but know that your investment will pay off. Montessori is not a quick fix. It is a long-term approach.

NOTE: We have preserved the original quotes from Dr. Montessori's writings, which are mostly gendered he/him as representative of her time and place.

FURTHER READING

For the science behind the Montessori approach and the ideas shared in this book, we refer the reader to:

- the comprehensive yet accessible work of Angeline Stoll Lillard, *Montessori: The Science Behind the Genius*
- the online appendix, "How Does Montessori Work?" by Mira Debs and Angela K. Murray (workman.com/montessori)

MONTESSORI IS FOR EVERY CHILD

We believe that Montessori can be applied in any home, with any child from any background, anywhere in the world, and regardless of their family constellation. Montessori is about learning how every child is unique, supporting their individual development, and making adjustments as necessary.

Montessori is not only for children who can sit quietly and bring their activity back to the shelf. It's also, and particularly suited, for children who need to move. They can move as they play, they can dance and sing, make music, discover rhythms, and make big and small movements. Montessori is for all types of learners. Those who are visual learners or aural learners or kinesthetic learners (those who like to touch and feel things to get to know them). It's for children who like learning through doing, and it's also for children who like learning through observing.

Dr. Montessori observed the potential in all children, including those who are neurodivergent (e.g., are autistic, twice exceptional, gifted, or have ADHD, sensory issues, or learning differences), have a disability (intellectual or physical), are deaf or blind or have (selective) mutism.

WHAT WE LOVE ABOUT
THE 3- TO 6-YEAR-OLD CHILD

The 3- to 6-year-old child is curious. While we might like to stay in bed all day, our 3- to 6-year-old cannot stop learning and moving. They have so many new things to discover and constantly ask "What?" and "Why?," hungry to understand the world around them. They want to know the names of things, relationships between people, and simple explanations of how things work.

The 3- to 6-year-old child picks things up effortlessly. Dr. Montessori described the child's mind at this age as an *absorbent mind* able to pick things up effortlessly like a sponge. We see children of this age learn multiple languages without any formal lessons; they absorb how to move and how to communicate and listen; they start to explore symbols like letters, numbers, maps, and flags; and they take in the social life of others. Where the absorbent mind of the child younger than 3 years old is *unconscious*, taking everything in without conscious effort, the mind of the 3- to 6-year-old is *conscious*, aware of what they are taking in and eager to crystallize all they have learned in earlier years.

The 3- to 6-year-old child takes things literally. They understand the world in a very concrete way based on what they see around them. This reality-based understanding is an important foundation for their growing imagination. It can make for some fascinating conversations too. For example, if you ask them what would happen if you didn't have a brain, a common response might be that your head would look squashed!

The 3- to 6-year-old child loves to communicate and express themselves. By the age of 3 years old, a child has mostly learned to express themselves verbally. From ages 3 to 6, there is increased vocabulary and an informal introduction to grammar. By around age 6, many children can express themselves (speaking and writing) and understand others (listening and reading). They also love to express themselves with dance, with music, and with art.

The 3- to 6-year-old child is busy matching, sorting, grading, and classifying impressions in the world around them through their senses. They are still a sensorial learner. This means they will learn and take in information through touching, smelling, hearing, seeing, and tasting everything they come across. Verbal instructions or lectures are less interesting; invitations for explorations to make their own discoveries are much more exciting. They are exploring the qualities of materials they come across—rough and smooth, long and short, soft and loud, hot and cold, light and dark.

The 3- to 6-year-old child will repeat and repeat a task. When a 3- to 6-year-old is working to master something, they will repeat it many times until it is mastered. In the classroom, we can witness a child tying bows, undoing them, and tying them all over again, or coming back to the same activity every day for 2 weeks and then moving on from it.

The 3- to 6-year-old child loves to be involved in daily life. Children of this age love what we call *practical life activities*. They like to learn how to look after themselves by brushing their hair, looking after plants or pets, or setting the table for family meals. They are learning a sequence of steps and refining their coordination and movements, and they love making a contribution. Through these daily life activities, they are also exposed to their culture through everyday objects (like the utensils we use to eat) and customs (like how we say hello).

The 3- to 6-year-old child is capable of more than we expect. They are able to cook pancakes, tie their shoelaces, make a map of Africa and label each country, and sew a decorative pillow. When they have an environment set up for them to be successful, the freedom to choose what they like, a patient adult or older child to ask for help if they get stuck, and the time to practice and master skills, children can take on and complete time-consuming and detailed tasks.

The 3- to 6-year-old child mostly lives in the present moment. While they are starting to get a better understanding of time than when they were toddlers, for them "yesterday" could be any time in the past and "tomorrow" any time in the future. They remind us to stay present, in the here and now, and not too focused on the past or future. They have things they are doing right now that are far more important.

WHAT WE LOVE ABOUT
THE 6- TO 12-YEAR-OLD CHILD

We can have a lot of compassion for the 6- to 12-year-old child. They are often criticized for being rude, disorderly, and answering back. We may wonder what has happened to our sweet child. Our child is entering a new stage of development (the *second plane*), and they will need to be supported differently.

The older child is driven by reason, imagination, and their developing moral values. They are attracted to working in, being in, and belonging to groups that aren't family. But adults still play an important role. They have an increased stamina and thirst for knowledge, and they want to make a difference in the world.

The 6- to 12-year-old child is more stable. The rapid rate of physical growth of early childhood begins to slow, and they become more stable and less volatile. They are losing their baby teeth and their round faces, and their legs are getting stronger. They are becoming more adventurous and daring and will share their feats with us.

The 6- to 12-year-old child has an enormous sense of justice. They want to make things as equal as possible for everyone. If there are ten cookies and six children, they would prefer that each child get one cookie and leave four on the plate than some children get two cookies. As they thrive on law and order, we can ask them to help create agreements for the home, which they will be happy to uphold and enforce. This also means they are trying to be truth tellers, eager to let us know when someone has done something wrong. They are trying to follow the rules and distinguish right from wrong.

The 6- to 12-year-old child loves being part of a group. They are learning how to be a contributing member of the group, exploring the idea of fairness, learning how others think, developing empathy, and feeling protective of those they perceive as "weaker." They are practicing being members of society and may need our help navigating some of these natural instincts toward sociability.

The 6- to 12-year-old child has an interest in secret languages. They may be fascinated by ciphers and hieroglyphics, or might invent their own language, a way for children to feel independent and separate from their family while creating their own society with friends.

The 6- to 12-year-old child is capable of big work (and big mess!). They will want to do work if it has a purpose, if it is with and for their group, and if it is aligned with their interests. They love sharing new knowledge and discoveries. They now need a wider environment to explore; they are not satisfied with only the home and school. We can give them the universe—not just math and grammar, but subjects like biology, history, geography, astronomy, and mechanics. They are learning that everything is interrelated and that everything in the universe (from a bacterium to a spider to themselves) has a *cosmic task* and its own special role to play.

The 6- to 12-year-old child uses their imagination to explore the universe. They are moving beyond exploring with their senses and can now apply their imagination to understand other cultures, environments, and things they cannot physically touch or see. Simone once heard this described as using "the eyes of the mind, not just the body." They might do this by inventing something, thinking of ways to solve a problem like pollution, or using their imagination to put themselves in another's shoes.

The 6- to 12-year-old child is building the foundations to grow into a contributing adult of society and be of service to others. They are learning that they can be of service to their class, their classmates, their family, and others in society; for example, by mowing the lawn for an elderly neighbor or writing a letter to the local authority to ask them to fix a crack in the pavement that might disadvantage those in a wheelchair.

WHAT OUR CHILDREN ARE TRYING TO TELL US

THE 3- TO 6-YEAR-OLD CHILD

THE 6- TO 12-YEAR-OLD CHILD

When they say, "No, you do it," they are ACTUALLY saying, "Will you get me started?" or "Will you sit with me while I do it?"

When they argue and yell, "It's not fair!," they are ACTUALLY trying to understand justice and how things really work.

When they ask, "What?" or "Why?," they are ACTUALLY wanting to take in everything about the world around them. Encourage them to do this.

When they tattle constantly, they are ACTUALLY checking the limits and consistency of right and wrong.

When they say, "But I don't want to go to bed!," they are ACTUALLY saying, "Do you mean it's really bedtime or are you so tired that you are going to let me stay up?"

When they make big messes, they are ACTUALLY exploring and making big work and are often putting ideas in order, though it may be hard to see.

When they cry, they are not pretending. They are ACTUALLY saying, "I'm not doing well right now. Can you help me to regulate myself? Then I'll fix what I've broken."

When they cry, they are not pretending. They are ACTUALLY saying, "Even though I'm older, I'm still not doing well right now. Can you help me to regulate myself? Then I'll fix what I've broken."

When they ask for help, they are ACTUALLY saying, "Help me to do it myself," so they can learn to take care of themselves, others, and the space around them.

When they ask deep questions, they are ACTUALLY asking us to help them think for themselves and give them tools and frameworks for exploring ideas and finding answers.

When they are not listening, they are ACTUALLY saying, "What you are saying to me does not align with what I want to do right now. Can you let me finish and then ask me again in a way that makes me want to do it?"

When they seem like they are not listening, they are ACTUALLY always listening. They might not respond or follow directions, but they did hear.

IMPORTANT MONTESSORI PRINCIPLES FOR THE 3- TO 12-YEAR-OLD CHILD

2

A BRIEF HISTORY OF MONTESSORI

Dr. Maria Montessori was an Italian medical doctor, anthropologist, and scientist who was interested in everything from women's rights to geometry and botany—and especially children.

Born in 1870, Dr. Montessori received an education and opportunities that were unusual for women of her time. She earned her medical degree and began working with special-needs children (then referred to as "delinquent children"), producing extraordinary results. (After working with the children, Dr. Montessori registered her students for a state exam. The majority passed, some receiving higher marks than the children without special needs.) As a result, Dr. Montessori thought children without special needs could be doing better.

In 1907, Dr. Montessori had the opportunity to test her ideas in the Italian educational system. She opened the first Casa dei Bambini (Children's House) for the children of working parents living in a low-income housing estate in the slums of San Lorenzo, Italy. The school became Dr. Montessori's laboratory. She observed the children, documented everything she saw, and supported their development. If the children appeared interested in something, she would provide it. If they stopped showing interest in something, she would replace it with something else. She followed their natural tendencies and modified the environment accordingly. Contrary to the commonly accepted belief at the time that children were stubborn, selfish, and unwilling to share, Dr. Montessori found that when children were in the right environment and their needs were being met, they were caring, capable, and eager to learn.

Dr. Montessori was unique in that she learned about children not by guessing, theorizing, or making assumptions but by simply observing them. What we call the "Montessori method" could really be thought of as the "children's method" because the children transmitted—through Dr. Montessori's observations—what they liked, what they preferred, and their characteristics at different ages.

Dr. Montessori worked with children around the world, testing, refining, and improving her method, until her death in 1952. News about her work spread, and the people (educators, parents, government officials, dignitaries) who came to observe and learn from her returned home and replicated her methods—setting up the environment, observing the children, and meeting their needs. Her methods were hailed for their positive and replicable results.

Today, over a century later, educators, parents, and caregivers around the world have applied the same approach and have found that the underlying characteristics of children—their human tendencies and their needs—haven't changed. Children are independent and capable; they are able to listen, they are able to follow instructions, they are able to share, and they are able to care. In fact, these traits are part of their nature. These methods are therefore as relevant today as they were during Dr. Montessori's life.

WHAT IS MONTESSORI?

One of the most frequent, and most challenging, questions asked by anyone encountering Montessori for the first time is "What is Montessori?" Montessori encompasses so much: It is an outlook, a lens, an attitude, and a form of wisdom.

> Montessori is a philosophy of life. A way of living, and of being with others but specifically, being with children.

Montessori as an outlook

The Montessori outlook or perspective is one of awe and wonder. It is living in awe of ourselves and those around us—including animals and plants, big and small. It is appreciating the Earth and its components, animate and inanimate; the universe; and the intricacies that contribute to our existence. It is wondering how everything came to be, what else is out there, and how it all works together.

This awe and wonder are often accompanied by joy. Montessori is joy. We (Junnifa and Simone) have experienced this joy in our parenting, in our work as educators, and, more generally, in our day-to-day activities because of this expanded view of life.

The Montessori outlook centers on stewardship and responsibility. On an understanding that there is an interdependence between things, and that our actions, conscious and unconscious, affect everyone and everything. It is the intention of approaching life with this awareness and acting with responsibility for ourselves, others, our society, and the environment. It is knowing to first look at ourselves before looking at others, especially children, when trying to solve problems.

This outlook affects everything we do because it colors the way we look at our interactions, homes, and the way we raise our children and the opportunities we explore for ourselves, our children, and beyond. It becomes the lens through which we view our children.

Montessori as a lens

When we look at children through the Montessori lens, we don't view them as empty vessels, ready to be filled up or made into whatever we desire. Instead, we view them as human beings, full of potential, deserving of respect, and capable of participating in their own development. Our role as educators, parents, and caregivers is to try to understand, nurture, and bring out what our children already contain.

We view children as unique, with their own individual strengths, personalities, capacities, and interests. We recognize that their journey, pace, and experience will be different from those of others. We do not see them as replicas of us or define them by their age and other general descriptors. We don't try to force them to conform to the actions of others or compare them to one another. Instead, we recognize and nurture their individuality.

We view children as capable. They are capable of constructing their own unique personalities and of doing so much for themselves at every stage. We recognize that they are capable of constantly improving upon their capacity. Instead of doing things for them, we give them the opportunity to do what they are capable of, and when they need help, we help them do it for themselves.

We view our children with awe and wonder. We notice their little conquests and are in awe of their amazing abilities. This awe and wonder make parenting and caregiving a joy instead of a chore.

Because we view children differently, **we also come to view ourselves and our role differently**. We are not sculptors or creators but gardeners. We are more guides than teachers. As Kahlil Gibran says in "On Children" (see the dedication page), "You are the bows from which your children as living arrows are sent forth."

Montessori as an attitude

Montessori is an attitude toward children as well as life in general. It is an attitude of respect, humility, constant curiosity, openness and acceptance, patience and trust.

Montessori is an attitude of respect. We approach the child first as a human being that deserves to be addressed and treated with respect. We allow even the youngest child to have and express their opinions, choices, and preferences. Instead of judging, we are open and try to understand. When a child is crying, for example, instead of seeing it as an annoying disruption, we try to understand what the child might be trying to communicate. Montessori encourages respect for the child's unique process of development and learning, their capabilities, and their growth.

We communicate with respect in both our tone and words. We are not patronizing. We don't label children or call them names. We don't speak harshly to them. We are conscious of the effects of our words. We also give them space to speak while we listen and consider, without talking over them. We give them opportunities to participate, and we acknowledge their contributions.

Respect is also evident in the way we handle and touch our child. We ask, first, for their permission and then use soft, gentle, noninvasive hands that consider their experience (unless their safety is at risk). We show respect by preparing our spaces in such a way that considers our child's needs and accommodates them accordingly.

Montessori is an attitude of humility and constant curiosity. Dr. Montessori's own curiosity and humility, her constant questioning to understand children, fueled the development of the Montessori philosophy. As the adults, we do not see ourselves as "sages on the stage" who have all the answers and fill our child with knowledge. Instead, we are "guides on the side," staying curious as we walk beside and collaborate with our children, learning from them and with them and staying open to new possibilities. And we stay humble, allowing our child to make their own discoveries and develop their intelligence.

Montessori is an attitude of openness and acceptance. We accept and welcome the children in our care the way they are, with curiosity about their needs and a willingness to modify our environments and expectations to allow them to bloom.

Montessori is an attitude of patience and trust. We are slow and deliberate in our interactions, taking time to model activities and behavior. We also wait and watch, so we can observe what our child is showing us. We give them time and space to do the things they've mastered, and opportunities to practice the things they have not. We are patient as they develop at their own pace.

Just as the gardener prepares the soil, trusting that the plant will sprout; feeds the soil, trusting that the plant will grow; weeds, waters, prunes, and cares for the plant, always with trust; we, too, trust that the child will develop. We prepare the environment and nurture the child with trust and with patience. We trust their abilities to do, to think, to be. We work with them to develop these abilities, and then we trust them to use them.

> Montessori is a belief in the potential and the abilities of the child. The belief that children are always capable given the opportunity and the right environment. The belief in the innate goodness of children and their ability to learn.

Montessori as wisdom

Of the many gifts that Montessori has given us, the most critical one is wisdom: understanding how children develop and how we can support them through their own metamorphosis.

The Montessori approach helps educators, parents, and caregivers understand and recognize the stages of our child's development. It teaches us to identify all changes—even when the signs are barely perceptible. The *human tendencies* and the *planes of development*, both Montessori terms, provide a valuable framework to help us understand, guide, and support our children as they grow and transform toward adulthood.

Dr. Montessori used the analogy of a caterpillar's metamorphosis from egg to caterpillar to chrysalis to butterfly to describe the child's development. Children go on a similar journey; at each stage, they are like completely different beings. They grow and change, physically and psychologically. Sometimes the changes are obvious, and other times, they are barely noticeable. Sometimes the changes are uncomfortable—for the child and for us—and hard to understand. But these changes are part of the natural path of development on the way to adulthood. To unfurling their wings to fly. (For a beautiful story about Junnifa and the children watching a butterfly's development, read "A Caterpillar's Journey" found in the online appendix at workman.com/montessori.)

THE HUMAN TENDENCIES

> "One of Dr. Montessori's great contributions to the subject of child study was that of the human tendencies. . . . The human tendencies are innate in man. They are the characteristics, the propensities which allowed the human being, from his first inception on earth, to become aware of his environment, to learn and understand it. . . . Each child, as he is born, enters, as did the very first human being, an environment created for him but unknown to him. If he was to live his life securely within it, he had to have a way of making a knowledge of it. This way was through the human tendencies."
>
> —Margaret E. Stephenson, "Dr. Maria Montessori—A Contemporary Educator?"

"Human tendencies" are the universal natural inclinations of human beings—the ways we think, act, and respond to adapt to our environment and meet our material and spiritual needs. When the human tendencies are nurtured, they aid our child's self-construction (how they take in and discover everything around them to create their personality) and "adaptation" (how our child becomes a citizen of their time, place, and culture). Human tendencies are a cornerstone of the Montessori practice. Our role as caregivers is to ensure that conditions are right for the human tendencies to be expressed and to remove any obstacles that might interfere with them.

What are the human tendencies?

Imagine for a moment that we have just gotten off a plane in a new country. What might we do first? Maybe we'd meet our family members or friends before getting a taxi to our hotel. We might then check in to our hotel, rest a bit, and head out to explore. We might visit places of interest, try the local cuisine, listen to some music, or go to a museum. We might stop at the store on our way back to our hotel and buy some things—we'd most likely do the currency conversions to make sure the prices make sense. We might plan to return to our hotel, so we can text our family back home to share some of our experiences. But imagine that when we came back, our hotel was no longer where we'd left it. We might hesitate to explore further until we had sorted out the situation.

This journey we just went on illustrates many of the human tendencies: exploration, orientation, order, communication, the mathematical mind, imagination, abstraction. We'll explore these further below along with the other human tendencies of movement, work, exactness, repetition, self-perfection, social development, and expression.

Exploration

We humans explore to become familiar with our environment. We search, investigate, and experience through movement, our senses, our intellect, and our imagination.

Physical, cognitive, social, and spiritual exploration comes naturally to children. In the early years, most exploration is physical—a newborn searching for their mother's nipple, a toddler touching everything in reach, a child climbing furniture. As our child gets older, their exploration becomes more cognitive and social and then, later, spiritual. It is through exploration that our child gains the reference points they need to explore even further.

There is so much that children need to know and explore as they go through childhood. *What are those things? How do I get around? How do I read? Write? What is appropriate? What do I enjoy? What is safe? How much of this is fun? How was this made? Oh, there were people even before my grandparents? How did they live? There are other countries, continents, planets? Where are they? What happens there?*

Children explore their environment to understand and master their place, time, and culture. To orient themselves. Once they adapt to their environment, they can work to change it or improve it.

Our role: We can support our children by providing resources to aid their exploration. When our child is jumping on the sofa, instead of simply stopping them, we can try to understand what they are exploring—perhaps the capacity of their body, or the sound of their jumping, or even what is allowed or not allowed. Then we can provide appropriate alternatives for their exploration.

Dr. Montessori believed that we should provide the child younger than 3 years old with the home, the 3- to 6-year-old child with the world, and the 6- to 12-year-old child with the universe. As the child gets older, we can incorporate new tools, agreements, or boundaries, as well as proper guidance, for exploration.

Orientation

Orientation is the tendency and ability to align or anchor ourselves—to place ourselves physically or psychologically in relation to our environment or situation. Orientation is usually the first step in exploration. When a child is oriented, they feel secure and have a starting point for exploration.

Humans have a need to know where they are and what to expect. It's important to observe our children and understand how much orientation they require to feel safe.

A newborn's point of reference is their mother's heartbeat or voices familiar from the womb. A young child in the park might look behind them for their parent or caregiver to orient themselves before gaining confidence and exploring more freely. If a child is starting a new school, they will want to be oriented on the first day to things like the toilets, where they store their belongings, eat lunch, and the general order of the day. An older child gains more points of reference, not just physical ones—they orient themselves with what they already know or believe about a subject they've previously explored as well as orienting themselves with rules or expectations.

Our role: We can prepare the physical, cognitive, social, and spiritual environment that our child will orient themselves around. We can provide opportunities for exploration so that our child develops even more points of reference. We can help our child understand the expectations and limits of their environments and ensure that they have anchors to count on throughout their day—in their home, their classrooms, and their interactions. We can be as predictable as possible in our reactions and interactions so that they can know what to expect.

Order

In Montessori, we often say "a place for everything and everything in its place." When there is physical order, we are more likely to have internal—psychological and cognitive—order. Order can also be a logical, predictable sequence in the child's daily life, one that they can rely on and that anchors them. For younger children, an anchor may be an action, like a song sung every morning. For an older child, the anchor might be a regularly scheduled event, like dinner at six o'clock. Order includes the tendency to classify and organize what we know and learn, including ideas, values, and feelings.

Our role: We create order in the child's environment and help our child create, maintain, and restore order. We can help them build skills, create systems, and guide them. We can ensure that they have daily, weekly, and seasonal rhythms and rituals, so they experience predictability.

Communication, expression, and social development

Communication is the natural inclination to share our ideas, experiences, and concerns, as well as to listen to and understand those of others. It supports the human tendency for social relations and collaboration. Babies are often born able to suck, swallow, and cry as a form of communication. By the time the child is 3 years old, they have usually learned the language(s) of their community and can express their thoughts fluently. Then the child develops the ability to read, write, sing, gesture, and create art and poetry, and may learn to speak additional languages.

We have a human tendency for expression, the desire to express ourselves through art, music, and dance. They are sources of happiness. Even babies move to the rhythm when they hear music. Most children from 3 to 12 years old are naturally drawn to open-ended art activities. They seem to naturally want to draw, paint, or arrange rocks and petals into designs. All of these are forms of expression.

As mammals, we have a desire to be part of a group, and we have a human tendency for social development. We have a need to belong and to collaborate. The social environment grows with the child—a baby is part of their family; then it extends to other caregivers; then perhaps to a nursery or a playgroup; then to preschool, grade school, and other activities and groups. We will look at their social development in detail in chapter 6.

Our role: Children absorb language easily, so we can prepare a language-rich environment by talking (or signing) to our children, reading to them, singing to them, sharing stories, and letting them watch while we interact with others. As our child grows, we can use even more precise and rich language—instead of "flower," we can say "red hibiscus flower." When our children want to share their experiences, thoughts, or questions, we can give them our time and attention.

We can provide opportunities for artistic expression and also the tools of expression, like pencil and paper, paintbrushes and paint, and music players, song lyrics, and instruments.

We can support the child's social development by teaching the expected rules, behaviors, and culture in our family and community. We can support our children as they learn how to interact and be members of our family group and then with other individuals and groups.

The mathematical mind

Humans are born with a very logical mind. We use our mathematical mind when we go to the store and keep a running tally of our items in our head. We see it in the baby estimating where and how far to reach to pick up an object. We see it when we offer a child two cookies and they pick the bigger one. The mathematical mind is always at work, and it supports and works with two other tendencies, imagination and abstraction.

Our role: We can provide opportunities for our children to use their mathematical mind. Opportunities for them to solve problems, to estimate, to guess, sort, categorize, measure, and engage in activities that require analysis.

Imagination

Imagination is the ability to see things that aren't in front of us, to create solutions that do not currently exist, and to meet our needs. This starts at a very early age. A young child will learn that they still have a parent or caregiver even when they are not present in the room. Older children are able to imagine what life was like for people in early civilizations or in other places even if they have never been there. And early humans noticed animals had thick fur that protected them from the elements and imagined clothing that would do the same—they pictured it and then they created it.

Our role: Imagination is built on concrete experiences. We can support our child's imagination by providing lots of activities for hands-on exploration and discovery of the world around them in the first 6 years. For our older children, we can share stories about life and times that are different from theirs and invite them to use their imagination.

Abstraction

Abstraction is imagination's cousin. It is the ability to take the essence of something and apply it to other things. It is the ability to see beyond the concrete, to interpret, and to generalize. While abstract thoughts are present in younger children, they become very active as the child gets to be 6 years old. Abstraction and imagination are optimized once a child has a strong understanding of reality. For example, when a younger child is doing addition with golden beads in a Montessori classroom, they put 5 beads and 4 beads together and count that there are 9 beads in total. An older child will be able to abstract when they see the numbers and a plus sign and will know to add them together to get the answer.

Our role: We can help them gain understanding of key concepts, provide them tools to understand, and revisit the concepts as much as they need to until they internalize it; for example, offering concrete objects, dictionaries, etc. We can also allow the child to use their imagination to create or bring their ideas to life. This is a form of abstraction.

Movement

Movement is the ability and need to use our bodies in our environment. This is how we explore our environment and eventually improve it. This tendency is very evident in children. How many times do we comment on how our child cannot sit still? The innate drive to move helps the child's development.

Manipulation, another kind of movement, is an important form of exploration. Dr. Montessori called the hands "the instruments of the intelligence." Our hands are an important tool in our mastery of our environment, and in our ability to modify, work with, regenerate, and improve it.

Our role: Instead of being an obstacle to the child's movement and activity, we can provide opportunities and activities that help develop and refine their motor skills. We can give them room and space to jump and run. We can offer them items to manipulate that require increasing abilities.

Work, exactness, repetition, and self-perfection

It is through *work* that we improve our environment and ourselves. Once we understand our environment, our mathematical minds usually see ways to modify it to better meet our needs. We can imagine these modifications and then bring them to reality through work. This could be as easy as oiling a squeaky chair or fabricating a toolbelt with pockets that hold special items.

Along with our inclination to work, humans have a tendency toward *exactness* and *self-perfection*. We have a need for precision. We see this in children learning to ride a bike, write, climb, or acquire any new skill they desire. Even when they fall or fail, they try again. Self-perfection is the desire to continually improve ourselves and do the best for ourselves and for others. We see exactness in the child's questioning. They keep asking, seeking for exact answers around what things are and how they work.

Repetition helps us master an activity. Mastering an activity gives us control of the environment and leads to confidence and contentment. When our children reach for the same activity over and over, they are acting on their human tendency, and we can appreciate the value of this repetition. An older child between 6 and 12 years old will also repeat but may not want to repeat it in the same way each time. Instead, they will look for ways to repeat with variations.

Our role: We can provide activities that are on the edge of our child's ability—not too easy and not too hard, and constantly adding new levels of difficulty—to support our child's work toward self-perfection. Children are often more focused on the process than on the product. We can support this by resisting the urge to help when they struggle and allowing them to repeat steps. Repetition requires time, so we can make sure the child has blocks of time in which they can explore and repeat without interruption.

OBSERVATION TO SUPPORT
THE HUMAN TENDENCIES

- Observe our child to see which tendencies are at work and how the child is acting on them.
- Prepare our environment to be rich with opportunities and activities that support the tendencies.
- If, over time, we do not observe a particular tendency at work, look for obstacles impeding it and try to remove them.
- Evaluate ourselves and our environment to see if and how our child's tendencies are being supported. What can we change or do better?

THE FOUR PLANES OF DEVELOPMENT

Dr. Montessori's *four planes of development* is a framework to describe how humans develop from birth to maturity (around 24 years old). We can use the four planes to understand the characteristics of our child at every age, so we can support them through every stage. Each plane is around 6 years long: ages 0 to 6 years (infancy), 6 to 12 years (childhood), 12 to 18 years (adolescence), and 18 to 24 years (maturity). Interestingly, Dr. Montessori included the ages 18 to 24 in childhood years before studies on the brain found that the prefrontal cortex (where rational decision-making is located) is still developing into our mid-twenties.

Dr. Montessori used the word "rebirth" to describe the changes that occur in the child as they move from one plane to the next. At each stage, it can feel like a new and different child emerges, one with new characteristics and needs, one who acts on their human tendencies in new ways and learns in new and different ways. Just like a caterpillar goes through many physical and behavioral transformations on its way to becoming a butterfly, so does our child as they mature.

Each plane builds on the previous one, with the acquisitions of each plane preparing and laying a foundation for the next. It is important to know that while Dr. Montessori noted that each plane lasts for about 6 years, the moment of transition is different for every child. For example, some children start to show the signs of switching to the second plane at 5.5 years and others at 7 years. Transitioning from one plane to the next is usually gradual, with the child sometimes having one leg in one plane and the other in the next. We can use the ages as guides and look out for the other signs and characteristics of transitioning, which we will discuss, to recognize when our child is moving from one plane to the next.

When we have an understanding of each plane, we can adapt our method, environment, and response to meet our child's needs. Our role as parents, caregivers, educators, or loving adults changes as our child moves through the planes of development.

CONSTRUCTIVE RHYTHM OF LIFE

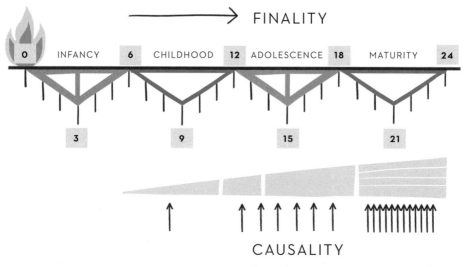

Source: Association Montessori Internationale (AMI)

This diagram was presented by Dr. Montessori in Perugia, Italy, in 1950 to explain the four planes of development.

- We see four repeated triangles. Each triangle represents a plane that consists of 6 years.

- The first and third planes are subdivided into subplanes; for example, the first plane of development is made up of the 0–3 subplane (the acquisition phase) and the 3–6 subplane (the refinement and consolidation phase).

- Dr. Montessori observed that humans develop in cycles, with periods of rapid development followed by periods of consolidation. This was counter to the more commonly held belief of the time that human development follows a linear or straight path where the youngest learners learn the least and the older learners are capable of learning the most. This traditional view of development is shown in the lower half of the diagram (blue triangles showing the amount of education starting from 6 years and increasing into the college years).

- The planes share similarities. The first and third planes have thick orange lines because they are dynamic, explosive, and dramatic periods of physical and psychological growth. The second and fourth planes have thin blue lines because they are calmer periods of steady growth. This is what we call in Montessori "parallel planes."

The first plane: 0 to 6 years, infancy

The first plane of development is marked by explosive growth and significant physical, cognitive, and psychological changes. The child at 6 years old looks very different from the newborn and knows so much more.

The child in the first plane is a sensorial explorer. They receive sensorial impressions from the environment and use them to build their intelligence and personality.

Because the child in this plane is focused on constructing themselves, while they may like being around others, they prefer to work on their own or side by side with another person. This will change radically in the second plane, ages 6 to 12.

The child in the first plane has what Dr. Montessori called an *absorbent mind*. From birth until age 6, the child takes everything in without effort and without discrimination. They absorb the sights, smell, tastes, behaviors, and culture around them. This is an unconscious process that doesn't involve our child's choice or effort. It happens automatically and with ease. Their mind is like a sponge that soaks up whatever liquid it is immersed in. It cannot decide what part of the water to absorb—it takes it all in. The things that our child absorbs become a part of their personality and their self.

The first subplane (0 to 3 years)

A child does so much in these years. They learn how to walk, talk, act, and be a person of their time and place. It is a period of great physical growth and transformation. Our child goes from having no teeth to a full mouth of teeth, from only drinking milk to being able to eat everything, from crying as a newborn to possibly speaking multiple languages. During these years, they go from instinctively kicking their legs to rolling, crawling, standing, walking, running, jumping, and enjoying a wide range of movement. From batting their hands to using a refined pincer grip (holding something between their thumb and index finger) for specific tasks like sewing and writing. From peeing and pooping by instinct to controlling the process and using the toilet independently. They go from not knowing much about the world to knowing how things work in their home and the world around them. They know how to think and solve some problems. They know some of the norms and cultures of their group and are beginning to understand what is appropriate. They can make connections and draw some conclusions.

The child at 3 years old, especially if they have been given the right environment, is a creator who has already accomplished so much. They have created what Dr. Montessori called their *psychic organs*—language, movement, culture, intelligence, and a will. The amazing thing is that they have done all this without realizing it or even remembering the process. This is why Dr. Montessori called the child at this stage *the unconscious creator.*

continued on page 28

SENSITIVE PERIODS

> "A sensitive period refers to a special sensibility which a creature acquires in its infantile state, while it is still in the process of evolution. It is a transient disposition and limited to the acquisition of a particular trait. Once this trait, or characteristic, has been acquired, the special sensibility disappears."

—Dr. Maria Montessori, *The Secret of Childhood*

A sensitive period is a time or stage in the child's life when they seem to be drawn to a certain aspect of the environment. We notice them constantly returning to an activity or repeating an action. Through this work over a period of time, they acquire a new skill or ability. The child may be able to make the acquisition at a different time, but it will require a lot more effort.

Sensitive periods are extremely active and concentrated in the first plane of development. Dr. Montessori called them *beams of light, vital impulses,* and *creative sensibilities.* While the absorbent mind allows the child to take in everything in the environment indiscriminately, the sensitive periods, like beams of light, focus the child on one aspect of the environment. The skills acquired in each sensitive period helps the child act on their human tendencies.

SENSITIVE PERIODS ARE TRANSIENT. They eventually disappear, whether or not the skill is acquired. This work can be done tangibly (physically) or intangibly (mentally).

SENSITIVE PERIODS WILL OCCUR NATURALLY FOR EVERY CHILD. However, they need an adult to support them by preparing the right environment and encouraging activity within the environment. For example, a child in a sensitive period for language is drawn to language and has the ability to develop language skills. However, if there is no language in the environment, they won't acquire the skill, and, eventually, the sensitive period will pass.

RECOGNIZING SENSITIVE PERIODS. Sensitive periods happen around the same time for most children, so they can be anticipated and identified by observation.

Some things that can be observed during a sensitive period are:

- An attraction to a certain element of the environment

- Increased activity and repetition leading to concentration

- A feeling of refreshment and satisfaction at the end of work

The sensitive periods that manifest strongly in the first plane are:

- Language
  - Spoken language: in utero to 2.5–3 years
  - Writing: from 3.5 years to 4.5 years
  - Reading: 4.5 years to 5.5 years

- Weaning: 6 months to 12 months

- Order: birth to 5 years (peaking between 1.5 years and 2.5 years)

- Tiny detail and small objects: from 1 year to 4 years

- Movement
  - Acquisition: from birth to 2.5 years
  - Refinement and coordination: from 2.5 years to 4.5 years

- Sensorial exploration and classification
  - Acquisition and accumulation of impressions: in utero to 3 years
  - Classification and organization of impressions: 2.5 years to 6 years

- Numbers and mathematics: from 4 to 6 years

- Manners and courtesies: 2.5 years to 6 years

- Assimilation of images (storing images/details in their mind): birth to 6 years

- Music: 2 years to 6 years

NOTE: 1. Ages are for guidance only; all children develop on their own timeline.

2. If a sensitive period is missed, the child will still be able to learn the skill but it will take more effort (like learning a foreign language as an adult).

The second subplane (3 to 6 years)

In the second subplane, our child goes from an unconscious creator to a conscious worker. Guided by the tendencies of repetition, exactness, and self-perfection, our 3- to 6-year-old child makes a more intentional and deliberate effort to refine and master the abilities they acquired in the first subplane.

From the ages of 3 to 6, our child is active, seeking to use their hands and master their environment. Dr. Montessori called this "the age of play" and described play as the child's work. Our child wants more precise language, more precise movement; they want to understand the world around them better and do things for themselves. If they could express what they want from us, they would say, "Help me to do it myself." They want tools that they can use, and they want to participate in life around them. These children are constantly asking "What?" and "Why?." They want to know the names of things and what they do. They want to do what they see the adults around them doing. They want to perfect the construction of themselves as an individual and forge independence through the ability to care for themselves—like eating and dressing themselves and using the toilet independently.

The adult and environment for the first-plane child

Our role during this stage is to give the child security and unconditional love, and prepare our home as recommended by Dr. Montessori in a way that allows our child to feel oriented and provides predictability. A home is a love-filled nurturing environment with a consistent caregiver. The environment is prepared with beauty and order, filled with rich language and sensorial impressions. Things for the child to see, touch, smell, taste, and hear. We can ensure that there are opportunities for the child to explore through movement, manipulation, and their senses, with opportunities to freely explore both the indoors and the outdoors.

In the first plane, our child will:

- Develop coordinated movement.
- Develop intelligence (an understanding of "What?," "Where?," and some "How?" around their immediate world). They are ready for the universe.
- Learn to order and classify their impressions (e.g., lightest to darkest, smallest to biggest, smoothest to roughest).
- Refine their sensorial perceptions in order to make judgments.
- Develop the language(s) of the environment.
- Develop functional independence (e.g., to dress themselves, care for their body).
- Develop a unique character and personality and adapt to their time, place, and culture.

Second plane (6 to 12 years): childhood

Unlike the busy, fast-moving first plane, the second plane is, according to Dr. Montessori, a "calm period of uniform growth." It begins with significant physical changes. Our child starts to lose their baby teeth and grow permanent teeth. They become leaner and taller, with more balanced proportions. Their hair texture changes and their feet grow bigger to balance their growing height. Most of the early childhood illnesses are behind them, and the hormones of adolescence have yet to kick in. So our child is strong and generally happy. Their body is capable of so much, and they know it, so they test and push their bodies. They want to see how fast they can run, how high they can climb, how many cartwheels they can do.

There are also psychological changes:

Social. Our 6- to 12-year-old child is confident and secure in their family, so they begin to seek more time with others. They want playdates and sleepovers. They want to be part of groups and are influenced by their peers. They want to explore farther away from home in the community. They may also lose some of their sweetness. Dr. Montessori and many of us who have children this age notice that they can exhibit a kind of hardness or toughness that can come off as unkind and even rude. (Dr. Montessori called this "the age of rudeness.")

As a younger child at the end of the first plane, they enjoyed being part of a social group and knew largely how to act within the group. The child in the second plane wants to create their own group, to determine the hierarchies, the roles, and the rules. At times, we may need to remind them of, and uphold, our family agreements (the freedoms and limits of our home), which provide them guidance and security about how to behave in social groups.

This is also a period of hero worship, as our child finds people to admire and be inspired by.

Cognitive. The child in the second plane outgrows the absorbent mind. Now they can move, speak, act, and express the culture of their environment. They are strong and capable, independent and intelligent, confident and articulate. They are a person of their time and place. They now need and use their *logical, reasoning mind*.

Our child is no longer a sensorial explorer; they are an intellectual explorer. They spend a lot of time abstracting and imagining, and there is no limit to their exploration— they only need opportunities and the right conditions. Adults tend to underestimate the abilities of the child in this plane. We can offer them wider contact with the environment to feed their hunger for knowledge and culture.

Dr. Montessori said that this is the plane for optimal learning, and she invited adults to sow as many seeds of interest as possible, to give our child culture, and offer them the universe to explore. Our child has the advantage of physical strength, good health, and interest driven by their logical inquiring minds. We are to share with them the world of nature and the accomplishments of humans over time. We tell stories and build their interest and curiosity, while also helping them make connections between concepts and ideas, and eventually building their own understanding of the universe.

Our child not only wants to know "what," they also want to know "why" and "how."

Moral. While the child in the first plane mostly accepts whatever we tell them is not appropriate, the child in the second plane wants to know what it means to be appropriate and why something is not okay. It may feel like they are always tattling and reporting someone for doing the wrong thing, but they are trying to understand what is right and wrong and what is fair and just. *Why is it right? When is it right? All the time or sometimes? How does one respond? Do they respond this way sometimes or all the time?* They are instinctively trying to develop their moral compass.

This is a sensitive period for justice. We hear them say "It's not fair" so many times. It is because they have a heightened sense of justice and want things to be fair. They have intense feelings and rebel against injustice, including to animals.

This is also a time when the adult must be conscious of being honest and morally correct in front of the child. Lying to the child while they're in this plane can break the child's trust in them. The child in this plane is a cultural explorer who encompasses the right and the wrong, the good and the bad. They don't just absorb the world around them; they seek answers.

Emotional. Children in this plane have an understanding of reality and how things are meant to be. They practice adapting their behavior to circumstances. They now have self-control, can self-regulate, and can delay gratification. When these factors are working together, the child becomes an integrated personality. They are able to research and learn things, control themselves, and question things while staying regulated.

While in the first plane the child had a high sense of physical and external order, the second-plane child may seem disorderly as their focus moves to internal, intellectual order. The first-plane child also exerted maximum physical effort, wanting to use a lot of energy, but the second-plane child with their logical mind wants to be efficient. They want to exert minimum effort for maximum results. The second-plane child's maximum effort is more intellectual and social.

The adult and environment for the second-plane child

We can sow seeds of interest and provide resources and opportunities for our child to pursue these interests. We can tell them stories and encourage them to use their imagination and their logical, reasoning mind. They need a lot of intellectual stimulation.

Our role is to still provide the love and security of home while also trusting and giving the child freedom and opportunities to explore beyond home. We can prepare them for interactions with other groups. School is a great way to extend the child's community, but they also need environments beyond school, like scouting groups or musical groups.

The second-plane child needs physical activity and social interaction, so this is a great time for group sports. They also need good role models and people to look up to. We can provide opportunities for the child to be a part of groups that work together on projects or activities. This allows them to learn how to work within a team and also figure out group dynamics. It is also a rich field for moral exploration. We can act as a guide for social interactions and help the child work through the inevitable conflicts that arise as a result of being part of a social group.

Our child will have come to the end of the second plane when we recognize that:

- They are strong and stable both physically and mentally.
- They are gregarious and have good peer relationships. They love being part of a pack.
- They are a social being able to participate and associate positively in groups.
- They can control their will and self-regulate and therefore also listen to instructions and adjust their behavior.
- They have developed a logical, reasoning mind. There will be critical thinking, cognitive flexibility, a great imagination, and love for exploring abstraction, whether in the form of ideas, formulas, or concepts.
- They are confident, knowledgeable, and responsible.
- They have a strong sense of justice and a strong moral compass and the ability to distinguish between right and wrong.
- They have a rich knowledge of the world and the universe. They can make connections and see interdependences—how things affect others— and out of this grows a sense of responsibility and stewardship.
- They have achieved intellectual independence. They have interests and the ability to explore and enrich them.

Third plane (12 to 18 years): adolescence; Fourth plane (18 to 24 years): maturity

The third plane is another explosive and creative period, similar to the first plane. This time, it is the adult that is being created. The fourth plane is the period between childhood and adulthood when our child enters the world, the *unprepared environment*. This again is a more stable period with fewer physical changes.

We'll look at the third and fourth planes more in chapter 9, "What's Next."

FIRST PLANE	SECOND PLANE	THIRD PLANE	FOURTH PLANE
0–6 years	6–12 years	12–18 years	18–24 years
We are planting the seeds.	The stem is growing tall and strong.	Leaves and blossoms unfurl, nearing maturity.	The plant is fully grown.
• physical and biological independence • absorbent mind • concrete understanding of the world • sensorial learner • working in parallel with small amounts of collaboration • rapid growth and change	• mental independence • using their logical, reasoning mind; developing their moral sense and exploring how things work and connect • more abstraction • learning through imagination • working in groups • more stable period	• social independence • developing social policy (how they would change the world) • sharing ideas and ideals with others • enormous physical and psychological changes (similar to the first plane)	• spiritual and moral independence • giving back to society • reasoning, logical mind • more stable period (similar to the second plane)

RAISING THE MONTESSORI CHILD

3

BEING THEIR GUIDE

Montessori educators are called "guides," not "teachers." This is central to the Montessori philosophy. A Montessori guide observes the children in the class, sets up the classroom environment to meet their needs, helps connect the children to it, and makes adjustments as needed. This is different from a teacher deciding what each child needs to learn based on an arbitrary timeline or curriculum and teaching it to them.

Similarly in the home, we are not our child's boss (nagging or deciding what they have to learn, do, or be) or their servant (doing everything for them) or laissez-faire (letting them do whatever they want).

Instead, we are the child's guide.

We want our children to feel involved in the home. We want them to become independent and responsible. We want them to learn how to contribute to the family and their community. And we want to cultivate a love of learning within them. They are so capable when we allow it.

- A guide prepares a safe physical and psychological environment.
- A guide develops agreements together with the child.
- A guide observes the child and seeks to understand their needs.
- A guide fosters independence and responsibility.
- A guide sparks the child's wonder in the world around them.
- A guide nurtures connection.
- A guide builds trust.
- A guide is a model for them.
- A guide cultivates slowness.
- A guide respects the child, loves them, and accepts them.
- A guide helps them become a member of the family and society.

There is now so much research showing that children who are engaged in their own learning are more likely to develop into independent, self-directed, and lifelong learners. Children who are respected learn to respect themselves, others, and their environment. And instead of having to conform to familial or societal expectations, our children are allowed to become their true selves.

It takes practice to let go of some control. To step back and only step in when our child really needs support. To allow them to experience all of their feelings and provide support if needed, like rubbing their back or helping them make amends once they are calm. To give them time to develop skills like dressing themselves, preparing their own lunch, writing a thank-you note, or making a repair with a friend.

It can feel brave to step in and calmly and clearly set a limit to keep everyone safe. To let them know that something they are doing or saying is unkind or hurts, not in an angry way, but by modeling how to set boundaries with others that are kind and clear.

It requires patience. This is a long-term approach, not a quick fix. We are laying a foundation of trust and connection so that our child knows they can come to us even when they are not at their best, that we will love them at their worst and guide them to become independent so that they can help themselves, others, and the world.

We will need to navigate the contradictions of raising children: keeping them close yet giving them space; sparking an interest but letting them take it further on their own; allowing them freedom while setting clear limits and responsibilities; fostering a secure attachment and also letting them go.

Our role as a Montessori parent or caregiver then is to allow the child to develop naturally to their optimal potential while helping them adapt to their family and society.

> "It is necessary for the teacher to guide the child without letting him feel her presence too much, so that she may always be ready to supply the desired help, but may never be the obstacle between the child and his experience."
>
> —Dr. Maria Montessori, *Dr. Montessori's Own Handbook*

LAYING A STRONG FOUNDATION

1. Make agreements for our home

In Montessori classrooms, there are clear freedoms and limits. These freedoms and limits—these agreements—are known to everyone and are predictable. In the 6 to 12 classroom, the children are involved in deciding what the agreements should be. Kim Anh Nguyễn Anderson, a Montessori educator of over 15 years, says that this process of making agreements together makes the learners feel safe and like they belong.

Together with our children, we can make agreements for our home. The more involved our child is in making the agreements, the more likely they are to be intrinsically motivated to keep to them. The goal is that everyone in the family agrees on, contributes to, and understands the agreements. Being specific helps. If an agreement is, "We treat each other with respect," we can clarify what "respect" means—waiting for someone to finish speaking before speaking ourselves, using a gentle tone of voice with each other, not making fun of each other, and so on.

These agreements provide a clear base to refer to. We can ask the child, "What's our agreement about rough play?" There is not much to argue with when they have been involved in making the agreements.

Make too many agreements, and it will be hard to keep track of them. And we should be mindful of changing them too often—our children need the agreements to be predictable rather than dependent on our mood or how much sleep we had the night before. However, they are living documents, and we may need to revise them if they are not working and as our children grow. If that's the case, change the agreements at a neutral (ideally, planned) moment, like at a family meeting.

Family meetings. For children from 3 to 12 years old, having regular but informal family meetings can be helpful. The family meeting can be a space in which to develop clear house agreements, to discuss what's going well for our child and where they may need help, or to look at what's coming up for the week ahead. Some families like to add something fun to the meeting, like popcorn, or have a family meal or movie after the meeting.

With a 3- to 6-year-old, the meeting is going to be short and more adult-led, but they may have ideas about where they'd like to go on an outing or their favorite meal as a dinner suggestion. We can practice respecting and valuing their contribution. By the age of 5.5 to 6 years old, they will be well on their way to being able to participate fully in the meetings.

EXAMPLES OF FAMILY AGREEMENTS

- **WE ARE KIND TO EACH OTHER.** Even if we disagree, we will not hurt each other physically or tease each other. This teaches children to respect themselves and each other and find ways to solve disagreements through discussion.

- **WE GET PERMISSION BEFORE TOUCHING ANYONE.**

- **WE SIT AT THE (DINING) TABLE TO EAT.** This keeps food to one area of the home and helps limit mindless eating while playing. It also gives families a regular time to be together and have conversation and allows us to get to know each other's friends better, too, when they are visiting.

- **WE CONTRIBUTE TO THE HOUSEHOLD.** No matter what our age, we help around the house, and our help is valued.

- **WE ENGAGE IN ROUGH PLAY ONLY BY MUTUAL CONSENT.** This is a mouthful for young children, but they understand its meaning. If someone says "stop," they are saying that they are not having fun anymore and the game needs to end.

- **WE ARE RESPECTFUL AND SAFE TOWARD OURSELVES, EACH OTHER, AND THE ENVIRONMENT.** That could mean singing as long as it doesn't bother others, uplifting and encouraging others, or using a bookmark rather than folding pages in order to care for our books.

If we are raising children with a partner or co-parent, it can be a good idea to have a separate meeting once a week to discuss things between the adults. Going over all the practical things that come up in the family during the week—appointments, commitments, meal planning, transportation arrangements—can bring calm to the upcoming days. It also allows any invisible load to become visible and equitably distributed. Periodic meetings can also be arranged with a grandparent or caregiver who regularly looks after the child or children to keep everyone on the same page (as much as possible).

Ad hoc agreements. Dr. Jane Nelsen, author of the Positive Discipline books, also suggests making ad hoc agreements, which we can kindly and gently hold them to. For example, if our child has some work they need to do, we can ask them what time they'd like to get it done. They love to choose exact times, like 5:33 p.m. If they need reminding, we can say, "It's 5:33" and wait for them to process what we have said. If they ignore us or say, "But . . . ," we can calmly repeat ourselves: "It's 5:33." We can hold them to the agreement they made in a kind and clear way.

2. Prepare the physical and psychological environment

Physical environment. We can set up a physical environment where our child feels welcome, where they can find everything they need, where they know where things belong and can put them away, where they can be independent, where they can find ways to entertain and challenge themselves, and where they can learn to care for these spaces. The environment will be adapted as our child grows. We go into this in more detail in the next chapter.

Psychological environment. We are also responsible for preparing the psychological environment of our home. This means a space in which our child feels emotionally safe and free to explore. We can ensure that our child feels safe coming to us when they are having a hard time. And we can be predictable, clear, and consistent, so they know what to expect. We want to create a home where they can feel "seen, safe, soothed, and secure," as described by Daniel Siegel and Tina Payne Bryson in their book *The Power of Showing Up.*

Safety and supervision. Our child relies on us to provide physical safety and supervision. Their prefrontal cortex, the part of the brain responsible for rational decision-making, isn't fully developed until their early twenties. So "it is our job to keep them safe," a phrase we learned from our Montessori friend Jeanne-Marie Paynel.

This doesn't mean wrapping them up in bubble wrap or being a helicopter parent, but we can find ways for them to do what they'd like to do and keep them safe at the same time. If a child wants to climb a tree, rather than saying no, we can help them choose a tree that is the appropriate size and has sturdy branches, explain how to test a branch, and show them how to climb down. We can allow our children to have friends over and make their own pizza. We can supervise to make sure they are safe but allow them to burn the pizza if they forget to turn on the timer, or ask them to wash up at the end even if the dishes don't get perfectly clean.

A child of 6 to 12 years old may want to do more on their own outside of the house. If we live in a city, we will likely need to supervise, but we can still offer our child more freedom. For example, we can let them research their route on public transportation, go with them but allow them to get on the bus going in the wrong direction, and then let them work out how to fix their mistake.

Removing obstacles. We can also identify and remove any obstacles to our children's development. We can address physical obstacles, such as placing their plates, glasses, and snacks in a low drawer so they are easily accessible or placing their toothbrush, toothpaste, and a mirror at their height to encourage toothbrushing.

A child from 3 to 6 years old might still be hanging on to things like a pacifier, a diaper, or a stroller that may be keeping them from moving on to the next stage of development. For a child from 6 to 12 years old, we might find that too many scheduled activities or too much screen time is limiting their development.

Other obstacles may include too many interruptions (we can set up a space where our child can choose to be alone), limited opportunities for hands-on discovery (we can provide some new and exciting opportunities for exploration), and too many new things competing for their attention (we can limit the number of activities available at one time).

Sometimes, *we* are the obstacle to our child's development. For example, by telling them what they should wear; not allowing them space to develop their own ideas; doing their homework for them; nagging them constantly; not allowing time for conversation, free play, or time outdoors; or not making them feel safe and accepted.

3. Nurture connection with our child

As Simone wrote in *The Montessori Toddler*, "Without connection, we get very little cooperation."

From the time our child is in utero, we begin to build a connection with them. We are learning who they are, and they are learning about us too. But within a few years, our relationship may become less about connection and more about accomplishing tasks and delivering instructions to get through a busy day. It is not surprising then that our child stops listening to us. If instead most of our daily interactions with our child are rooted in connection, then our (less frequent) requests for cooperation are more likely to be heard. As our child gets older and their world and social circles expand, it's even more important to maintain a strong connection.

Connecting with our child can look like:

- Snuggling up with some books first thing in the morning, before getting ready for the day
- Taking time for family meals and sitting at the table together (no screens allowed)
- Showing an interest in our child's passions even if we don't necessarily share them
- Finding time for conversation, particularly in instances where we don't need to make eye contact—while biking or in the car, cooking or washing dishes
- Not judging what they tell us so they feel they can come to us without being subjected to a lecture or unsolicited advice
- Making a list of things we enjoy doing together—and then doing them
- Putting on music to dance to in the kitchen or sing along to together

- Having family rituals—Sunday-morning pancakes or a weekly outing with the whole family
- Creating a set of family values (e.g., being environmentally friendly, connecting with nature, or giving to the community), perhaps made into a poster and hung on the wall
- Turning off our phones, putting them away, and being truly present with our family
- Responding in a predictable way in moments of conflict
- Being a reliable guide when outside the home ("Use your eyes to look at the fragile things in the store.")
- Finding moments of one-on-one time with each child in the family
- Allowing space for them to finish what they are saying ("I'll first finish listening to Oliver and then I'd love to hear what you have to say, Emma.")
- Having a sense of humor (including some potty humor!)

4. Build trust with them

A large part of raising a Montessori child is trust—if we show our child that we trust them, they build trust in themselves and learn to trust their environment.

Learning to trust themselves might look like a baby batting a ball and making it move (*I did it!*), a toddler wiping up some milk they spilled (*I can clean it up!*), a preschooler feeding the family pet (*I can care for others!*), a school-age child developing ways to help society (*I can make a change!*).

As the adult, we show our child we trust them by:

- Allowing them to do things for themselves (e.g., fetch something from a tree while we hold the ladder).
- Giving them opportunities to do things they are capable of (e.g., serve a cup of tea to a visiting grandparent).
- Respecting their opinions (e.g., by making them feel heard).
- Giving them responsibilities and not nagging them (e.g., for a younger child, trusting that they will brush their teeth when they are ready; and for an older child, letting them decide when to do their homework and follow through by themselves).
- Letting them overhear us telling others that we trust them (e.g., standing up for them if someone does not believe them). One morning at church, Junnifa's son missed out on sweets that had been passed around. When he asked for one, he was told by the caregiver that he had already had one. Junnifa stepped in to say that she trusted her son, and if he said he had not yet received one, she believed him. This was a huge deposit in the trust bank with her son.

- Valuing them as contributing members of the family (e.g., relying on them to empty the trash or to help ready the home for visitors).
- Involving them in making and sticking to agreements (e.g., about whether they are allowed screen time and how much).
- Allowing them times to be in charge (e.g., for a younger child, to choose on the map which animals we will visit at the zoo; and for an older child, to use a map to lead the way on a hike).
- Being understanding about their mistakes (e.g., doing our best to stay calm if our child breaks something while giving them an opportunity to repair the object and make it up to us).
- Resisting the urge to rescue our child when they make a mistake (e.g., delivering a forgotten sports bag or nagging them to do their homework so they don't get in trouble at school). We can trust that the child will feel the consequences and learn to adjust their behavior for themselves.
- Being honest with our child (e.g., giving them age-appropriate, clear, and direct answers to their tough questions about things like death, divorce, sex, sexuality, race). See chapter 7 for more of these conversations.

For those of us used to taking control, we can take the role of hands-off supervisor rather than micromanaging boss. We can let go of societal expectations about how and when our child should develop and trust that they are growing on their own timeline. It takes trust to believe that our child will become interested in reading or mathematics or sports even if we don't force it. We can focus on how they are developing as a whole human and contributing in the way they were meant to.

5. Be a model for them

We ask our children to be kind to each other, to speak softly, to wait their turn, to be honest, and more. But remember, our actions speak louder than our words.

Here are some examples of things we can do to be a model for our child:

- Care for ourselves and our environment, such as by keeping our clothing and spaces neat and organized.
- Take time to move and care for our bodies.
- Rest and have some items in our home to invite resting, like an eye pillow, a cozy blanket, a yoga mat, or a floor cushion.
- Care for others—bake something for a friend or neighbor, stop to talk with someone asking for money, help an elderly person with some shopping or housework.
- Be mindful with our movements (difficult for some of us). We can apologize if we bump into someone.

- Resolve conflicts in front of them so they learn how we repair a rupture.
- Let them know when we learn that something we thought was true is actually misinformation. Learning, unlearning, relearning.
- Take and give space in terms of how we use our voices, how we pause and listen.
- Spend less time looking at our screens and more time looking into others' eyes.
- Be careful how we talk about our work and friends. Our children will observe our work and social habits, our focus, and our joy.
- Say thank you, accept compliments, and graciously receive feedback.
- Apologize when we get it wrong ("What I should have said is . . . " or "What I should have done is . . .").
- Be lifelong learners and exhibit a love of learning.

LEARNING WHO OUR CHILD IS

1. Observe them

As a parent, it's hard to be objective about our own child because we are so connected with them. Observing allows us to step back and more clearly see who our child is, how they are unfolding, how their needs are changing, what skills they are practicing, and which skills they still need to learn.

It's easy to get activated by our children (they don't seem to listen to us, do something careless, or appear to lack appreciation), and observing can give us the space to pause, see things clearly, and respond rather than react.

Observing is not easy. In the *1921 London Lectures*, Dr. Montessori talked about the need to prepare our eyes to observe, to draw a bead across a string every time we want to interfere, to practice being silent and motionless, to observe everything in our field of vision, to be patient, and to pay attention to uninteresting things (because we don't know what will become interesting).

"It is not always imperative to see big things, but it is of paramount importance to see the beginnings of things. At their origins there are little glimmers that can be recognized as soon as something new is developing."

—Dr. Maria Montessori, *Education and Peace*

SOME THINGS TO OBSERVE

When we observe, we see our child with fresh eyes without any preconceptions or judgments. We can take a notebook and pen and do a 5-minute observation, pretending to be a scientist who has never met our child before. We can make a running record of what we see, be like a video camera recording all the details. Even the smallest moments can provide valuable information. Some ideas what to look for:

- MOVEMENT: how they walk, stand, sit, climb, skip, etc.; how they hold a pencil, a book, scissors, or an object they are using, etc.

- COMMUNICATION: aspects of their speech; their articulation; the speed at which they talk; their vocabulary; their body language, etc.

- SOCIAL DEVELOPMENT: how and when they interact with ourselves and others; their body language; whether they initiate contact or reply when spoken to, etc.

- INDEPENDENCE: when they ask for help; what they can manage by themselves; if/how they react when something they are doing themselves becomes difficult, etc.

- ACTIVITIES: what engages them; what they do if they are bored; what breaks their concentration (sometimes this is us interrupting), etc.

- EMOTIONAL DEVELOPMENT: how they react when they are sad, happy, frustrated, or angry; how they solve problems, etc.

- SELF-OBSERVATION: how we react/respond to our child; how our hands move; what activates us, etc.

- IN CHALLENGING MOMENTS: e.g., how our child reacts; how they calm down; what helps them; when this happens; whether there are any patterns, etc.

From these observations, is there something new we learned about our child? Is there anything we would like to change as a result? Something in the environment? Another way we can support them? Obstacles we can remove? Including our own intervention? Observe joy!

2. Understand their needs

As we explored in chapter 2, the needs of a child in the first plane of development can be quite different from those of a child in the second plane of development. They will still have the same human tendencies, but these will look quite different.

When we have a child transitioning between planes of development, we may observe characteristics of both. For example, Simone remembers a friend talking about her 6-year-old. Sometimes the child was asking for more responsibility and sometimes they were being very emotional about something that seemed very small. They wanted to be "big" and "small" at the same time.

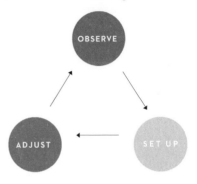

We observe the child to understand their needs, we set up our environment and prepare ourselves to support them, and then keep adjusting.

3. Respect them

Respecting children is a fundamental part of the Montessori approach.

Some examples of this respect are:

- How we physically handle them when needed: gently and with their consent
- How we step back when they can manage themselves and are available when they need guidance
- How we allow them to develop their full potential, without projecting onto them our own ideas of who they should be
- How we allow them to speak for themselves
- How we listen to them with our whole body and heart
- How we communicate kindly with them
- How we find ways to cultivate cooperation rather than using threats, bribes, or punishment
- How we work with them rather than making demands all day
- How we are clear and kind when communicating limits
- How we solve problems together so that everyone in the family can have their needs met

4. Love them

We can love our children deeply, show them empathy, and allow space for everyone in the family in a fair and equitable way.

Love is infinite and can be shown in so many ways. We recommend reading *The Five Love Languages* by Gary Chapman to remind ourselves that people receive love in different ways—and not always in the ways we give it.

If we find it fun to show love through food or presents or taking our children places, then we give and do these things unconditionally. Unconditionally means we are not doing it for their thanks or their love, to be a good parent, or so they do something for us in return. Giving with resentment is not how we show anyone our love.

We do these things because we love giving in this way or we love how others light up when they receive in this way.

5. Accept them

We accept our child for who they are. We are not molding them. We believe in, respect, and value our child and their unique potential. We are their guide as they explore who they are. We let them be themselves.

Accepting means dropping judgment or catching ourselves when we're judging. Accepting means not testing them ("What color is this?"), showing them off ("Tell Grandma what you just won"), or comparing them to other children ("Why can't you be more like _____?").

To accept our child fully is to also allow them all their feelings. If we were raised in a more traditional way, we may have been told "Don't worry," "It doesn't matter," "Don't cry," or "It's not so bad." We may have learned not to express our feelings or to feel understood by our loved ones, or how to manage emotions like anger and sadness when they come up. Instead, we try to see things from our child's perspective. Because all behavior is communication.

The Montessori approach to raising children can be described as being in service to our child's spirit. We prepare ourselves and the home intentionally, then allow them to *construct themselves*. They are laying down their personalities, finding out how the world works, and discovering their abilities.

We are learning to "follow the child." To let them unfold into their full capacity. To support their interests. To blow flames on their fire, not dampen their spirit. To be their guide when there are skills to build in difficult areas. To give them clear limits when needed.

We let them lead the way in their life, we lead the way in ours, and we travel the path together, alongside each other.

"I have helped this life to fulfill the tasks set for it by creation."

—Dr. Maria Montessori, *The Absorbent Mind*

SELF-DISCIPLINE AND INTRINSIC MOTIVATION

When we observe a Montessori classroom, there are children working in different parts of the classroom, on different activities; some by themselves, some in pairs or, in a classroom of 6- to 12-year-olds, in larger groups. There is a hum of activity and movement that looks to the observer like a dance as the children go about their work, the adult quite inconspicuous in the classroom. For someone who went to a school where we sat in a classroom with the teacher at the front telling us what to do, it's hard to believe that no one is telling these children what they need to learn, that they are choosing to work on long division, or taking care to walk around another child's work that is laid out on a floor mat, or watering the plants and wiping up any spills they may make.

This system works because it's not freedom *from* rules. It's freedom *to* do things—to move, to choose, to express themselves—with the associated responsibilities. The children are being told that they can do something, rather than that they can't. For example, they can move freely as long as they are not hurting themselves, someone else, or the space. They can choose what they want to work with as long as it isn't being used by someone else. They can express themselves by talking, writing, or even singing and dancing, as long as they do not use words that are hurtful, use a volume that is okay with everyone, and do it in a space where others won't be disturbed. Carla Foster, an AMI Montessori trainer, refers to these options as "rules, not prohibitions."

In our homes, we can also offer such freedom and responsibilities and prepare an intentional space for our children to explore. The child can make themselves a snack when they are hungry, or help themselves to a glass of water when they are thirsty, and leave the area tidy when they are finished. They can play quietly if they wake up early, as long as they don't disturb others. They are free to talk and contribute their views at mealtimes, waiting for others to finish talking and taking their turn.

Rewards, bribes, and punishment are extrinsic motivations—our child complies with our wishes only to avoid being punished or to receive the bribe or reward being offered. While we all may have used them, these strategies do not build self-discipline. In the Montessori approach, one of our roles as their guide is to cultivate the child's intrinsic motivation. We want our child to do things because they feel capable, they want to contribute, or they want to help another. We give the child freedom, and they learn that with that freedom comes responsibility.

Did you know that the root word of "discipline" is "disciple," meaning "to teach and learn"? Every time something happens, be it a fall, an argument, a disappointment, or a child lying, we don't have to be afraid. Instead, we can see it as a fresh opportunity for learning for our children and us.

The Montessori approach to raising our child is all about building self-discipline and encouraging their intrinsic motivation. It is a different, very respectful way to approach the child. To assume the best in them, to make and uphold family agreements, and to have clear conflict resolution strategies.

FOSTERING INDEPENDENCE AND RESPONSIBILITY

Dr. Montessori heard a child say, "Help me to help myself," and this phrase was soon adopted as a tenet of Montessori education and one we can use at home. We can help our child learn that they are capable and in charge of themselves and their bodies (*physical independence*) and that they can think for themselves (*mental independence*).

When a child is independent, they also learn responsibility for themselves, others, and their environment. They will want to make a contribution to the family and society. They learn to wait their turn, help a friend, or take care of a plant. They are intrinsically motivated to do so.

Self-discipline arises when we create opportunities for independence and mastery and when children learn the skills to be in community with others. We show our child we trust them, and they thrive on the chance to be responsible. It could be carrying their own plate to the table for their meal; using a sharp knife once they have learned to do so safely (with supervision); thinking to prepare something special for a child with a food allergy when inviting them to a birthday celebration; learning to light candles safely at dinnertime; or being in charge of looking up the train times for a family outing and buying the tickets from the ticket machine.

"Following some inner guide, they occupied themselves in work different for each that gave them joy and peace, and then something else appeared that had never been known among children, a spontaneous discipline. This struck visitors even more than the explosion into writing had done; children were walking about, seeking work in freedom, each concentrating on a different task, yet the whole group presented the appearance of perfect discipline. So the problem was solved: to obtain discipline, give freedom."

—Dr. Maria Montessori, *Education for a New World*

Scaffold skills. Children do not learn skills overnight. We might start with modeling, then collaborating, then allowing them to take over more steps themselves. As they master things, we can add more difficult steps. If our child forgets some steps they knew before, we can show them again until they have mastered them. Skills take practice before they become fully integrated.

Break skills into small parts. We can break down the skill they are learning into small parts that are easier to master. For example, for a younger child, by slowly showing them the steps for undoing and doing up a button or tying their shoelaces; older children can follow a note with instructions to get dinner started when they arrive home.

Step in as little as possible, and as much as necessary. It takes practice to trust, to observe, to wait, to let children make mistakes. Then we are rewarded by those moments of satisfaction, or deep concentration, or when they clap for themselves, skip off happily, or smile, having mastered something themselves (*I can do it*).

If we see that they are struggling and are about to become too frustrated to get further, instead of taking over, we can first ask, "Would you like some help?" or "Would you like me to show you?" or "Would you like me to give you a tip?" Then we can give the smallest amount of help, and let them continue.

Some children will refuse our help, and we do our best to be okay with that, too, knowing that they will keep trying and will get it in their own time.

Set up the environment for success. Our children can help themselves independently when they can access a choice of clothing, or reach the plates to set the table, or have their activities arranged in baskets or trays, or have a broom or mop at the ready. Older children will know where to find their sports equipment or musical instruments and have art materials like scissors, a stapler, and paper at the ready.

Allow time. It takes more time for a child to dress themselves, to have them help prepare dinner, or to stop to listen to a long story they want to share. When our schedules are less full, we are allowing more time for them to master skills, make discoveries for themselves, engage in rich conversation, and connect with us and others. They need time to get bored, to get creative, and (particularly for older children) to work on big projects.

Slow hands, omit words. When we are showing a 3- to 6-year-old child how something works (e.g., opening a combination lock on a bike, putting on an item of clothing), we can say, "Look!" then stop talking and make very slow and precise movements to demonstrate. This makes it simpler for them to learn. Jeanne-Marie Paynel, a Montessori parent educator, uses the acronym SHOW (slow hands, omit words) as a friendly reminder. Once our child is 6 and older, we can use a lot of words!

Help them become a member of the family and society. We want our child to become the best version of themselves while being respectful of others and the environment. Raising children in a Montessori way does not mean letting them do whatever they like (e.g., letting noisy kids run around a restaurant is disrespectful to the other people eating there). Nor does it mean being so strict that the child has little autonomy and either becomes subservient, passive, or compliant or goes behind our backs so as not to get caught. We are offering freedom with responsibilities, supporting them to become members of the family and society. We'll explore this more in chapter 6.

RAISING CURIOUS CHILDREN

As a child's guide, we can inspire them, wonder with them, and spark their curiosity. We can also provide them with a community of folks they can learn from, including our family, friends, peers, experts, and those in the local community.

Respond with curiosity to their questions. Rather than always giving our child the answer, it's fun to say, "Let's find out together." It's easy to look something up on the internet, but it can be a richer experience to look it up in a book or encyclopedia (we can come across wonderful things while we are searching), call an expert/professional/grandparent/family friend with knowledge of the subject, or plan a visit to a museum. Children will learn that when they don't know the answer, they can find it out.

The 3- to 6-year-old child has a *conscious* absorbent mind and therefore has lots of questions. They ask us, "What is this?" and "Why?" They are looking for simple explanations for the things they see around them. We can respond patiently even if they repeatedly ask the same question, because we want them to never stop being askers of questions! We could reply, "I remember speaking with you about that earlier. Do you remember what I said?" or "Why do you think?"

The 6- to 12-year-old child has a reasoning mind and the power of imagination, so their questions are now around "How?" and "Why?" They want to know not only the facts but the cause and effect of things. Dr. Montessori wrote in *The Absorbent Mind* that the 6- to 12-year-old "is not satisfied with a mere collection of facts; he tries to discover their causes."

When our child asks questions about topics like race, sex, war, or violence in the news, it can be hard to know how to answer. Britt Hawthorne, an antiracist and antibias educator, speaker, and advocate, suggests we do the following:

- Ask them what they already know.
- Ask them what they are wondering.
- Tell them we are glad they asked.
- And if we don't know the answer ourselves, agree on a time to come back to them to discuss it together. See chapters 6 and 7 for more help with answering tough questions.

A "wonder wall" is another idea we love. It comes from Julie Bogart's book *Brave Learner*, which we learned about from Montessori educator Pilar Bewley. When our child asks a question, rather than giving them the answer or immediately looking it up on the internet, we can write it down on a sticky note and put it on our wonder wall. Then these questions become topics to do a deep dive into, use as inspiration, or seek answers to at a later time.

Respond with curiosity to their statements. Sometimes children will repeat things they hear or say something we know not to be true, or we think they are saying one thing when they mean something else entirely.

It's easy at these times to shame them or correct them, but this could cause them to say less, or be scared to talk about these things in the future, or make them think we don't talk about these things. Britt Hawthorne suggests that if we instead respond with curiosity, they'll know that there is no embarrassment in getting things wrong; we can help them to correct it, or we may find that we simply misunderstood what they were saying. They will also learn to check whether they understood something correctly themselves.

WAYS TO RAISE CURIOUS CHILDREN

ASK OPEN-ENDED QUESTIONS:

"I wonder what would happen if . . . ?"

"Can you guess what that is/does?"

"I'm curious about _____. Why do you think that's the case?"

WHEN READING A BOOK TOGETHER, WE MIGHT ASK:

"What do you think the characters are thinking?"

"What do you think might happen next?"

WHEN THEY SHOW US SOMETHING THEY MADE, WE CAN ENCOURAGE THEM TO SAY MORE:

"Ooh. Tell me about it."

WE LIKE TO AVOID QUIZZING OR TESTING CHILDREN. We could instead use this question from Paula Lillard Preschlack's book *The Montessori Potential*:

"What do you remember about . . . ?"

We could ask, "Could you say more about that?" or "Let me just check that I understood you correctly; what did you mean when you said _____?" They may need more information, they may need to know that we don't say unkind things about people's ethnicity or skin color. For a 6- to 12-year-old child, we can explore further; for example, by asking, "Can we think about it in a different way?" or saying, "Let's consider how this might impact _____." Or we may have misunderstood what they meant and find that they weren't saying anything problematic. Curiosity allows us to clarify what support is or isn't needed.

Challenge them to question things and become critical thinkers. We can help them be critical thinkers about the media that we consume, to learn how to find reliable sources, and to question information from different perspectives. This applies not just to information but also to societal expectations and systemic thinking.

Children from 3 to 6 years old will see us being agents of social justice, and together, we can question things around us. From the ages of 6 to 12, children will become even more active in these conversations and may feel inspired to take action. (For more on moral development, see chapter 6.)

Become a storyteller. This may not come naturally to everyone, but we can learn to be a storyteller. Storytelling has the power to spark a child's curiosity and capture their imagination. When sharing information, our family history, or our sense of wonder about the world around us, let's think of how we can create an engaging and meaningful story. It may take some practice, but we have plenty of time to develop our storytelling skills. We can also use concrete objects, books, and art as springboards for our stories.

Our child may then be inspired to make their own storybook, comic strip, or stop-motion film. They might do some research at the library, conduct a survey, or interview a neighbor. Or they might just enjoy a good story, well told (and perhaps aspire to become an interesting storyteller too).

Link them to the environment. In *The Absorbent Mind*, Dr. Montessori described the prepared adult as one who offers "warmth, enlivens and invites." We can link children to things in our homes; to the wonders of nature; to the community, society, and eventually the world and the universe.

We never force them to do something, but we can introduce new ideas through conversation, with concrete materials, by working on something ourselves, or perhaps by presenting some well-selected media like an article or TED-Ed talk. We can fill our home with a curated selection of books, encyclopedias, beautiful objects, and artwork to inspire further research or inquiry.

Then we can encourage creativity by making time for free exploration, interrupting as little as possible, and leaving it up to our child how and with whom they might like to explore these ideas.

Teach by teaching, not by correcting. Who hasn't had someone correct them and immediately felt their heart sink? If we are working from an understanding that our child is doing their best and that mastery requires practice, then when we see them make an error, we can make a note of the skill they are missing and make time to teach it to them again. This could apply equally to a cognitive skill (e.g., how they've divided up their marbles) or a behavior (e.g., slamming a door, which we could have fun showing them how to close it as quietly as possible at a more neutral moment later). They are learning to be friendly with making mistakes.

If necessary, we can scaffold the skills, and teach them one step at a time. If we notice a 3-year-old with their shoes on the wrong feet, we could say, "I see you put on your shoes all by yourself!" Then at another time, we find a way to show them how to put their shoes on the correct feet. Then, we might make them a mat with the outline of each shoe to use as a guide.

Go slow. Slowing down is one of the easiest places to start. It allows us to:

- Take the time to observe and see things clearly—not just what we think we see.
- Pause before stepping in to help them with something they can manage themselves or allow them to learn from their mistakes.
- Respond (by pausing first) rather than reacting (acting before we think).
- See details that we would otherwise miss.
- Show our child how something works by slowing down our movements, talking less.
- Make time for connection, conversation, exploration, independence.
- Look after ourselves so we can more fully show up to care for others.
- Listen completely (to their words, their actions, their facial expressions).
- Be intentional in setting up our home and activities.
- Incorporate calmness into our homes.
- Move at the child's pace.
- Make an investment in the future by giving the child the time to learn to do things to care for themselves, others, and the environment (this takes longer in the short term but yields long-term gains).
- Model for family and other caregivers how we give our child time to master things for themselves.

> "Slow down . . . the small steps lead to extraordinary outcomes."
>
> —Catherine McTamaney, *The Tao of Montessori*

The Montessori principles we have discussed in this chapter help our child move from seeking extrinsic motivation (looking outside themselves) to nurturing their intrinsic motivation (doing something because they want to do it, they want to master a skill, or they want to care for someone or the environment). We are helping them become self-motivated citizens of the world. For more about supporting their intrinsic motivation, see the online appendix "40 Ways to Build Self-Discipline and Intrinsic Motivation."

JUNNIFA, UZO, SOLU, METU, BIENDU, NALU

Nduoma Montessori
Nigeria

"Montessori to our family is our enjoyment of the little things and the little moments. In our observation of the world around us. Noticing the buds and the bugs, the changes in season, the bird building its nest and working with its partner to watch their eggs, noticing the nestling and the fledgling. Noticing the eggs, the caterpillars, and the butterflies and truly enjoying the experience. Montessori has made us more mindful, intentional, and peaceful in our daily lives."

"I also really enjoy observing my children. I am fascinated by human development and just watching to understand them. I like to see how their unique personalities reflect in their everyday life as they act and also in their interactions with each other. Observing them helps me understand them and appreciate their individuality."

"We spend a lot of time with our extended family and in so doing share our culture, values, and customs. We attend a lot of cultural events around music and art. Concerts, exhibitions, celebrations, fairs, and just things that introduce our children to aspects of our culture and bring up questions that can be dug into. In our home, we play music, put up art, have clothing and food that reflect our culture while still exposing them to other cultures through travel and other experiences. We also share stories and read books. My dad enjoyed sharing stories of his childhood."

SETTING UP
OUR HOME

4

Our home is our child's base, the soil in which they put down roots and from which they take nutrients and sprout. It is the base from which they explore all other environments, the anchor that keeps them grounded. When we prepare our home intentionally to meet our child's needs, they can take all they need from it and blossom. The environment we prepare for our child can be a way to demonstrate our love, regard, and respect for them.

Dr. Montessori said that the absorbent mind takes indiscriminately from the environment and uses whatever it takes to construct the child. The things our child absorbs from the environment become a part of our child. Knowing this, we can consider what our child will see (colors, shapes, cleanliness, beauty, and order); what they will smell (plants, other natural scents); what they will hear (quiet, sounds of nature outside, wind chimes); and what they will feel (the temperature, the ambience).

Just as our children grow and change, our prepared environment can adapt to our growing child and their changing needs.

THE PREPARED ENVIRONMENT FOR EACH STAGE

THE NEEDS OF OUR CHILD FROM AGES 3 TO 6:

- Movement
- Space and opportunities for physical exploration
- Order
- Rich sensory input for all senses
- Opportunities to absorb our culture—through art, objects, and so on
- Beauty
- Encouragement toward functional independence

THE NEEDS OF OUR CHILD FROM AGES 6 TO 12:

- Systems to support order
- Space and provisions for big work
- Resources for intellectual exploration
- Items and spaces to spark their curiosity

THINGS TO CONSIDER IN PREPARING
THE PHYSICAL ENVIRONMENT

Accessibility: Our homes can be set up to encourage our child's autonomy and help them feel confident and respected. We want our child to be able to see, reach, and use the things in our space. When possible, we can have child-sized furniture and tools, or we can adapt things to support, encourage, and ensure accessibility: providing a stable stool or portable stair to use in reaching higher surfaces, lowering light and fan switches and door handles if needed, adding faucet extenders, placing their items on low shelves, and choosing furniture that is light enough that it can be picked up and moved by our child when necessary.

We can be aware of the way our child will interact with our space and the things in it. We want them to be able to move through their space with ease and not have too many areas that are out of bounds or things that we must constantly prevent them from touching or using. Things that are not appropriate for kids—such as fragile family heirlooms or expensive computer equipment—can be moved to less trafficked areas of the home. If a child has a physical disability, we can ensure that the space is adjusted to allow them as much independence as possible.

Functionality/independence/autonomy: Our homes can be a place where our children learn to act, think, and make choices for themselves. We want them to be able to open doors; turn lights on and off; and reach dishes, cutlery, snacks, clothes, toys, paper, pencils, paint, and tape. We want them to be able to take care of their basic needs: get water when they're thirsty, make a snack when they're hungry, and rinse their plate and cutlery. We want them to be able to solve simple problems for themselves, like getting a Band-Aid for a small cut. We can create possibilities for movement and exploration, both physical and intellectual. For example, a child who encounters a word they don't understand can have a dictionary in reach to check its meaning. We can provide them with things to touch and feel, to wonder about, to measure, to inspire them, and to use.

From age 3, a child begins to develop their personality and sense of self separate from their parents or caregivers. When we provide opportunities for independence, we acknowledge this separateness and support their development. As they acquire more awareness of their capabilities and capacities, they become better able to assess their limits and assess risks.

From ages 6 to 12, our child is very capable and can do a lot for themselves and for others. Our home can be designed to support these capacities and stretch the child's abilities. They can be given opportunities to use knives; cook on a stove; employ a tool to fix something; change a light bulb; run the washing machine, dishwasher, and other appliances; and use an iron.

Comfort: We can make choices that will allow both adult and child to feel equally comfortable in our home—this can include paying attention to furniture and the way our space is organized, ventilated, decorated, and lit.

Beauty: Beauty is subjective and can be a way to transmit culture to our children. We can create our spaces with elements that reflect our culture, our preferences, and our values, and in so doing, transfer these to our children. From ages 3 to 6, our child is still in the period of the absorbent mind and so this beauty will become one of the building blocks for their personality. From ages 6 to 12, our child is exploring the world. Their imagination is in full bloom, and so our home can become a canvas for this exploration and creation.

Order: A core Montessori principle is "a place for everything and everything in its place." This means designating different spaces for different activities: a place to cook, a place to eat, a place to sleep, bathe, and so on. And establishing a place for our everyday objects and possessions: a place for shoes, a place for books, a place for the sponge and for the soap.

Our spaces can have consistent points of reference to meet our child's need for orientation and a sense of order. (The couch is always in the same place even if the pillows might change.) Consistency and predictability lend a sense of safety to children. When changes need to be made, we can notify our children and involve them in the process. It can be an opportunity to contribute to the home and practice decision-making.

The 3- to 6-year-old child has a need for external order—we can support this by preparing the space so they can find everything and know where to return things, and can begin to take responsibility for keeping the house tidy for everyone. The 6- to 12-year-old child places less importance on external order, but it will come more easily to them if they understand where things go.

Simplicity: A simple space often encourages order. It also supports independence in our children because it is usually easier to maintain. We can avoid clutter and choose items for our home which are both beautiful and functional. We can have storage for things that are needed but not currently in use. Toys can be rotated, and extra supplies can be stored neatly away. When we prioritize simplicity and a minimalist outlook, we also start to see new uses for the things we already have. When we bring into our home only the things we need (making sustainable choices when we can), we are also showing our children to limit overconsumption.

Richness of sensorial feedback: Children from 3 to 6 years old are interested in categorizing and classifying, comparing and contrasting. We can provide opportunities for this in our home. We can choose sheets, curtains, or containers that show a gradation of colors; planters, light fixtures, or containers with different geometric shapes; a set of nesting tables that are graded in height and size; rugs, couches, and blankets with different textures; kitchen containers made of different materials. We can plant different flowers that have a range of colors, leaf shapes, and scents. All of these differences provide an opportunity to enrich our child's language as we give them specific vocabulary for them.

Accommodation: Every room in the home can accommodate both adult and child, supporting our child's need to communicate, socialize, and spend time with their loved ones. They may not want to interact with us all the time, but they do want to be close and feel our presence.

Safety: We will want to keep hazards such as poisonous substances, electrical wires, choking hazards, sharp objects, and medication out of reach. However, the 3- to 6-year-old is very capable and reasonable and can be shown how to use things appropriately. Instead of eliminating danger, our goal is to help our child become masters of their environment, making good judgments about what is and is not safe. We do this by watching, guiding, and showing. We can label things a safety hazard and show our child what is okay to use and what is not, how to use it and how not to, and in doing so, we can allow them opportunities to learn, grow, make judgments, and build and understand capacity through practice. Children in Junnifa's school have access to a room with sharp tools, and even the 3- to 6-year-old children learn how to use the tools safely, with care and consideration for themselves and others.

Storage: In order to have calm and engaging spaces, effective storage will be an important part of our home. We keep out only a few well-selected activities for each child in the family and store things that are not being used (or for a younger child to use when they get older). Ideally, this storage will be easy to access and keep organized. When things are difficult to reach, we are less likely to store and rotate the activities. Toy rotation can continue until the children are no longer playing with toys (around 12 years old).

ROOM BY ROOM

Here are some ideas and considerations for preparing each room of our home. These lists encourage us to look at our spaces with fresh eyes to see what we may be able to add, adjust, or perhaps subtract.

Entryway

This is a space that welcomes every member of the family into the home and bids them farewell on their way out. It could have:

- A place to sit to take off shoes and a place to store them.
- A place for keys and to hang up bags and coats/jackets/raincoats.
- A basket for umbrellas.
- A full-length mirror to check themselves in before heading out the door.
- Tissues and sunscreen at the ready.
- Plants to add color and a natural ambience.
- A place to pause, set down the burdens of the outside world, and transition into the refuge of home. It could be a doormat to wipe our feet on, indoor shoes or slippers to switch into, or a sign or piece of art that reminds us that we are home.

Living room

The living room can be the heart of the home, the locus of family connection. Every member of the home feels welcome here and has a sense of ownership of this space. Play spaces can be created in the living room as this is the space where the family "lives" and spends their time, which means children often spend their time here playing. There may be space for a separate play room, but it is not necessary. The living room could have:

- Comfortable seating for adults and children to sit or lie down on for conversation, reading, watching a family movie, hanging out with guests, or spending time together.
- A low table for games and other shared activities.
- A music player and/or instruments for shared experiences with music and dancing.

- Toys and other items that promote collaboration, such as building blocks, train sets, puzzles, Legos, games, supplies for drawing or painting, and books that can be enjoyed by old and young. These can be kept accessible on a low shelf.

- A place to display our child's art—both made and found. This can be a designated spot on the wall for hanging art, or a table, basket, frame, or shelf for displaying found items. We can display them for a while, then replace them with new treasures.

- A flower, rock, or leaf arrangement that showcases our child's creativity and (found) seasonal items while also adding beauty and character to the space.

- Plants that can be taken care of by our children

- If the family has a TV, monitor, or projector, it can be in this space but preferably not as the focal point. Specific shows can be watched together as a family and discussed. As our children get older, the family can choose to have designated shows or screen time, but more time can be given to other activities that actively engage the senses.

- A rug and/or the ability to easily move furniture to open up the floor space for floor play, "indoor camping" and other floor-based activities, and big work for a 6- to 12-year-old.

- Floor mats that can be rolled out to mark an area where the children are playing. Using a mat also keeps blocks, Legos, and loose parts in a contained area.

- Items that lend comfort and coziness, like blankets and pillows.

WHEN THERE IS MORE THAN ONE CHILD

- We can use lower shelves for items that are safe for any younger siblings, such as blocks, baskets of animals, vehicles, and Magna-Tiles and higher shelves for things for an older child that may have small or fragile parts.

- For small parts, use containers that are difficult for a younger child to open.

- Create clear spaces where each child can go to be alone; for example, the dining table or a tent made from a blanket and two chairs with a sign that says "Do not disturb."

See also pg. 67: Considerations for small, shared, and large rooms.

ELEMENTS OF A PREPARED ENVIRONMENT

Here are some ideas to incorporate into our spaces in the way that works best for our family with our space, budget, and style.

Kitchen sink with a modification to allow child to reach water

Sectional sofa in living room that can be moved around

Accessible art/craft materials

Instruments at the ready to play

Shelves—three or four shelves are useful.

Table and chairs appropriately sized for our child

Large spaces to play/work

Somewhere to keep shoes, bags, and keys in the entryway

A place to hang a daily routine, timetable, or calendar

Uncluttered storage for sports equipment and musical instruments

Accessible wardrobe with labels

Shelves above the bed for our child's special things or collections

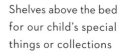

A display of some of of their schoolwork as artwork

A work/study area

Space to move

A place to read

A workshop

A display of cleaning supplies

Accessible cleaning supplies

Kitchen and dining area

The kitchen is an important space in the life of our child. So much learning, sensorial experience, and connection can happen in the kitchen. It is another space that can be shared by and adapted to every member of the family. We can set up our kitchen to allow collaboration with our children, and nearness when not collaborating. Meals are opportunities to connect and share—we can share our culture, history, and values with our children, and we can learn about their experiences and foster trust. Our kitchen can be set up to include:

- A work space that allows for our child's participation. This can be a low table or a stool to extend our child's reach.
- Child-sized tools and utensils like a cutting board, serrated knife, choppers, and other tools, like an egg slicer or carrot peeler.
- Tools for the older child to explore, like a blender, mixer, juicer, mechanical peeler, pasta maker, bread maker, ice cream maker, toaster/toaster oven, or measuring scale.
- Access to the oven and stovetop (with supervision).
- A snack area in a low cupboard or on a low shelf to encourage independent snack making. A level in our fridge can also be assigned to things our child needs for snack preparation. We can also have a snack table that is our child's size. They can set the table for a snack, pour drinks for themselves or siblings, and wipe up when done.
- If possible, a space for our child to sit with an activity when not participating in meal preparation. This is especially helpful for families with multiple children.
- Plates and utensils suitably sized for children and available at their height.
- Access to the dishwasher if we have one, or a cart for dirty dishes if the washing-up area or dishwasher is not accessible to a child.
- Ingredients for our child to use in making simple meals kept in accessible areas of the kitchen cabinets, pantry, and refrigerator. We can make sure containers are easy to open and a suitable size. For example, a small jug of milk for a younger child instead of a gallon jug.
- An accessible area with cleaning supplies like a broom, brush and dustpan, napkins, a feather duster, sponges, a mop, and rags to allow our child to contribute to the care of the home and clean up after themselves.
- An adjustable chair like the Stokke or a cushion or booster to help our child eat in a comfortable position when sitting at the dining table for family meals.
- Supplies to set the table for meals, again at their level. These can include tablecloths or place mats, dishes, and cutlery. Special table runners, flower arrangements, candles, and name cards can add ritual and ceremony to the process. Children who are learning to read and write will enjoy making and placing the name cards. Older children might enjoy learning different and more challenging ways to fold napkins.

Children will like the responsibility of making a meal and making it feel like a special occasion. They will also remember the ritual of setting the table when relatives or friends are visiting for a meal. It is a chance to add more cutlery for different courses like soup and dessert.

- Drinking water that our child can reach independently during the day. This could be in a dispenser, a refillable pitcher, or a water bottle.
- A large calendar where important dates and appointments can be noted, and also an interactive one for younger children where they can turn a disc or a block daily, weekly, and monthly. This supports their growing awareness of time and also provides an anchoring ritual.
- A clock to use in keeping track of time and routines.

Child's bedroom

If choosing a room for our child in a new home, we can consider our child's view from the windows and choose a room with good light and opportunities to observe nature, such as trees swaying, birds (and possibly birds' nests), the changing light as the day passes, the moon, and the signs of the seasons. If building a house, consider lower windows and even bay windows when possible.

The design and layout of our child's room can convey warmth, security, and comfort. This room is our child's space, where they can feel most centered, anchored, and balanced. We can consider what will transform the room from being any child's room to being our specific child's room. It can reflect their preferences and interests as much as possible. These can come through in color choices, fabric choices (sheets, curtains), wall hangings, art, and accessories. The room can be arranged simply and in an orderly manner with a consistent place for everything.

> "We must give the child an environment that he can utilize by himself: a little washstand of his own, a bureau with drawer he can open, objects of common use that he can operate, a small bed in which he can sleep at night under an attractive blanket he can fold and spread by himself. We must give him an environment in which he can live and play; then we will see him work all day with his hands and wait impatiently to undress himself and lay himself down on his own bed. He will dust the furniture, put it in order, take care to eat well, dress by himself, be gracious and tranquil, without tears, without tantrums, without naughtiness."
>
> —Dr. Maria Montessori, *The Child in the Family*

Preparing the environment for sleep

- An accessible bed allows our child to climb in and out on their own. A small twin frame is great for the 3- to 6-year-old child, or a bunk bed for a shared room. A larger bed can accommodate shared experiences like cuddling with or sleeping with a sibling, or lying together with us while we're reading bedtime stories or putting them to bed.

- A comfortable chair or rug could provide a spot for shared time with us and other adults.

- A fitted sheet and a simple blanket or quilt allow our child to make their own bed. If our child is still working on nighttime toilet independence, a waterproof sheet would protect the mattress and support independent cleanup.

- A bedside lamp is cozy for reading, and a night-light is useful for helping our child navigate any middle-of-the night visits to the bathroom.

- An end table or nightstand can hold accessories, a book that is being read at night, a cup or bottle of water for the night, or any belongings by the bed.

Getting dressed

- A regular closet can be modified with most of the clothes hanging or folded higher up and a few options for them at our child's eye level. We don't want the closet to be cluttered or too full; it should be easy for our child to take out and put away their clothes.

- It helps our child's sense of order to have a designated place for each category of clothing, such as shirts, sweaters, pants, skirts, dresses, socks, and shoes. Drawers, baskets, or boxes are great for this categorization. They can be labeled with pictures, name tags, or both.

- It is useful to have a few clothes that go together, like a capsule wardrobe that can be combined in different ways. This allows our child to make choices that are suitable for the season and occasion.

- A small chair, stool, or rug for sitting on to put on clothes can be helpful. As always, observe what works best for our child.

- A laundry bag or basket for dirty clothes accessible to our child. As our child gets older, we can provide options for sorting laundry into white clothing, colored clothing, dark clothing, and delicate items.

- A mirror that allows our child to see their full self from head to toe supports independent dressing as well as a sense of self.

Considerations for play, work, and other activities

- A music player to listen to and enjoy music and audiobooks.

- A place for books, maybe a small reading corner. Some options include a small standing shelf with a comfortable seat, a floating shelf on the wall for a few books, pockets hanging from a bed or chair, or a book basket.

- If the bedroom is also a play space, a shelf for a few (quiet) toys or activities that can be rotated.
- A table and chair, and a rug or open floor space for playing.
- A few pieces of furniture that are easy for a child to move so they can create forts, tents, and tea parties. These self-made spaces can be opportunities for a child to use their imagination and create private retreats.

Considerations for small, shared, and large rooms

- If the room is a shared space, each child can have some designated space that feels like theirs alone. We can paint the wall by each child's bed a different color or add wallpaper. They can each have a shelf by their bed for their special things, artwork near their bed around their interests, a special blanket on their bed, and a selection of books that they are reading on their bedside table. Dressers can have assigned drawers.
- In a small room, the bed can be elevated like a top bunk and the space underneath can be used as a work/play area.
- A large room can be arranged to still feel cozy and personal. Nooks and corners can be created for different purposes, like reading, resting, and sleeping.
- In a room shared by children in different planes of development, their individual needs will have to be considered. The older child could have belongings on higher shelves that cannot be reached by the younger child. Tables can be adjustable or have different levels to be used by different-age children or to grow with them.
- In a shared room, we can provide opportunities for privacy (especially as the children get older), like a curtain that can be drawn or a sign to indicate when they do not want to be disturbed.
- In small spaces, hang sports equipment, shelves, storage systems on the walls; remove pieces of furniture that are not used often; look for furniture that can be used for multiple purposes; paint storage cupboards the same color as the walls to make the space feel larger.

Adjustments in the bedroom for 6- to 12-year-old children

All of the above also applies for the 6- to 12-year-old child, but there are some extra things to consider as they grow.

The 6- to 12-year-old will want to be involved in setting up their room. They may have opinions about the furniture, colors, fabrics, layout, and art. If it is possible to make changes to their room as they grow, we can include them in the decision-making.

At around age 6, or when our child begins to tell time, they can have a wall or tabletop clock that is easy to read. A weekly or monthly calendar to note the passing of time and keep track of dates important to them such as birthdays, activities, and due dates could be added to the room.

It is also lovely to have something living they can care for. It can be a plant, a terrarium, or a family pet. A small animal like a fish, turtle, or hamster can live in their room or in other shared spaces.

If our child has toys or games in their room, a shelf with compartments will help maintain order. Our 6- to 12-year-old child is working on creating mental order and is not as concerned with external order. This means that they can be messy! Knowing this, we can create systems that help our child maintain their room in an orderly way. They can have fewer things and keep them in labeled containers. A time can also be agreed on (daily and weekly) when they tidy up and return their belongings to their designated places. They may need us to guide them in this process to break it down into smaller manageable tasks if they are feeling overwhelmed.

If our child has specific clothing, equipment, instruments, or materials for their extracurricular activities, we can provide designated storage spaces for these items with a checklist to help them stay organized.

Bathroom

The bathroom is a space that our child uses multiple times daily. We want it to be comfortable and offer support for our child's developing independence and sense of self. We need to ensure that it is accessible and safe. We can provide:

- For a younger child, a stable step stool to use in reaching the sink and low hooks or rods for a towel, washcloth, and other hanging items.
- A wall-mounted or pedestal mirror to use when brushing their hair and teeth.
- A small container for accessories and pocket treasures that might be removed in the bathroom.
- A container or accessible shelf to keep self-care tools like soap, a toothbrush, toothpaste, tissues, toilet paper or wipes, and a shower cap within their reach.
- A few water toys or other things that make bath time enjoyable, such as a hand shower, bubble bath, and bath bombs.
- A small bin that can be managed by our child.
- A toilet brush, mop or towel, and any other tools needed to clean up the toilet and bathroom after use.
- In a shared bathroom, visual prompts to remind each person to flush the toilet, wipe the seat, put down the lid, and wash their hands. Different-colored toothbrushes, hairbrushes, and hand towels can also help each child find the one that belongs to them.

Adult's spaces

Even older independent children who have their own room enjoy spending time with their parents or caregivers. This is usually in the morning, at the end of the day, and on weekends. Accommodations can be made to allow our children to feel welcome in our rooms, such as our work space or our bedroom. We may want them to feel comfortable in bed with us and/or provide a rug, a couch, or a chair where they can read a book or do an activity. That way, they are close.

Part of preparing our personal spaces for our children is setting and sharing our expectations and limits with them. There might be a time before which they are not allowed to enter our room or an expectation that they will knock and wait for a response before they enter or that they only enter when the sign on the door says they can. We need to communicate this to them. We can also provide some guidance for when it's time to leave or when privacy is wanted. These boundaries need to be defined.

If our children have access to our rooms, it is important to consider things in our room that might be unsafe or inappropriate for them; these will need to be out of our child's view and reach. We can also set boundaries around what they are allowed to touch in our room.

Considerations for a shared room (parents and child)

- In Montessori, independence extends to sleeping. However, some families choose to have a family bed or share a room with their children. This is a personal decision for each family.
- In the room where adults sleep, we can add a sleeping corner with a mattress that can be folded up or a convertible couch. Our child can come to sleep on this during the night if they are feeling sick or scared or are having trouble sleeping.
- In a shared family sleeping room, we can think about how each child can have their own space if needed, including clothes storage, a space to go to if they want to be alone, and a place to get dressed. The same can be done for the adults who share the space.

Playroom

If space allows, the considerations in setting up a playroom for our child are the same as in the other areas in our home, including beauty, order, and accessibility:

- Each activity has its own place. Toys with multiple pieces can be put together in a basket or container; keeping the components together allows our child to manage for themselves and makes it easy for our child to put them away when they are finished.
- We can provide seating and floor options for play and work, as well as a table and work surface.

- We can factor in the kinds of activities our child will be doing in this space. Perhaps we put a rug in part of the room and leave the floor bare where they do activities that might require cleanup, like painting or clay.

- Shelves can be used to display toys and games and art supplies. With children of mixed ages, we can designate the lower shelves for items suitable for all of our children, and activities with smaller pieces or fragile items can be placed on higher shelves out of reach of the younger children.

- Shelves don't always need to be placed side by side along the walls. We can create areas and nooks by placing shelves at a right angle to each other, creating cozy corners within the room. We can designate areas for different kinds of activities, such as making art or playing musical instruments.

- We can create an art supply area where they can find paper, pencils, a stapler, tape, yarn, and so on (see the Activities Appendix for ideas for activities' supplies).

- Art on the walls where our children can see it, sculptures they can touch, and found art from nature can become inspiration for their art.

For the 6- to 12-year-old child, we may not need to prepare activities. Instead, we can display interesting items for exploration and trays or baskets for gathering them. That said, it can still be valuable to display activities for older children rather than expect them to open a cupboard to find something of interest.

Outdoors

The outdoors is an important part of the home environment and can be prepared for our child's enjoyment, development, and safety. It's nice to have space and opportunities for movement and activities such as walking, running, riding a bike, skating, jumping, skipping, climbing, and playing catch and other ball games.

We can look to make space for a small atelier or woodworking shed where our child can build, create, and use their imagination, as well as their growing mathematical and analytical skills. We can hang safety goggles and tools at the ready, with a clear place for everything to be safely stored, such as a hammer, drill, saw, gloves, measuring tape, wood glue, and containers for small nails and screws. We show our children how the tools are used safely, we collaborate, then we step back and let them manage independently, providing supervision as needed. Woodworking can also be an opportunity for collaboration and shared activity with an adult.

Also allow space and opportunity for observation, exploration, and appreciation of nature. This can be in the form of:

- A vegetable garden or container garden to tend to while observing the life cycle of plants, their parts, and their functions, as well as the needs of different plants, and their soil.

- A flower garden or a few flowerpots to attract birds and insects and offer the beauty, colors, shapes, and scents of flowers
- Logs that can be climbed on or lifted to find little ecosystems such as frogs, worms, ants, termites, and other living things like mushrooms, moss, and algae

A small outdoor space can include potted plants, flowerpots, a bird feeder or birdbath, and other things that attract and reflect nature. If you have no outdoor space, make time to get to the local park, woods, or any nature spot nearby to offer these experiences.

We can provide ways for our child to document their observations, express their imagination, or capture inspiration found from being outdoors with materials, such as: art supplies for drawing and painting, an analog or digital camera, a nature journal, a leaf or flower press, and a jar in which to keep rocks, shells, or sticks.

We can provide places to rest and relax outdoors, for example, the shade of a tree, a hammock, a shaded outdoor space, a chair to sit in to read or simply to enjoy looking around, mats to lay out, or grassy space to lay on.

We can provide specialized equipment like a swing set, jungle gym, trampoline, bicycle, scooter, skateboard, wheeled cart, rollerblades, or roller skates. If we are near the seaside, we could look for a secondhand boogie board or surfboard. If there is a place to ice-skate in the winter, ice skates or strap-on skates could be useful.

Other tools to aid interaction with and care for the outdoors could include gardening tools (such as a watering can and a child-size rake, hoe, and spade), a water hose, a wheelbarrow, binoculars, a telescope, a magnifying glass, a bug catcher and holder, or a microscope to use in examining samples found outside.

Activities like painting, weaving, woodworking, gardening, upcycling, or crafting with recycled objects are great for the outdoors.

As much as possible, we can make the outdoor area safe so that children can be given freedom to explore it independently. We can prepare or provide appropriate clothing for different weather conditions to allow our children to enjoy the outdoors in every season. We can provide sunscreen, bug repellent, hats, and any other items that make for safe enjoyment of the outdoors accessible.

As our child gets older, the outdoor environment is not limited to the immediate space outside their home. They might visit friends, use community parks or playgrounds, ride their bikes or skate down the street, walk to a neighborhood shop, or hike a nearby trail. At this stage, part of the preparation of the outdoor environment becomes preparing our child to use and enjoy the outdoors.

We can show them how to:

- Pack a bag for an outing, perhaps helping them make their own checklists so they don't forget anything
- Safely cross the road
- Ride a bike
- Take a bus or other public transportation
- Greet people and ask for directions
- Spot signs of danger
- Take action in times of uncertainty or danger
- Memorize important phone numbers and addresses

Ideas for enhancing outdoor space in our home environment include:

- A walking path, either paved or made of rocks or stone slabs. At a Montessori school in rural Mexico, educator Meg McElwee used smooth rocks to create a beautiful spiral, labyrinthine walking path. At the entrance, there was a small chair where the children would sit and take off their shoes before entering the labyrinth barefoot.
- A sand pit.
- A balance beam made with a log, a wood plank, or a raised board.
- Hand-built hills or other variations to the land.
- Climbable trees.
- An easel for doing artwork outside.
- Space to play sports, like soccer, basketball, or badminton.
- A water source.
- Containers for collecting water.

In cases where there is minimal access to an outdoor space, here are some suggestions:

- A balcony can be set up be to child-friendly and safe. It can include an easel, or a table to sit at and paint or play, some plants to care for, a bird feeder, or a simple chair to sit in and watch the world go by.
- A little window garden or compost bin can bring some nature in.
- A younger child might be able to ride a small bicycle in our home's hallways.
- Soft balls to kick or throw into a basket or hoop or to one another, which can be used inside.
- Pillows, cushions, rugs, and other floor coverings can bring opportunities for gross-motor movements into indoor living spaces. These can be used to set up obstacle courses. An area can be provided for practicing cartwheels, somersaults, or yoga. A small trampoline or climbing wall can be added to the space.

PSYCHOLOGICAL PREPARATION

The psychological environment is the intangible part of our home. The atmosphere within our home, how our child and others feel there—this, too, needs to be prepared.

Love: Our home can be a place of emotional safety for our child. The love is tangible and intangible. We can express our joy and enjoyment in our children through the time we spend with them and our attitude on seeing them and being with them. We smile, laugh, have conversations, hug them, listen to them, and are present, in the moment, with them.

Acceptance and belonging: We can create a feeling of acceptance by the way we prepare our home with consideration for our child in each space. Also by the way we speak to and react to our children. Accepting them for who they are and not trying to change them into who we want them to be. Involving them in decisions that affect them as well as the family.

A friendly attitude toward mistakes: Our attitude toward mistakes also affects the psychological environment. We want our home to be a place where it is okay to make mistakes. Accidents happen, and we help our child learn how to fix it and try again.

Trust: Our trust in our child's ability as well as their trust in us also constitutes the psychological environment. We show our trust in them in the way we encourage them to build their independence by allowing them to do things they feel they are capable of instead of insisting on helping. We also allow them to participate and contribute to our home even when it is not convenient and their effort is not perfect. Most times it is easier, faster, and more efficient to do things ourselves, but when we include our children, they build trust in themselves and in us.

Our emotional and mental state: Another part of the psychological environment is the adult's emotional and mental state as well as the relationship between the adults in the home. When we are stressed, angry, unhappy, anxious, fearful, or frustrated, our child feels and absorbs these emotions. Children are very perceptive and sense when things are not okay. It is important to know this and ensure that we take care of ourselves and our relationships to promote a positive atmosphere and make sure they see us resolve any conflicts.

We will discuss this preparation in detail in chapter 8, "Preparation of the Adult."

NUSAIBAH & NOAH

Rumi Montessori
UK & Malaysia

"There's a huge emphasis in the Montessori philosophy about respecting and trusting the child. For me, as a Muslim, I see this as part of our faith; we should already trust and respect the child. With my work in Islamic Montessori, it's not so much about trying to make Montessori Islamic, but more about trying to understand that all these Montessori principles of love and respect are already part of the teachings of our Prophet. As Muslims, we should be people who have this trust, love, honor, and respect for the child, and we should strive to follow the natural development of the child, their fitrah."

"I knew he was autistic from when he was quite young. I decided to take his autism as a gift, and embrace it positively with all that it comes with, rather than taking it on as a challenge. I found the art of observation to be the best tool that's helped me as a mother to an autistic child. When observing, we learn to be objective; we get to find out what is really happening rather than seeing our own narrative. This is where I learned so much about Noah's needs and how I can support him. He was interested in birds of prey for 2 years, we had so much fun exploring this interest. He was very unique and did many things differently. Through observing, we got to find his triggers and understand his challenges. It was always interesting for people to observe him and say, 'I've never seen anyone do anything like that.' It was truly amazing."

"The fruits of all the work we put in as Montessori parents really blossom in the adolescent years. When you have an adolescent who has been through the Montessori philosophy from birth, they're very self-directed: They know who they are, they know who they want to be, and they don't get swayed by peer pressure as much because they have their own concept of who they are and what's right and what's wrong. They have a strong moral sense and clarity on what they want to do and not do. It becomes a pleasure to see them grow into these wonderful young adults who are ready to take part in society and make a positive impact."

MONTESSORI ACTIVITIES FOR CHILDREN

5

In the previous chapters, we learned about our child, their characteristics and needs, and how they develop. Now we are going to look at how we can support their development. Our goal is not to replicate a Montessori classroom. We are looking to find ways to support our child's interests, seize upon learning moments that occur naturally through daily life in a fun way, and encourage our child to become a lifelong learner.

When many think of Montessori, they think of specific materials and toys. While these Montessori activities are valuable, there are more important things that can't be purchased but can make all the difference in our child's development. That is where we'll start.

CONSIDERATIONS FOR SUPPORTING OUR CHILD'S DEVELOPMENT

Time

The first way we can support our child's development is by giving them time. Just like a plant that grows from a seed, our child needs time, nurturing, and warmth to grow and thrive. We can set aside some time each day to connect with and focus on each of our children. This time spent together is how they learn to feel secure in our love.

Children need time to explore. This is time when they are free to choose how to occupy themselves, indoors or outdoors (and ideally both). This is undirected free time when they can follow their inner guides. They need time to explore their environment with all of their senses. To make messes, chase butterflies, and roll in the grass. To sit quietly and read a book, or work on an activity, or share a game of hide-and-seek. To get to know themselves and others. To make friends, build relationships and memories.

Children need time to experience boredom. We might worry about our child being bored and feel like we need to entertain them or ensure that they are always engaged in an activity—but children actually need periods when they have nothing to do. This is when they can reflect and figure out for themselves how to fill their time. As children get older, and especially from ages 6 to 12, time to be bored is usually what spurs big work. So when our child comes to us and complains of boredom, we can tell them it's okay to feel that way and that it's a good time to come up with new ideas.

Children need time to observe. As we know, the child from 0 to 6 years old has an absorbent mind that soaks in everything they observe. For the 6- to 12-year-old child, observation is how they make connections and find things to question and understand. Junnifa remembers her children stopping during walks to watch ants carrying food, watching a stock person stack boxes at the grocery store, or watching a plumber fix a leak in their house. This observation is part of their self-construction, so it's okay to slow down for them to observe and not interrupt them. When our child observes us, we can be conscious of our movements and do things carefully so that they can take in the details when we're working, cleaning, cooking, or writing

Children need time to repeat. Repetition is the way that humans perfect their skills and abilities. Many times, we'll notice our child finish doing something and choose to do it again immediately. Children, especially those from 3 to 6 years old, are less focused on the outcome than on the process, so they will repeat an activity over and over again, or possibly repeat just one step of the activity. We might see a child tie a shoelace and immediately untie it to try again, or ask us to read the same book over and over. Repetition can be a clue to what sensitive period they might be in or to an interest they might be working on. It can be a sign that they are concentrating. The 6- to 12-year-old repeats, too, but not necessarily in the same way each time; they often repeat with variations, like making paper airplanes again and again but making them slightly different each time.

Children need time to solve their problems. Dr. Montessori said to "never help a child with a task at which he feels he can succeed." This means that we first assess whether the child actually thinks they can do it. There's usually a thin line between struggle and frustration, especially with younger children. We observe our child when they are struggling, and if it seems they are tipping over into frustration, we can step in and ask if we can help. If they accept our help, then we need to *help them to help themselves*—giving just enough help and showing them how to do it themselves. For example, an older child might be struggling with an idea or question that they're trying to understand. Instead of giving the answer, we can show them how to use a dictionary or encyclopedia. A young child might be getting frustrated trying to unbuckle their shoes. If they accept our offer to help, instead of taking off the shoes completely for them, we can show them how to pull the strap to undo the buckle. We can encourage them if they need it: "I think you can do it!" or "Keep trying" or "You can do hard things." We offer just enough help to still allow the child to experience and own their success.

Children need time to rest. They need time to sleep, to be quiet and still. A lot of consolidation happens while children rest and sleep. We can build quiet time into our child's day. This can be a nap or just a time to lay down and rest their bodies. As much as possible, it is also important for children to go to bed early. For children between 3 and 12 years old, 7:00 to 8:30 p.m. is a reasonable time in general.

Children need time for communication and connection with us. We stop to listen, to take turns in conversation, to ask questions, to allow them to ask questions, to use rich language, to be together, and to be a safe place for them to express themselves. We will also need time to practice grace and courtesy, which we will cover more in chapter 6.

Purposeful activity

Children need purposeful activity. Dr. Montessori wrote in *The Absorbent Mind* that the child from 3 to 6 years old needs such hands-on purposeful experiences to perfect, enrich, and understand all they absorbed in the first 3 years and to see their effect on the environment. We can set up our environment to encourage spontaneous and natural activity as well as prepare activities based on our child's needs and interests; for example, their need at this age for movement, language, and refinement of the senses.

When we offer purposeful activities, we see our child find meaning in their work; they feel like they are making a contribution, we see deep concentration, and when we offer them real objects and experiences, they know we trust them.

> "So we must have interest first and then work with an intelligent purpose,
> work which is freely chosen by the individual."
>
> —Dr. Maria Montessori, *The 1946 London Lectures*

Purposeful work for the 6- to 12-year-old child involves thought, problem-solving, and the building of new understanding and connections. The child's goal is intellectual independence, so purposeful work helps direct and strengthen thought. For example, pre-measured ingredients for baking might be purposeful for a child younger than 6 years old, but a more purposeful setup for a 6- to 12-year-old would involve them figuring out what ingredients are needed. This can be by reading a recipe, gathering the ingredients, and figuring out the measurements.

Process versus product

Notice that when doing activities, the child from 3 to 6 years old is more interested in the process than the product, and they will often focus on one part of the process, repeating it many times.

The older child from 6 to 12 years old is different. They are no longer driven by just the desire for movement; they are interested in the product or result. They like responsibility and can be given freedom to execute tasks in ways that reflect and display their abilities. They want to be involved in aspects of running the family, like creating a meal plan for the week, researching a vacation, making a list for grocery shopping, or planning the daily routine or schedule. All of these tasks also provide opportunities for the child to acquire and refine physical, cognitive, and social skills. They build responsibility and prepare the child for life.

Follow the child

An important note: There are so many ways we can support our child's development; it can seem overwhelming! The suggestions outlined in this book are not meant to be done all at once or even at all. Remember, we follow our child's interests and their timeline, and use them as a starting point for exploration. That said, a child does not leave school for the day and stop learning. We hope to give you support on how you can help your child develop a true love of, interest in, and wonder at the world around them and want to make a difference in it.

Other tips

- At home, children might choose to work with multiple activities concurrently and might not return each activity before bringing out a second one. This is fine as long as they do not have so many things out that it becomes chaotic, disorderly, or overwhelming to clean up. We can set limits on the maximum number of things that can be out before we pack some up and help them notice and recognize when things are getting out of hand.

- A younger child may want to have everything they need on a tray and at the ready. Then we will notice when they are also able to collect the things they will need onto a tray themselves. For example, fetching a tray, choosing some paper and a pencil, and bringing the tray to the table to work.

Choosing toys

When choosing toys, it's ideal to choose "passive" toys that the child needs to actively manipulate and explore. Avoid "active" toys, which are designed to entertain the child and the child is mostly passive, like a toy that sings a song when the child pushes a button.

We also want to select toys that are aiding their development. We can look at what skills our child is showing interest in and working to master. We prefer toys made from natural materials, which are often more environmentally friendly than those made from plastic and also provide more and richer sensorial qualities in areas like color, weight, size, and texture.

We want to choose toys (and furniture) that will grow with our child, items that can continue to be used over time, can be used in a new way, and can later be sold or passed on to another family. We can look for toys that invite both individual and collaborative play with friends and/or siblings; encourage thinking, problem-solving, and analysis; and foster concentration and focus.

We want to be mindful of consumption and not buy lots of materials. Most of the suggestions in this chapter and the Activities Appendix to support our child's development do not require additional materials or can be made using things we already have in our homes.

We can buy secondhand, go to thrift stores, reuse packaging for art materials, rent rather than buy toys, set up a sharing community, search freecycle groups, borrow items from the library and share with friends, and repair rather than replace.

Our favorite way to source materials is to head out into nature and find items there. Have fun being creative while inspiring our children to be caretakers of our Earth.

WHY MONTESSORI ACTIVITIES ARE IMPORTANT

Dr. Montessori said that the child develops through "means of their own activity." We can support this by making a wide range of activities available to our child. When choosing activities, we call to mind our knowledge of the *human tendencies*, the characteristics of the *planes of development* that our child is in, and the *sensitive periods* we observe them in.

We see children in Montessori classrooms calm, focused, and at ease. When a child is engaged in an activity that meets their needs and interests, they experience what psychologist Mihaly Csikszentmihalyi calls a flow state. When in a flow state, a child is calm and regulated. The more often they experience a flow state, the easier it is for them to come back to calm when dysregulated. If we do not find activities to challenge our children, they will challenge us.

Activities for the 3- to 6-year-old child

We know that the human tendencies for exploration, orientation, order, communication, movement, work, repetition, and self-perfection are dominant in the first plane. We also know that the child from 3 to 6 years old is consciously working on refining the acquisitions they made in the period from 0 to 3 years old and that they are in the sensitive periods for movement, language, and the refinement of senses. All of these are considerations when providing opportunities and activities for our 3- to 6-year-olds.

We can provide our child with opportunities to experience things with all of their senses. They can classify the world around them: grading pine cones from biggest to smallest; refining their sense of smell with smelling jars or while cooking in the kitchen; or putting on a blindfold and exploring different textures.

When they ask us "what?" we can give them rich vocabulary to understand the world they are absorbing. When they ask us "why?" we can help them look up the answer in a book or encyclopedia, or find an expert to ask, or create hands-on experiences for them to discover the answer for themselves.

Introducing a new activity to a 3- to 6-year-old

Some of the activities we set up for our child will be intuitive and easy for them to figure out on their own. Others will require us to model or demonstrate to get them started. The following are some considerations and steps for modeling or introducing new activities.

- Ensure that we have set up all the required items or parts of the activity and that they are logically arranged. These may be displayed on a tray or for the child to fetch the parts needed.
- Practice in advance to make sure we understand the sequence we want to follow.
- Set up the activity on a shelf or where we would like it to go.
- Choose a time when our child is calm and when we have the time and attention to immerse ourselves fully in the activity.
- Invite our child: "I have something interesting I want to show you." We shouldn't force them to join us; we should respect their decision not to if they are not interested.
- Go with them to retrieve the activity from its location so they know where to return it to when they are finished.
- Let the child know that we will show them and then they will get a chance to do it too. This encourages them to wait patiently while we show them the activity.
- Sit in such a way that the child has a good view of our hands. Ideally, they sit on our nondominant side because we will mostly be using our dominant hand.
- Introduce them to the activity, giving vocabulary for the activity, parts, and steps.
- Demonstrate the activity, making sure to minimize words when demonstrating so that the child can focus on the actions.
- Let the child have a turn. Be careful not to correct or interrupt. If we notice something that needs correction or emphasis, wait until they are done, then ask to take another turn and emphasize the necessary steps.
- When the child is working independently, step away and allow them to repeat the activity as many times as they want. We can remind them to pack up and put it away when done.
- We can observe from a distance.

Activities for the 6- to 12-year-old child

The 6- to 12-year-old child now uses their logical, reasoning mind, which asks "Why?" and "How?" They want to understand how the world works, how things fit together, the origin of things, and the workings of the universe. Their imagination is active, and they are able to conceive of a different time and place. This is a great time to:

- Encourage big work (projects that take a long period of time and/or take up a lot of space).
- Go out into the community to learn about areas of interest.
- Challenge and promote their critical thinking skills: Ask them questions; explore their questions with them; get them to back up their opinions; encourage them to research and debate topics arising in current affairs.
- Share stories (including fantasy stories).
- Help them develop their language for classification and observation.
- Honor their love of hero worship by delving into history, civilization, great inventions, and people who made or make a difference.

Cosmic education

For the 6- to 12-year-old child, cosmic education becomes very important. Cosmic education is the idea that everything in our cosmos—people, animals, plants, etc.— has a purpose (its cosmic task), and that everything in the universe is interconnected. The child learns to develop respect for, and be gentle with, all living things (even those that may sometimes annoy them like flies, wasps, ants, or spiders).

With their love of big ideas and big work, curiosity, imagination, and interest in social and moral development, the 6- to 12-year-old will enjoy exploring this concept. They will also learn that they have a special role to play, as well as an opportunity to make a difference in the world, be it in their family, school, or local or global community.

We can begin to introduce these concepts to the 3- to 6-year-old child. We can discuss with them what plants need to grow and why we are gentle with insects they find, and talk about the water cycle, the sun and moon, and anything else they show interest in as they explore the world around them.

An example of cosmic education would be talking with our child about the food we eat and all the people and factors that made it possible. The person who planted the seeds and nurtured them. The soil in which it grew, the water that nourished it, the worms that made the soil nutritious, the insects that pollinated it. The person who harvested it, the one who transported it for processing, the person who processed it, packaged it, sold it,

WHAT WE CAN OBSERVE

- Interests: topics they talk about; observations they make while exploring; which activities they are drawn to, etc.

- What movements they are mastering: how they hold their pencil; how they climb, swing on monkey bars, etc.

- Activities they choose: how long they work with each activity; how much of the activity they do; what they do with the materials; whether they have mastered the activity.

- Where they use the activity: how they retrieve the activity from the shelf; how they carry it to a mat or table; whether they return it to the shelf when finished.

- Independence: whether they choose activities independently; what aids their independence; any obstacles (including ourselves) to independence; how they ask for help; if they accept help, etc.

- Focus: Look for moments when they are deeply focused as well as when they are distracted by someone or something but still able to come back to the activity. Note when their breathing is smooth; when they are regulated; when they look satisfied at completion.

- Concentration: what breaks their concentration; where they concentrate best; how we support their concentration (mostly this is by not interrupting; at times we can step in to help a little then step back again to let them get further).

- Repetition: if they repeat an activity; if they repeat in the same way or with variety.

and cooked/prepared it. The person who will pick up the trash when we throw away the leftovers, the bugs that will break it down. They can learn all these interdependencies and that everyone has a role. They will enjoy finding more connections like this.

Interdisciplinary education

While in many non-Montessori schools, subjects are taught separately, in our Montessori classrooms, we recognize that all subjects are interconnected. For example, while focusing on science, we also touch on math, geography, culture, language, and more. We can help the child to realize that everything in life is interrelated.

TYPES OF MONTESSORI ACTIVITIES

IN THE ACTIVITIES APPENDIX, which begins on page 232, we provide dozens of activities for everything from reading and writing to sensorial experiences to learning about the natural world to music and art. We can pick the ones that speak to our child's interests at the moment and return to the list when we see that they've entered a new interest, sensitive period, or stage of development.

IF YOU'D LIKE INSPIRATION BASED ON THEIR INTERESTS, you can refer to the online appendix titled "Activity appendix based on interest" at workman.com/montessori to get you started. Montessori is a truly holistic approach to the child, and one area of interest can be a springboard for many areas of development. For example, an interest in rainbows could cover art, science, language (vocabulary, books, poetry), etc.

SOME COMMON QUESTIONS ABOUT SUPPORTING OUR CHILD'S DEVELOPMENT

How can we nurture our child's concentration?

We can help build their concentration by:

- Minimizing interruptions—we can wait as long as possible before interrupting them to offer them help, to ask them a question, or call them for a meal.
- Allowing boredom—long blocks of unscheduled time allow them to get bored, come up with creative ideas, and take these ideas deeper and further.
- Minimizing devices—limiting the availability of screens will keep them as active learners for more of the day.
- Modeling concentration—we can take time to pursue our own hobbies, like sewing, gardening, or building.
- Observing—when the choices available in our home follow their interests based on our observation, they will be more focused on these activities.
- Learning what concentration looks like for our child—for example, is their breathing smooth when they are concentrating? Do they stick out their tongue? Do their eyes stay focused on the activity and do they not notice what is going on around them? Do they go back to their activity even after being distracted?
- Preparing the environment—have a table facing a wall, a place they can go where they won't be disturbed, or a work mat that can keep everything together for them to focus on.

How can we make the activities inviting?

How we arrange the activities in our home will often determine how our child uses them. Here are a few helpful tips:

- **Storage.** It helps to have a place to store toys that are not currently in use. We can use tubs or boxes to separate different categories by types, interests, and ages.

- **Shelves.** It helps to have open shelves where our child can easily see what is available. This is preferable to a big toy box, where it can be difficult to see what's available and often the contents get dumped out onto the floor, leaving a mess.

- **Order.** We can arrange the activities on the shelf from easiest to hardest. This helps the child orient themselves. If an activity is too difficult, they can try an easier one to the left; if it's too easy, they can try a harder one to their right. We can also arrange materials so that our child's movements are from left to right as indirect preparation for reading and to give them practice crossing the midline. In countries where we read from right to left, we can set up the activities for the child to move from right to left.

- **Group similar items together.** This helps them to know where things belong, and it can also help manage the energy in different parts of our home. We may have a quiet reading area next to activities for fine-motor-skill coordination like puzzles and some climbing equipment near other activities with larger movements like music.

- **Less is more.** It is easier for the child to choose an activity when there is a curated selection for them to choose from. If we have everything stored in a cupboard or toy box with things on top of other things, it is difficult to see what is available. Similarly, having too many toys out at one time makes it more difficult to choose and find those things that are available. We could select as few as six toys per child and rotating those activities that are not being used.

- **Containers.** Look for baskets, trays, and boxes to display the activities that are made of natural materials and that the child can manage themselves. We can use clever wall storage to hold jars filled with materials for arts and crafts.

How can we help our child with homework?

If our child is at a non-Montessori school and receives homework, we may need to help them from time to time. Our goal is to provide as little help as possible and as much as necessary.

If our child is having a problem understanding their homework, we can look to create a hands-on opportunity for them to understand it more clearly; help them create a science experiment to bolster their comprehension of the topic; go to the library or find an expert whom they can interview to find out more about the subject.

Helping them with homework will then take longer than answering the question for them because we are helping them to understand the concepts and learn how to find answers to things they don't know.

Depending on our child we can check in daily or weekly to see if they need help with their planning. We can scaffold these skills until they are able to plan their homework and any study independently.

How can we cultivate imagination and creativity?

Some people have the impression that Montessori limits creativity because of the focus on activities with defined purposes and because we focus on reality over fantasy in those first 6 years. In fact, Dr. Montessori spoke a lot about imagination. One of our favorite quotes of hers on the topic appears in *To Educate the Human Potential*: "The secret of good teaching is to regard the child's intelligence as a fertile field in which seeds may be sown, to grow under the heat of flaming imagination. Our aim therefore is not merely to make the child understand, and still less to force him to memorize, but so to touch his imagination as to enthuse him to his inmost core."

Here are some ideas for cultivating creativity and imagination in our child:

Start with reality. In the first 6 years, we help our child explore the real world with all the senses. They are still working out the difference between reality, pretend, and fantasy, so when we come across a book with a dog driving a car, we can help guide them. "Do dogs really drive cars? No, that's pretend." Once they have a strong foundation in reality in the first plane, everything they have explored will become a springboard for their imagination in the second plane. If in the first plane the child has seen many towers in person and in books, in the second plane they may come up with a design for their own tower that is beyond anything they have seen or experienced.

Allow them to process all they have taken in. We will see the 3- to 6-year-old child doing a lot of pretend play with objects around them. They will pretend to bake a cake, go to school, nurse the baby, or be a dog. We don't discourage this play. We observe them and see them processing and making sense of what they have absorbed around them. We also don't have to give them prescriptive items for such play, like a doctor's kit or a firefighter's hat. We can give them open-ended items like scarves or blocks for them to explore in their own way.

Let them explore with the eyes of the mind. Once they are 6 years old, the children want to explore the universe, beyond what they can touch and feel and instead explore with their imagination. This has been described as using the eyes of the mind, not just the body—such a rich description of the 6- to 12-year-old child's imagination.

Encourage them to solve their own problems. Montessori children learn to solve problems for themselves. They are not given solutions or formulas but come up with these themselves from manipulating materials, doing calculations, and undertaking research and experiments. When they don't know an answer, they look for ways to find out.

Promote working with others. They also look to come up with creative solutions with others. In chapter 6, we explore this social development in detail, learning to be part of and to serve their community.

Provide a rich environment. In our homes, we set up interesting invitations and materials for them to make discoveries, and as much as possible, we have beautiful, good-quality art materials for them to use. There is beauty around them in the form of flowers, plants, and artwork. We include a lot of natural materials, and they also have opportunities to connect with nature outside the home. They have their culture represented as well and perhaps access to a workshop or atelier. All this makes their environment a space for creativity and using their imagination.

Avoid prescriptive workbooks and coloring books. A variety of papers and materials will help them come up with their own ideas, rather than follow someone else's. We don't prescribe to them that the sky has to be blue or the grass green. We show them how materials are used and then let them use their own imagination.

Prepare ourselves. We can ask, not tell. "Would you like to tell me about what you made?" We can allow long stretches of uninterrupted time to play and get bored, a breeding ground for creative ideas. We can focus on the process rather than the result. "I see you were working for a long time positioning things carefully and gluing them in place." And we can be okay with things being a little messier as the child gets creative.

Go outside. Spending time outdoors or in nature provides endless inspiration and can be a source of interesting treasures that can be brought home and used in projects. We can also attend dance and music performances and visit art galleries and other cultural spaces to admire others' work, meet creative people, and get new ideas.

YULIYA, KLAAS-WILLEM, YVANN, NATASHA

Welcome to Montessori
Netherlands & Ukraine

"Now that our children are in the second plane, we can really see how their world is expanding. Our 10-year-old is particularly interested in world affairs and news. He's trying to understand how and why certain things happen, is more curious about travel to places he learns about, etc. It's magical to watch his world grow from our small village to the whole world, and more!"

"Our home is a mixture of so many cultures and languages at any time. My first language is Russian (I speak this to the children), my husband speaks Frisian (a regional language in the Netherlands), and when we are all together, we tend to speak English. I cook Russian/Ukrainian food at home, we watch movies and read books in Russian, and we keep up with some traditions that I grew up with, too. We just try to offer exposure without forcing anything."

"Our family has benefited from Montessori in so many ways, especially after I became paralyzed. We really see the independence and trust that comes with Montessori at home. When I was first injured, I lost my independence and had to relearn how to do everything. I saw how so many people would take over tasks for me or make assumptions about what I could or could not do. My husband and I talked so much about this, and he helped to set up our home in a way that allowed me to be completely independent. Especially when one is in a wheelchair, the

limited mobility can mean that our spaces will look different or we need help with preparing the environment. It's okay to do things differently than what one sees on social media."

SUPPORTING OUR CHILD'S SOCIAL AND MORAL DEVELOPMENT

6

Montessori is known for fostering independence in children. Less understood is that the purpose of raising independent children is to build a stronger society. In this chapter, we will explore how our child can become a person in society, confident in themselves, aware of and accepting of others, able to recognize injustice, and empowered to take action.

> "One can speak of a true community only when each member of the group feels sufficiently free to be himself, while simultaneously restricting his own freedom for the sake of adjustment to the group. It is in seeking an optimal solution to this tension between personal independence and dependence on the group that the social being is formed. Too much individual freedom leads to chaos, too much uniformity, imposed by adults, leads to impersonal conformity or to rebellion."
>
> —Mario M. Montessori Jr., *Education for Human Development*

FOSTERING SOCIAL DEVELOPMENT

The day our child is born, they are in community with others. Their first community is their immediate family. Then comes their extended family, any other caregivers, and the people they meet in their daily life (at the library, the market, a playgroup, etc.). When our child is between 3 and 6 years old, their community will often expand to include their preschool, where they are working out how to live in a mini society with others. They may also visit friends' homes and attend classes or participate in activities with or without us. From ages 6 to 12, our child sees their society extend to their school, neighbors, friends, and the wider community.

Our child's *social development* is how they interact with others, how they get along with others, and how they understand other people and their needs.

Children learn social behavior from their environments. Ideally, our child is spending time in caring environments and experiencing positive social interactions. We can prepare them to navigate new or different environments by offering them lessons in grace and courtesy. We can help them learn how to be respectful, how to understand the social norms of our culture, and how to behave in certain social situations. As the adult, we can also model these things—being intentional with the language we use and in our daily manners, and when showing respect and care for ourselves, our child, and others.

OBSERVING OUR CHILD

To understand how we can best support our child with their social development, we can observe the following:

- **HOW THEY INTERACT WITH OTHER CHILDREN.** Do they initiate play or conversation? Do they prefer parallel play? Do they seek out others to play with? How do they respond when children would like to play with them?

- **HOW THEY RESPOND TO NEW SITUATIONS.** Do they take time to warm up in social situations? Do they walk in and immediately find something or someone to play with?

- **HOW THEY RESPOND TO US AND OTHER ADULTS.**

- **HOW THEY RESPOND IN A GROUP.** Do they listen to instructions? Do they like doing group sports? Do they know how to wait their turn?

- **HOW THEY RESOLVE CONFLICT.** Do they find solutions with their siblings/ friends/other children on the playground? Do they need assistance? Do they come to ask for help when needed?

- **HOW THEY TAKE OTHERS INTO CONSIDERATION.**

- **WHAT OPPORTUNITIES THEY HAVE FOR SOCIAL DEVELOPMENT.** This can be friends of the same age or different ages, siblings, cousins, adults, after-school activities, visits to the playground or community center, volunteer work (for younger children, volunteering with us; for older children, perhaps helping a neighbor or working at an animal shelter).

Dr. Montessori talked about the importance of developing *social cohesion*—when a community works together for the good of everyone. We can help our child consider not just what is good for them but also what is good for others around them—children on the playground, people in the supermarket, passengers on the train, or our neighbors.

We can help our child explore their cosmic task—a Montessori term that broadly means "one's purpose"—and the cosmic tasks of others. We can help them understand how all life on Earth is interdependent. We can help our child think beyond their role in our family or their classroom. We can encourage them to think about the planet and their responsibility to protect it; to serve others in our community and, as the child gets older, further afield; or to participate in such events as the Montessori Model United Nations—a forum where children from around the world act as ambassadors of different countries and present their policies—if the resources or a scholarship are available.

FOSTERING MORAL DEVELOPMENT

"Moral education is the source of the spiritual equilibrium on which everything else depends and which may be compared to the physical equilibrium or sense of balance without which it is impossible to stand upright, or move into any other position."

–Dr. Maria Montessori, *From Childhood to Adolescence*

As parents, we want to raise children who have a strong moral compass, who can discern between right and wrong. We want our child to do the right thing even when it is difficult. We want them to do the right thing because it is right and not because they want to be praised for doing it. We want to raise our child to have a strong character and to listen to their inner guide. We want our child to be secure in their beliefs and their abilities. To have a strong awareness of self and the ability to relate to others.

During the first plane of development, our child is absorbing more than just language and culture—they are also soaking in the values and beliefs that will become the foundation of their moral development. If we want our child to be kind, polite, courteous, patient, determined, generous, honest, optimistic, charitable, flexible, and inclusive, we must reflect these values in our attitude toward them and toward others. We can try to ensure that the communities where our child spends time—school, friends' houses, religious spaces—also share our values.

We can also explicitly tell our child what we expect of them. Different societies have different behavioral expectations—we are responsible for helping our children understand the expectations of our family and community. Of course, no one is perfect (even parents!), so we can also expect our child to hold us accountable when we do not live up to our values. We can encourage our children to question things they don't understand, to not blindly obey, and to learn to make good judgments.

If we have religious beliefs, these will also become a part of our child's moral development. We can share our beliefs with our child and help them develop their own sense of right and wrong.

EXTRA CONSIDERATIONS FOR THE 6- TO 12-YEAR-OLD CHILD'S SOCIAL AND MORAL DEVELOPMENT

The time from ages 6 to 12 is when our child's morals are solidified, but first they go through a period of testing and questioning our rules and values, poking to find any holes and exceptions. Our older child uses their logical, reasoning mind. They want to understand the whys and hows. The "how much" and "how often." They want to know the limits, conditions, and exceptions to all things, including morals.

Dr. Montessori called the years from ages 6 to 12 "the age of rudeness." We may observe that they are inclined to "tattle" or report on others. This is exploration—our child wants to see our response to help them judge whether something is right or wrong. They also may push the limits, with rude behavior and language. When this happens, it is important for us to respond respectfully and consistently with the understanding that they are experimenting and collecting data that will help them make their own choices in the future. We want to take time to explain the whys, give them opportunities to listen and act on their inner voice, and allow them to experience natural consequences as much as possible.

Children from 6 to 12 years old also have a strong sense of justice and are very concerned with fairness. As adults, we want to be fair and consistent, because our child is a keen observer and will catch any trace of injustice. This is a good time to have conversations about equality vs equity and fairness. (There is an excellent graphic made by the Robert Wood Johnson Foundation that shows how giving all members of a family the same bike would be an example of equality but not equity. Equity would look like a balance bike for a toddler, a child's bike for a school-age child, a three-wheeled bike for someone in the family with a disability, and an adult-sized bike for an adult.)

The 6- to 12-year-old child is very social. Belonging to a group or participating in group activities helps our child see the effect their actions or choices have on others. In addition to the group work and play they will likely do at school, we can provide them with opportunities to collaborate in and outside of our home. This is a great time for team sports or groups like scouts or guides. They will learn social skills, how to compromise, how to lead, and how to follow.

The child from 6 to 12 has the gifts of their logical, reasoning mind, and an imagination. We can invite them to empathize, to analyze, and to explore different behaviors, actions, reactions, and possibilities. They can explore events in the news and in politics and discuss different sides or viewpoints. Books (including mythology) and movies are also opportunities for discussions. We can introduce our children to good literature, music, and art that reflect the values we want them to acquire. We can talk about what we are reading and seeing and listen to our child's impressions, helping them fine-tune their understanding of complex issues.

In a Montessori classroom for 6- to 12-year-olds, particular attention is paid to people's contributions to the world and how they are connected. This interconnectedness is something we can highlight at home, developing gratitude for others and cultivating in our child a desire to contribute. We can wonder about the engineer who installed the traffic light that helps us drive safely or the farmer who planted the cotton from which our clothes were made or the person who invented the light bulb. We can help our child see that they, too, can work to have an impact on others in their community and the world. In this way, they start to explore their cosmic task.

As our child learns about people who have made an impact on the world, they will start to identify mentors and people who can be examples and models to them. Hero worship is a characteristic of the second plane, and our child may seek out idols who inspire them. Knowing this, we can expose them to models, whether fictional or real, who align with our family's values. We can also help them explore how humans can have both a positive and negative impact on the world around them. We can discuss what it means to use one's power responsibly.

An important part of supporting our child's moral development is giving them the opportunity and freedom to make their own decisions. This freedom means that they will likely make some bad decisions, and this is okay. It is better for them to make these decisions while they are still in our care, so we can walk through the repercussions together. This practice in decision-making and taking responsibility for one's choices will prepare them for the bigger decisions they will make down the road. Experience, not words, is the best teacher.

FOSTERING GRACE AND COURTESY

In Montessori classrooms, the children are given lessons on what is called *grace and courtesy*. The 3- to 6-year olds learn that while they have individual freedom, that freedom is limited by the needs and preferences of the group. For example, our child might like to sing loudly while knitting, but this might disrupt others. These lessons help the children learn how to respect one another and how to act around one another.

At home, we can help our child begin to recognize that they have to consider others in their choices and decisions. We can show our child how to recognize and express their feelings. We can show them how to respond to common situations, both positive and negative. What do you do when you want to do an activity that someone else is using? How do you react if someone offers you something you do not like? Or something you really like? Instead of assuming that our child "should know better," we can take the time to share with them what they need to know. We can practice these skills with them at neutral times and keep practicing until they become natural for our child. It does not need to be forced, and the best way for them to learn is for them to see us using these social graces and courtesies.

> "The adults do not insist on manners and courtesies but maintain an attitude of mutual respect and model expected manners and courtesies."
>
> —Judi Orion, AMI trainer, lecture in Switzerland, 2018

Grace and courtesy lessons still apply for the 6- to 12-year-old child, but they will look different. Our older child may be interested in the reasons behind the skills they are acquiring. For example, where did the custom of shaking hands come from? (It was a way for early people to show they didn't have a sword in their hand and meant no harm!) There is also less overt "teaching" with the 6- to 12-year-olds. Instead, we can make observations: "I've noticed that there are towels on the bathroom floor after you shower." We can see if they have observed the same, and invite them to explore the best way for their towel to dry. We can ask them to report back at the end of the week to let us know how it's going. When we hand the responsibility over to our child and give them space and time to sort it out for themselves, eventually it will come naturally to them.

As the adult, we define for our children the boundaries of appropriate behaviors. Grace and courtesy will reflect our family values, our culture, and our time and place. If we observe our child being rude to a friend or a caregiver or even to us and we ignore it, we have communicated to them that it is appropriate behavior. It is important to set limits and be consistent in maintaining these boundaries. When we do this, we are helping them develop knowledge and confidence in their world. There is a security that comes from knowing what is appropriate and what is not.

It is okay to say no to our child and stop them from behaving in a way that is antisocial. It is okay to take our child and leave the store or park if they are not behaving appropriately. We don't have to lose our cool or yell. We can count to 10 in our head to calm ourselves down first. We can say, "We are leaving now because this is inappropriate behavior/ because there are other people here whom we need to consider/because the library is a space for people to read and study quietly."

When possible, we can prepare our children in advance so that these kinds of situations are avoided. Before visiting a friend, we can orient them by telling our child how we will let them know when it's time to go. We can then give them advance notice when it will soon be time to leave and allow time for transitioning.

Grace and courtesy lessons we can give at home:

How to greet family members, friends, and strangers. We can model how to greet people in a way that is appropriate for our specific culture and environment. We can practice these greetings with our child. If in the moment of greeting someone, our child forgets, we can gently remind them. If they purposely refuse, instead of putting them on the spot or getting into a power struggle, we can discuss it with them at a later time.

How to welcome a friend or visitor. We can show our child how to welcome a friend or a special guest into our home. They can make a flower arrangement or a nice welcome sign. If culturally appropriate, we can show them how to offer a handshake, a hug, or a bow.

How to tell a friend you would rather not share a special toy. We can respect our children's wishes when they prefer not to share. We can show them how to put their special toys away before a guest comes over. We can teach them how to politely say they would rather their friend not use that toy. We can show them how to offer an alternative to their friend.

How to own up to a wrongdoing. Sometimes it can be hard to own up to a wrongdoing. We can help our child feel more comfortable by role-playing with them and showing them different ways to take responsibility for their actions.

How to apologize. We can show our children ways to apologize that communicate genuinely that they are sorry. In Junnifa's family, they are encouraged to say, "I am sorry that I _____ . I was wrong. Next time I will _____ . What can I do to make you feel better?" (For more on helping children make a repair, see page 154.)

How to express gratitude. We can make appreciation part of our family culture. We can start with saying thank you. Then we can teach our children to write thank-you notes or make little thank-you gifts. They can thank people for things like a meal or a gift; or they can thank the people in their life, like a postal worker who delivers packages.

How to give constructive feedback. Children can be blunt with their feedback, which can come across as insensitive. In our Montessori classes, we teach a "sandwich" approach, which can also be used at home. First, we acknowledge what we like or what the person did well; then we point out something they can improve upon, with specifics on how; and then we end with positive feedback. (For example, "Look how colorful your painting is. Maybe you could try to stay more on the paper next time. I can tell you worked really hard on it. You look pleased with it.")

OTHER GRACE AND COURTESY ACTIVITIES

MANNERS

- How to say please, excuse me, sorry, thank you, and pardon me

- How to open and close doors quietly

- How to excuse themselves from a group

- How to get the attention of a friend, parent, or stranger

- How to hold the door while someone passes through

- How to sneeze (into one's elbow)

- How to graciously accept or decline a hug, a gift, or an invitation

- How to express excitement

- How to disagree

- How to question a thought they don't agree with

- How to invite a friend to an event

- How to accept rejection

- How to give and receive a compliment

- How to talk or not talk about another person's features

- How to introduce oneself to an audience

MOVEMENTS AND INTERACTION

- Walking carefully (e.g., around furniture or where someone is working)

- Opening and closing a door or window

- Striking up a conversation

- Offering someone something

- Getting past someone who is in their way

- Meeting someone for the first time

DINING

- Setting the table

- Dining etiquette

- Manners—saying please and thank you

- Asking someone to pass them something

- Not speaking while eating

- Excusing themselves from the table

- Pulling out and pushing in chairs

GOING OUT

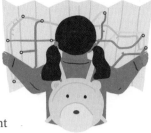

An important part of supporting our child's development is in going out into the community. In a Montessori class for 6- to 12-year-olds, the children arrange their own outings and an adult accompanies them as a chaperone. The children are responsible for making appointments, booking tickets, looking up transportation routes and timetables, and sending thank-you notes.

We can allow our children to do this as well. Some ideas include visiting a museum, the library, the train station, a bank, or the post office; doing community service or volunteer work or helping a neighbor; visiting an expert, a local business (e.g., a bakery), or a recycling depot. They learn so much from getting out into the community, expanding their horizons, and taking on the organizational responsibilities.

HOW TO HANDLE COMMON MORAL AND BEHAVIORAL CHALLENGES

The following are some moral and behavioral challenges that often come up in childhood.

Lying

Somewhere around the age of 3, children start to experiment with lying. For a 3-year-old, the lies may be very obvious or over the top. It is still important to address these lies and help our child practice telling the truth. If we address the behavior when they are young, it will likely stop for a while. But we shouldn't be surprised if the inclination to lie appears again in the 6 to 12 age range as our child begins to explore morality.

When our child lies, it is usually not malicious. Sometimes it is spontaneous self-preservation. Sometimes they are testing us to see if they can get away with it. Sometimes we know our child is lying, and we may be inclined to confront them or put them on the spot.

Junnifa learned this lesson the hard way in her elementary class. A child who had very neat handwriting was working on a project and for some reason wrote very messily on it. When Junnifa saw it, she said, "This couldn't possibly be Karina's." Karina was put on the spot, so she lied and said it wasn't hers. Karina later found Junnifa and confessed that it *was* hers, explaining that she had been embarrassed because Junnifa had already announced that it couldn't possibly be hers. It's in this way that we can unintentionally put our children in positions where they feel uncomfortable and then resort to lying.

However, it's important not to punish, overreact, or embarrass our child, especially if we see that they were lying to try to protect themselves. Instead of asking, "Did you do this?" we can help them verbalize it on their own in a nonthreatening way: "I see that the vase got broken. Let's talk about what we can do to make it better." We can offer alternative ways to handle the situation, always emphasizing the importance of honesty and trust. It is also important to show children how to make amends or restitution when they have done something wrong. (See more about making repairs on page 154.)

It is also important for us to model honesty by always telling our children the truth and also keeping our word. "I said I'd be home by 5:00 p.m., and I wasn't. That's not okay. I understand if you are upset, and I'd like to make it up to you." It is important not to exaggerate and to be careful when we are joking because the child may take our joke literally and think we are lying.

Siblings

Sibling relationships are some of the most important and lasting relationships our child will develop over the course of their lives. Here are some ways to support the development of a positive sibling relationship:

Start early. We can start while the younger sibling is still in utero. We can involve the older sibling or siblings by having them talk to the baby and read books and sing to the baby in the womb. We can involve our older child in the preparation for the new baby's arrival, such as helping to set up the baby's spaces. When the baby arrives, we can find age-appropriate ways to involve them. Allow them to carry the baby (for older children) and have them help with the care of the baby (for any age sibling). All of these actions build a bond with the baby.

Nurture our connection with the older sibling/s. When the baby is young, we can find ways to nurture our relationship with our older children while also helping them understand the needs of the baby. We can make sure to have some daily quality time when we are focused on our older child or have our partner and other family members give them more time and attention. We can also be careful not to give them too much responsibility. We can say things like "Can you look after each other while I visit the bathroom?" reminding them to care for each other regardless of birth order.

Do not compare them to each other. Each child is unique and will develop their own unique personality. Our own personalities can also affect the way we perceive our different children. We may be drawn to the child who is more like us or be activated by a child who reflects something we don't like in ourselves. Whatever our feelings are, it is imperative to not compare our children. When we do that, we give one child the impression that we prefer the other child, which can sow seeds of discord. We can encourage their uniqueness and strengths without putting anyone down.

As they grow, provide opportunities for them to do things together. While individual rooms might be attractive, a shared space is a lovely way to support sibling relationships. They will negotiate, discuss, laugh, play, and grow together. We can also provide activities that invite collaboration. Routines and rhythms, celebrations and rituals also support positive sibling relationships. We can develop family rituals around birthdays, holidays, or even meals, eating together, conversing about our day, and acknowledging each other's experiences.

Remain neutral when they disagree. It is normal for siblings to disagree or bicker, and it is important not to take sides or blame one child (often the older one). We can resist the temptation to interfere or to moderate every argument. When we do step in, we can try to remain neutral, acknowledging everyone's feelings, help our children clarify what they are feeling, and help them sort out the issue for themselves. All parties can be responsible for the solution. This avoids any resentment, and the children learn that they are part of a family that works and solves problems together.

It can also be helpful to have house rules or agreements about how members of the family interact with each other. (See page 36 for more on making agreements and page 153 for resolving conflicts.)

Connect with each child on an individual basis. When children aren't getting the attention they need, they will seek it by any means—including negative behavior. (See page 39 for ideas on how to connect.)

Prioritize equity over equality. We want to be fair, but instead of equality, we can aim for equity (see page 93). Sometimes one child needs more attention at a particular time, and that's okay. We can learn how each of our children perceives love and make sure to give them what they need. Some children need more touch, others more quality time, others words of affirmation, other acts of service, and others gifts; sometimes they need a combination. (For more on love languages, read *The Five Love Languages* by Gary Chapman.)

Encourage them to express their feelings to each other. We can give them the words: "I love you." "I appreciate how you _____." We can have discussions about what each child values, their love languages, and the language of apology. We can help each child learn how to fill the other's tank.

Observe when there is a lot of arguing. If our children always seem to be bickering and disagreeing, it is important to take time to observe and see what might be leading to the disagreements. Sometimes, when children are in different planes, their needs and perspectives are just different. Our once loving 6-year-old might become quite impatient with a younger sibling. We may need to provide them with tools to act better or modify our environment to ensure that each child has what they need. We can provide opportunities to be together as well as time apart; shared spaces and private spaces. (See chapter 4 for more tips about setting up the environment for siblings.)

Sharing

In a Montessori classroom for 3- to 6-year-olds, there is only one of each activity, and the children must take turns with it. They know an activity is available when it is back on the shelf, complete and ready for the next person. Dr. Montessori believed that this encourages the children to develop patience and to learn to respect someone else's work, whilst eliminating competition.

In our homes, if we have similar clear agreements about how things are shared, the children know what to expect and are able to solve problems with each other.

- What is the agreement about sharing activities in our home?
- What about special items for each child?
- Before visitors come over, can we involve our child in setting aside anything special they do not feel like sharing that day?
- How do we solve conflicts when they arise?

We can help our children learn how to negotiate sharing outside the home. For example, at the playground, we can help them learn how to stand up for themselves: "It's my turn next. You can wait behind me." "That's my bucket. You can have a turn when I'm done." We can also help them understand that there may be different rules at the playground than at home, and we let everyone have a turn. "Let's count down from ten so that someone else can have a turn on the swing now."

For a younger child, if they have taken something from another child and that child is upset, we may need to step in to translate for both parties. To the other child, we can say, "It looks like you are sad. That's your toy, and you weren't finished playing with it? I'm sorry my child took your toy. They really wanted to play with it, but it was not okay for them to take it." Then to our child, we can say, "This child was still playing with this, but it will be available soon. Can you please give it back, or do you need my help to give it back?" Similarly, if our child wants to bring a toy to the playground, we can remind them that other children may want to use it and check to see how that feels to them.

For the 6- to 12-year-old children, they are likely to come up with their own collaborative solutions, particularly if we encourage this and do not interfere.

How to interrupt politely

From the age of 3, a child can learn ways to interrupt us politely if we are in the middle of something. We can teach them to put their hand on our shoulder while they wait for us to finish. We can then put our hand on their hand to connect with them and acknowledge that they are waiting for us. We can keep our hand there until we are ready to give them the attention they need. This is something we can practice—for example, role-playing making a phone call and letting them practice getting our attention. When they forget (and they will), we can quietly tap our shoulder to remind them.

We can also be mindful of how we interrupt our child to tell them it's time to leave or that it's time for dinner or to ask them a question. Is it possible to wait until they are finished with what they are doing before saying anything? If we do need to interrupt them, how might they like to be interrupted? With a knock on the door? By our playing some music? With a timer or alarm? By placing our hand on their shoulder? How much time do they need in advance to transition from what they are working on?

If our child has a tendency to talk over us or others, we can help them learn to wait their turn by saying, "I'll finish my turn, and then you can talk." Or "We want to hear what you have to say once your brother has finished talking."

How to apologize or make it up to someone

Junnifa once observed the following exchange in a classroom: Toward the end of the day, as a child was carrying an activity back to the shelf, he got distracted looking out the window and bumped into another child. She began to cry and said, "Aslam bumped into me!" Aslam just stood there. A teacher asked him if he would like to apologize, and he did not respond. The teacher then said, "Emame is hurt. Would you like to bring some ice for her?" Aslam immediately went to get the ice. When he brought it to Emame, he looked concerned for her and helped her press it to the spot that hurt. He then said to her, "I really didn't mean to bump into you. I saw my mom's car go past, and I was distracted. I didn't even see you." And she replied, "It's okay. I feel better now." No one said the word "sorry," but both children had a clear understanding of what had happened and how the other person felt, the conflict was resolved, and each person left feeling better.

Often when children are forced to say they're sorry, they may not mean it, and it may not mean anything to the person on the receiving end of the apology. Instead of forcing our child to say they're sorry, we can encourage them to talk through their conflicts and guide them in coming to a resolution. When we feel an apology is necessary and our child is not being forthcoming, we can apologize on behalf of our child and then talk to our child later. Sometimes our child may need time to process an event before they can take responsibility. (More on repairs on page 154.)

Bullying

What if our child is being bullied? If our child complains about being bullied, we can first empower them to speak up for themselves. We might guide them on how to bring the issue up to their teacher if it is happening in school or directly to the perpetrators if it is happening elsewhere. If we do need to step in, we can do it in such a way that our child still feels empowered and is part of the conversation (e.g., we can ask them if they would like us to go with them to speak to their teacher to support them if necessary), instead of being relegated to the position of victim (we speak to the teacher for them). In a Montessori school, we recognize that a child who bullies generally does not feel like they belong. If possible, we can work with the school to make sure that they find a way for the other child to be seen, heard, and understood, so our child can be safe there.

What if our child is the bully? It is important to get to the root of the behavior. Children who hurt others are often feeling hurt themselves. Perhaps our child is feeling insecure or disempowered. It is important to address these needs as well as make our child understand that bullying is unacceptable. We can also hold them accountable and guide them in making a repair.

When our child appears bossy or shy

Some children enjoy telling everyone—including the adults—what and when and how to do things. These children may have a spark, initiative, and leadership qualities that we do not want to quash. But we also want them to build the skills they need to live and work harmoniously with others—to learn to wait, to respect and listen to others, to understand that everyone has their own will. Rather than labeling our child "bossy" (which can be a hard label to grow out of), we can help them identify their underlying need and build any skills they still need to learn.

Similarly, with a child who hides behind our leg in new situations, takes time to warm up to new people, or needs a lot of time alone after social engagements, we can accept them for who they are while still helping them build the skills they will need to live in society. We can help them learn to say hello in a way that makes them feel comfortable, to ask if they can join a group to play, and to excuse themselves for some quiet time when needed. We can stop calling them "shy" (again, such a label can become self-fulfilling) and instead guess how they may be feeling: "Do you need some time to warm up right now? Would you like to say, 'I need a bit more time to watch first'?"

Friendships

Children start to cultivate friendships in the first plane. We can provide opportunities for them to interact with others. They can also observe us modeling the elements of building positive relationships. We offer them language and opportunities for communication, showing our child how to express themselves, empowering them to stand up for themselves respectfully, and encouraging but not forcing collaboration.

Ideally, by the time our child has reached the second plane of development, we have helped them set a good foundation of values and morals that will guide them as their friends begin to have more influence over them. We can remind them of their values and discuss the choices that they're making. In order for these conversations to have an impact, we need to have built a relationship based on connection and open communication.

When we see signs of changes in our child's behavior with a particular friend.
We can bring these changes to our child's attention and have a conversation about them. We can listen to how they feel when they are with the child and why they might behave differently around them. Perhaps we need to do some work with them on their sense of self or give them tools to help them when they feel pressure from this friend. If this doesn't improve things, we can consider limiting their time with the friend by having more family time or playdates with other children. We can be careful not to come across as punitive, as this can also lead to rebellion or resentment from our child. As much as possible, we can remind our child of the values that matter in our home so they can have something to measure or compare other people's behavior against.

When things go wrong. When our children do something wrong in the presence of others, it's important to be calm and we can wait until we are alone with them to have a conversation with them about their behavior. It's important to always check our motives and make sure that we want our children to do the right thing because it's right and not because we want them to conform or because we care what others will say. Children are perceptive, and they absorb everything, including a feeling of wanting to please others.

Helping our child build skills with friends. If we observe that our child might need to develop some skills, we can play or practice with our child. For example:

- If our child likes to give hugs, we can teach them to check with the other person that they would like one.
- We can teach them to say "Stop" or "I don't like that" if someone does something they don't like or they want to stop rough play.
- If our child is sad that their friend doesn't want to play with them, we can teach them to ask if they would like to play another day, about games they can play by themselves, how they can ask to join another group's game, while also acknowledging our child's feelings.
- We can help them learn when to ask for help from an adult.

The competitive child

There is nothing wrong about a child enjoying competition. It is only a problem if our child has difficulty losing, or when their competitive spirit negatively affects other children. The Montessori classroom creates a noncompetitive peer learning environment. Even with the youngest children, we nurture working together as a community. Encouraging collaboration over competition reinforces the idea that everyone belongs and contributes.

If we have a child who is showing competitive behavior at home, we can look at the following:

Are we encouraging competition in our home? Do we ask, "Who can get ready first?" "Who can be my best helper?" "Who ate all their dinner?" Instead, could we encourage collaboration? "Let's see how quickly we can get ready for school." Those who are ready first can help the last ones if they need help.

When they compare themselves to others, can we focus instead on the individual? When our child moans, "It's not fair; they got two and I only got one," instead of lecturing or moralizing—for example, by saying, "Things don't always go our way"— we can acknowledge how they feel: "It sounds like you really wanted more. I can see why it must have been frustrating that there weren't enough for everyone to get two." When they boast, "I'm the fastest/strongest," we can respond without building up competition and focus on the individual: "It sounds like you love running fast/feeling strong!"

Can we focus on the process, not the result? This can help a child who wants to be best to focus on all the steps along the way, not only the outcome. "You've been training hard for the competition this weekend and not missed a single practice."

Does our family have an abundance mindset? In a Montessori classroom, every child can achieve their best and it's not at the expense of someone else. There is enough time to learn, there is enough space for each child, and every child is valued. This is an *abundance mindset*.

Can we practice sporting conduct—whether we win or lose? When children are playing a sport or a game, we have an opportunity to teach them sporting conduct—balancing their desire to do their best and build the skills to excel while keeping in mind ideas like equity and fairness. We can focus on playing our best, trying to improve ourselves, rather than always needing to win. We can practice the grace and courtesy of saying "Congratulations" to the winner and "Better luck next time" to the loser. We focus on how we all played, rather than on who won. This takes a lot of repetition and practice! If our child is upset when they lose, we can offer comfort: "It's hard to see you sad when you lose" or "It can be hard to lose when you really tried your best." This can help you to maintain connection even when they are having a hard time.

BECOMING SOCIAL CITIZENS

In our Montessori classrooms, we see every child as unique, we accept every child for who they are, and we ensure that every child feels they belong in our community. We can do similar work in our home. Raising antiracist, antibias children is intrinsically linked with raising a Montessori child. It stretches from how we spend our money, to how we show up in our communities, to finding ways to take action in the face of injustice.

A helpful framework for this work is the four antibias education goals developed by Louise Derman-Sparks and Julie Olsen Edwards.

Goal 1: Each child understands and values their own identity. We are all made up of an intersection of identities, including race, ethnicity, gender, religion, economic class, family structure, neurodiversity, differing abilities, languages, and so on. The child from 3 to 6 years old with their absorbent mind will pick up attitudes (positive, neutral, or negative) about parts of their identity from us and others around them. The 6- to 12-year-old child takes this further and will question how they or their family are the same and different from others.

To build a strong sense of self, we can help our child see themselves (their skin color, hair type, family structure, language, etc.) represented in:

- Books and storytelling
- Artwork, posters, and photographs
- Toys, such as dolls and puzzles
- Art materials, such as skin-tone crayons or paints they can mix to replicate their own skin tone
- Songs, dance, music, and instruments

Part of understanding who they are is also recognizing any privileges they have. Which of their identities gives them access, ease, or "invisibility" and which identities do not?

Goal 2: Each child understands and values others' identities. We can build on the work we have done on Goal 1 by helping our children get to know other people in our community, through real experiences.

We can look for toys, books, artwork, exhibitions, and other media that represent human diversity and center Indigenous children, Black children, children of color, Asian children, families with same-sex parents, people who are disabled, and members of the LGBTQIA+ and neurodivergent communities.

> "Children learn prejudice from prejudice—not from learning about human diversity. It is how people respond to differences that teaches bias and fear."
>
> —Louise Derman-Sparks and Julie Olsen Edwards,
> *Anti-Bias Education for Children and Ourselves*

We can go further and try to ensure that our friends, doctors, and other people in our daily life and communities represent a broad spectrum of identities. We can venture outside our communities to other neighborhoods or towns that are different from our own. We can notice what things are the same and what might be different.

Our 3- to 6-year-old children will take all of this in with their absorbent mind. The 6- to 12-year-old child will explore the similarities and differences under the lens of their moral compass and their intellectual growth, and ties to their interest in how people live in different places and at different times in history.

Goal 3: Each child can identify injustice and recognize that it hurts. We can help our child recognize injustice, unfairness, and stereotypes that are aimed at them or others. We can help them become critical thinkers by asking questions like "Who is not in the room?" or "Who does this disadvantage?" We can model asking questions when we hear something in the news, read an article or social media post, walk past a billboard, or overhear our children talking. Antibias educator Britt Hawthorne encourages us to help our child identify the problems in the system rather than the individual. When our child asks, "Why do those people live under a bridge?" it is an opportunity to talk about things like the cost of living in our city and how our city hasn't invested in affordable housing.

We can help our child challenge binary categories and learn to center others. They can learn to appreciate other cultures, not appropriate them. We can acknowledge the native landowners where we live and explore ways in which individuals and society can redistribute resources. As our child learns about who holds power in society, they can also learn to critically analyze the effects.

Goal 4: Each child feels empowered to take action in cases of injustice. We can ask our child what action they'd like to take. We can help them draft a letter to the local government. We can encourage them to stand up for themselves or someone else if they see prejudice or discrimination. "That's unkind." "That hurts me/them when you say that." In times of crisis, they may want to donate money they have saved or find hands-on ways to help and support individuals in our community who may be living on the margins.

We can help our 6- to 12-year-old child develop their sense of fairness and empathy. But these conversations can happen far earlier, with our babies, toddlers, and preschoolers. As their adults, we need to educate ourselves so that we can guide them in these critical conversations and model calling people in and out when we see or experience injustice.

Here are some useful phrases from *Speak Up at School* by Learning for Justice:

- "That offends me."

- "I don't find that funny."

- "I'm surprised to hear you say that."

- "What do you mean by that?"

- "What point are you trying to make by saying that?"

- "Did you mean to say something hurtful when you said that?"

- "Using that word as a put-down offends me."

- "Using that word doesn't help others feel safe or accepted here."

A note on books

We learned from Britt Hawthorne that there are different types of book collections. There are affirming books (in which children sees themselves represented), books for diversity (which represent many types of different children, people, and families), books for social justice (including books that include harmful stereotypes or other content that we want to critically analyze together with our child), and books for activism (about how others have taken action in the past and how we can take action now). We can think about the purpose of the books and how we will use them as we add to our book collections and when visiting the library. Some books we will want to make sure we read with our children so we can discuss what we see, and others we will be able to leave on the shelf for our children to explore on their own.

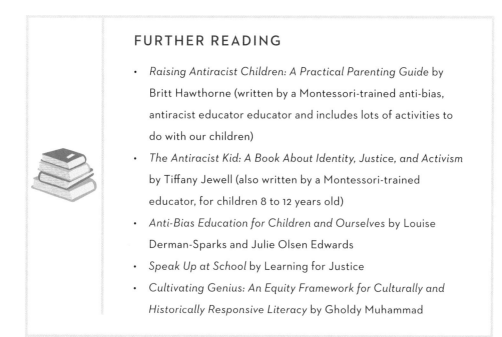

FURTHER READING

- *Raising Antiracist Children: A Practical Parenting Guide* by Britt Hawthorne (written by a Montessori-trained anti-bias, antiracist educator educator and includes lots of activities to do with our children)
- *The Antiracist Kid: A Book About Identity, Justice, and Activism* by Tiffany Jewell (also written by a Montessori-trained educator, for children 8 to 12 years old)
- *Anti-Bias Education for Children and Ourselves* by Louise Derman-Sparks and Julie Olsen Edwards
- *Speak Up at School* by Learning for Justice
- *Cultivating Genius: An Equity Framework for Culturally and Historically Responsive Literacy* by Gholdy Muhammad

BUILDING OUR FAMILY CULTURE

We can build a conscious family culture in our home. Colleen Wilkinson, of Trauma Informed Montessori, writes of mirror neurons: "We are a social species; if one animal senses danger, the entire group becomes alert, survival increases; calmness, safety, well-being are also contagious." We can be intentional then to offer our children such calmness, safety, and well-being.

- We want our children to feel safe in our home, physically and psychologically.
- They will receive our care, and they will learn to show the same care to others in the family.
- We can develop clear family agreements (see p. 36).
- We can talk about what respect means, such as using kind words, listening to each other, using our bodies to listen, and giving each other space to talk, move, and rest.
- And we can have fun. Simone knows a 10-year-old who who came up with a new way for their family to connect through pizza. Each person wrote down what toppings they wanted on their personal pizza and placed the paper in a hat. Everyone picked someone else's request and made it for them.
- We can ensure that each member of the family feel like they are special and belong in our family.

JOSHUAA, KALEB, KATERI

@ndnslp & Faculty of Johns Hopkins
Bloomberg School of Public Health
Diné & Acoma Pueblo, New Mexico,
on the Navajo Nation

"There's been a lot of problem-solving activities that I've done with my kids, like taking them outdoors and showing them cause and effect through the irrigation canal, like what happens when you fill up the water and it flows over."

"I also think about how I teach vocabulary to my kids, like being in the Kiva as Pueblo people, or out hunting and using those opportunities to tell them about what's happening and to provide that language facilitation through real-life conversations."

"I think Montessori is like real-life learning. Learning by doing, learning by experiencing, and learning by feeling and eating, by actually seeing it too. So that's really how I would explain Montessori and coming from an Indigenous lens to it, we're all about connection. Connectedness is such a key piece of our existence as humans, is connection to our children, and the other way around, connection to our parents, and then even connection to what's around us, living things, nonliving things, to Earth, all these things."

"Children that have been given those opportunities to learn a skill set, like starting a fire, respecting it, learning about it, why we do it, and how it's used, at a very early age, start to do some of those things on their own. Like putting the fire together, like being able to know what needs to be dried, starting with small pieces, and when to use something big."

"As a speech language pathologist, and as a parent, this approach works very well for young Native children, who are very unique learners and are in this stage of learning more about their culture, relearning their language, but also working through generations of trauma as well to where inadequate learning spaces were a contributor to increased anxiety and reduce academic self efficacy."

PUTTING IT
INTO PRACTICE

7

PART ONE

APPLYING MONTESSORI IN DAILY LIFE

DAILY RHYTHMS

Children thrive on knowing what comes next, which gives them a measure of control in their otherwise unpredictable days. Studies show that children have better cognitive and psychosocial outcomes when they have choice and control in their day, with predictable times for things like getting dressed, eating meals, and going to bed.

Often life seems to sweep us along, but it can be useful to be intentional about what our days, weeks, and months look like. Rather than the word "routine" or "schedule," we like using the word "rhythm," which we learned from Eloise Rickman, author of *Extraordinary Parenting*. Rhythms allow some flexibility to be able to follow the child's pace, with the predictability of knowing what comes next and how it will be carried out.

Most children like to know what the general plan is for the day. During breakfast, we can check in with the family to see what the day is going to look like. On vacations or weekends, this morning check-in can also help our child plan their activities. If we are heading out in the afternoon, they know they have the morning to themselves. If we have the whole day free, they might start work on a bigger project that needs more time and space. This gives them some choice in and control over their days.

When plans change (and they will), we can give them a heads-up. "You know how we were planning to go out soon? I've just seen that there is a delivery coming before lunch, so would it be okay if we go after lunch instead?"

TO OBSERVE

- Is there a clear rhythm in our home on weekdays?
- How is this similar/different on weekends?
- Is there enough time? Or are we always in a rush?
- What can we take out of our schedule to allow more free time in our week?

A daily rhythm

A daily rhythm is not a rigid schedule but more like large blocks of uninterrupted time for certain activities, with mealtimes at pretty regular times every day.

It's hard to generalize because families vary so much, but here is an example of what a daily rhythm might look like for a child of 3 to 12 years old:

WAKING

- Reads or plays quietly on waking
- Cuddles and reads or talks with parent

GETTING READY

- Brushes teeth, combs hair, washes face
- Gets dressed
- Helps prepare breakfast and eats with the family
- Packs lunch (if needed)
- Packs schoolbag

LEAVING THE HOUSE

- Puts shoes on
- Adds layers of clothing—coat, hat, gloves, scarf—if needed
- Applies sunscreen if needed
- Takes schoolbag and anything else they'll need for the day (clothes for playing a sport, a musical instrument, library books to return, etc.)

MORNING

- Attends preschool/school/a morning activity
- Lunch—eats at school or at home or has a picnic lunch

AFTERNOON

- Engages in after-school activities, such as:
  - Spending time in nature—going to the playground, park, beach, mountain, or forest
  - Spending time with the community—visiting family or friends, volunteering in the neighborhood, or going to the library
  - Playing sports or having a music lesson (not too many days in the week)
  - Engaging in free-play at home—reading, exploring, inventing, building, baking

LATE AFTERNOON

- Helps prepare dinner
- Sets the table
- Does any homework
- Tidies up

DINNER

- Eats with the family at the table (this will include learning grace and courtesy practices and engaging in family conversation)

AFTER DINNER

- Enjoys quiet activities or family walk
- Takes a bath or shower
- Brushes teeth
- Gets into pajamas

BEDTIME

- Reads books or tells stories in bed
- Debriefs about the day
- Snuggles
- Lights out

There are so many opportunities in our daily rhythm for our child to build their independence, take responsibility for themselves, and make their own choices.

We also check the needs of our child. If we have a child who prefers to be at home and we have had a lot of outings, scheduling a pajama day will give them time to decompress. If our child is overtired, we can look at our rhythm and see how we can create more rest for them.

When problems arise in our daily rhythms

It can be quite frustrating when our toddler who was interested in dressing themselves and getting ready now shows disinterest or seeming laziness, or expects us to help them. This is common from the age of 2.5 to 3 years and older. They no longer find it an interesting challenge to master, yet also want more autonomy over themselves. It can be a frustrating stage for both adult and child.

Always start first with observation to collect some objective information, including looking for any bottlenecks—points of resistance—that recur on a daily basis.

It might be that after breakfast, they need to go back to their room to get dressed, but they get distracted by the toys in the living room. We might be able to change the order so they get dressed upon waking, and then help prepare their breakfast.

It might be that siblings wind each other up and distract each other. We could try to have them get ready separately until the skills are in place again and then move toward their being able to get dressed at the same time.

Lessen the battles by being clear about what is happening (such as when we'd like to leave and what needs to be done), using positive ways to encourage cooperation, and not taking on the problem as our own. (See pages 141–146 for tips to cultivate cooperation.)

Slow down the pace and allow enough time. Both the 3- to 6-year-old child and the 6- to 12-year-old child generally do not like being rushed. They want to feel in control of how they leave the house. It can be a useful exercise for our child to record how long it takes to do everything to get out of the house (a younger child might need our help with this). We can then allow an extra 5 minutes on top in case someone cannot find their gloves or something unexpected arises.

Make a checklist or use routine cards. With a child from 3 to 6 years old, one way to ease morning and evening rhythms is to have the child help make a checklist of everything that needs to be done. (It's important to choose a neutral time to make this list, not when we are trying to rush out the door or they are bouncing around in their pajamas avoiding bedtime.)

Together, we can think of all the necessary steps that need to be done and document them. We can write a list, make a chart with simple drawings, print out some routine cards, or print photos of our child doing each step. These visual cues can be hung with tape, on a string with clothespins, or on a magnetic board that allows the child to choose or change the order of the routine. Then, instead of having to nag them, we can simply point to the chart, ask "What does the chart say is next?" and let them take responsibility for getting ready. We are working together. Often after a week, the rhythm has been restored and our child will rely less on the checklist.

For children ages 6 to 12, we could discuss at our family meeting ideas to help everyone leave on time in the morning. They might choose to set a series of alarms, agree to an earlier bedtime, organize things the evening before, or ask us to check if they are awake. Then we can make a time to come back to see how the new plan is working out.

Prepare the environment. We can review the principles in chapter 4 to prepare the enviroment so that the child knows where everything can be found, everything looks appealing, and they can do things with less help. The child younger than 6 years old likes it when everything is in the same place each time they look for it; and the 6- to 12-year-old needs some order in the external environment as it doesn't come so naturally to them.

To get out the door on time, observe the following:

- Is it easy for our child to choose clothing for themselves?

- Are the cupboards or drawers too full so it's hard for them to see what is available?

- Do we need to store out-of-season items to make it easier for them to choose appropriate clothing?

- Do they need a special place to sit to get ready?

- Would they find it fun to choose some clothes the night before and lay them out in the shape of a person?

- Is everything that they will need to leave by the front door? Shoes? Bags? Sunscreen in warmer months? Gloves and hats in colder seasons?

- Would a checklist of things they need to pack in their bags, including sports equipment or a musical instrument, be useful?

Help them to do it themselves. It may initially take a little longer to teach our child how to put on their shoes and tie their shoelaces than to do it for them, breaking it into small steps for them to practice. In the long run, however, we will then have a child who can do these things by themselves and no longer needs our help.

Give as little help as possible (and as much as necessary). We start by scaffolding the skills, but we can take down the scaffold when it is no longer needed.

For an older child around 5 years old, if they still need cues like "Now you need to put on your shoes," we may have forgotten to take down the scaffold. As we make the transition to doing less, we might need to keep ourselves busy. Our role is to support, not make it all happen. We can be responsible for things like ensuring that our child has clean clothes available and that there's healthy food in the fridge. Then we can trust our child to manage getting ready with just a little help like saying "bag" if we see that they are headed out the door without it.

Let them learn by experiencing consequences. A child leaving the house without their coat on will feel cold. A child who jumps in puddles will learn that their feet get wet. A child might go to school in their pajamas if they are not dressed in time—warn the school beforehand so they can provide support on their end and try to act completely normal so as not to shame the child but let them learn from the natural consequences. We do not need to lecture (avoid "See, I told you so"); we can let the consequences speak for themselves.

Get their agreement. Make it clear what the departure time is and ask if they need anything from us to make it happen. Let them know when it's 5 minutes before departure. Instead of calling from another room, go over to where they are, and, as much as possible, try not to interrupt them. Wait until they have finished their activity so they will be more likely to hear us. If it looks like they may not have time to finish what they are working on, we could say, "It is leaving time in 5 minutes. Would you like to start finishing up your game? Or you can put it somewhere to finish it when we get back."

Some last tips

- A playful reminder ("5 minutes, bakers!" if they have ever seen a cooking show) can be less stressful than a demand to hurry up.
- Allow time for them to process any requests. It is worth counting to 10 slowly in our head (not aloud, which can stress out our child) before repeating ourselves. While we think they are ignoring us, they may still be processing what we said.
- For the most relaxing start to the day, wake up half an hour earlier. Even better if it's before the rest of the family wakes up—we then have time to ourselves to shower, get dressed, and be ready to help the others if they need it.

Continued on page 118

TALK IN A WAY THAT HELPS THEM LISTEN

GIVE THEM A CHOICE	"Would you like to put on your coat or shoes first?"
GET THEM TO THINK	"What do we need to do before we leave?" "Where are your shoes kept?"
DESCRIBE THE PROBLEM (WITHOUT JUDGMENT) AND LET THEM WORK OUT THE REST	"I see you have bare feet, and we are about to go outside."
USE ONE WORD INSTEAD OF A LONG EXPLANATION	"Shoes" (if they need to put on their shoes). "Light" (as a reminder to turn off the light). "Plate" (if they have forgotten to take their plate to the sink).
WHISPER	This is a surprising way to get their attention and to bring down the energy levels in the house.
WRITE A NOTE	"Please don't forget me!" (taped to a pair of shoes) (Even if the child can't read, they are sure to ask you what it says.)
USE A CLOCK OR TIMER	"Let's see if we can get ready before the big hand gets to the 12/before the beeper goes off." We can see how fast we can go as a family (avoid a competition between children) and those ready first will be able to help the slower ones, even us—the adult—if we are the last to be ready.

- Fill their emotional bucket first thing in the morning—snuggle in bed, read books, give lots of hugs and tickles. Those lovely minutes spent connecting with our child will pay off in cooperation during the morning routine.

- Prepare the night before—it can help to pack lunches, lay out possible clothes choices, and check the weather. Rise and shine, and we will be ready to go.

- We can ask our child how they would like us to remind them if we notice they are short of time. It's hard to watch them be late, but we can stay calm knowing we have helped them, and they will do the rest.

- If a child is refusing to go to school, we can be clear that not going to school is not an option and be compassionate at the same time. "It sounds like there's something going on that is making you not want to go. We'll work together to make it as easy as possible for you to get to school."

If there is still resistance . . .

- Do not get into a power struggle.

- Remain calm.

- Let them know it's time to go using a kind and clear voice: "We need to leave now, and it's important for us to leave together." Please do not threaten the child by saying, "I'm leaving without you." This erodes the connection we are building.

- Assist a younger child if needed: "You tried to put on your shoes all by yourself. We've run out of time today, so I'll help you finish, and you can try again tomorrow."

- If the child becomes upset, we can give them a cuddle, and guess at their feelings. But as hard as it is, keep moving forward. We could say, "It looks like you wish you had longer to finish that" as we keep moving with them toward the door.

We can show appreciation for their cooperation by describing what they have done. "I see someone who is ready to go out and play in the park. You have your shoes on, your coat done up, and your mittens and hat on to keep you warm. It was helpful how you got yourself ready while I packed our bag. We make a good team, huh?"

SEASONAL RHYTHMS

Who remembers the smell of their favorite dish cooking at a special time of year? Or the sounds of crunchy autumn leaves? Or going on a scavenger hunt to find signs of spring? The taste of salt on our lips at the ocean? The touch of cold snow on our tongues or hands? Seasonal rhythms provide foundational memories for our child.

Our seasonal rhythms will depend on where we live and the places we visit. They will also reflect our culture and beliefs. We can be mindful to build our culture into our seasons. To think about the music we play, the food we cook and eat, the songs we sing, the dances we teach, the art on our walls, the poetry we read, the sacred places we visit, and the stories we tell. No Montessori family will be the same, but our seasonal rhythms can reflect our past, our present, and our future.

In Junnifa's family, they study their bibles and pray together every evening. They travel to their hometowns every Easter and December to spend the vacation with the extended family. On Christmas Day, they cook and bake and share with members of their community who do not have the means for a Christmas dinner.

Incorporate rituals

Rituals can be built into our daily, weekly, or monthly rhythms, from a slow Sunday breakfast to birthday traditions practiced year after year and cultural celebrations like Shabbat, Eid, Christmas, and Holi. As with rhythms, the child enjoys the familiarity of these events happening in the same way each time and imprints them into their soul.

We can also make space for surprise or novelty—filling up their room with balloons on their birthday, slipping a poem into their lunch box, or dressing up to go for afternoon tea.

Birthday celebrations

Celebrating birthdays is a beautiful opportunity to create rituals in the family. Our child does not need much to feel special on their big day. Here are some ideas to get you started:

- Make a birthday crown from felt with the age they are turning on it.
- Use a wooden candleholder, adding a candle every year.
- Make their favorite cake.
- Hang up birthday bunting for decoration.
- Go for a meal at a favorite local café or restaurant.
- Arrange a party for a handful of their close friends—one suggestion is to invite as many friends as the age the child is turning.
- Some of the best parties are at home with either nothing planned or activities to explore or a scavenger hunt.

GIFTS

We want to teach our children to be thoughtful about what we consume. Instead of new toys, we can give our child an experience, like an annual pass to a local museum or art gallery, or a trip to a water park with a friend or two.

It's harder to navigate gifts from other people that may not align with the Montessori approach. We can first try to prevent this by sending out a wish list or guidance in advance when the gifts are anticipated, such as for birthdays and graduations. We can do this in a gentle way, advising that these are things we are saving toward. If there is a theme, this may help people focus on things that would be helpful to receive; for example, things for the garden, crystals or rocks, animal figurines for our child's collection, or items related to the solar system. It is helpful to include a variety of price options as well as a variety of both material items and activities—for example, books, toys, sports, and outings.

If our child does receive a gift that doesn't align with our values:

- We can remember that if a family member or friend chooses their own gift, they have done so with good intentions and because it is something they think our child will like.

- It is important to still appreciate the gift and model gratitude to our children. They can call or write a note to say thank you.

- We can then decide what we want to do with it.

- Some gifts can be kept for a while and then taken out of rotation.

- Some gifts can be repurposed to have a more Montessori friendly use; for example, some battery-powered toys can become passive if batteries are not put in. When an item is taken apart, a piece of it might serve a different purpose.

- We can save for later what is not age appropriate. If it is something that might become obsolete, like an iPad or smartphone, we might explain that the child is not old enough for it yet and suggest an alternative.

- We can regift or donate what we think others might appreciate.

- If it is completely unacceptable or inappropriate, we can donate it or dispose of it.

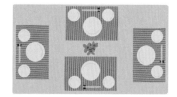

EATING AND MEALTIMES

We can impart to our children a few important principles around food.

We respect food. Children learn to respect food when they learn how much goes into having fresh food available for their meals. We can smell the food at the market and get excited by the delicious array our local stores provide. We can talk about who grew the food and all the steps it takes to get to us. We can prepare only as much food as we will eat so as to not waste food. We can be clear at mealtimes that food is not to be played with; it is for nourishment. We can express gratitude for our food. We can grow our own food to show our children the time and labor that goes into providing food.

Meals are for connecting with the family. Meals are as much a social occasion as they are a time for eating and nourishing our bodies. Connecting every day at the table means that we are prioritizing our connection and relationship as our children grow. We are passing on oral histories, checking in with each other, and learning to listen and take turns in the conversation, as well as having family jokes and building memories. The research shows positive outcomes for children in families that eat meals together, with children feeling better physically and mentally.

As much as our schedule allows, we can try to have as many family meals as possible. As our children grow and may wake later on the weekend, we can join them at the table with a coffee or tea (or a second breakfast) while they eat.

We learn to listen to our own bodies. Rather than insisting that our child finish everything on their plate, we can help them listen to cues from their body that tell them that they are hungry or full. Rather than preparing a plate, we can place the food on serving dishes and have everyone help themselves. They can take as much as they would like (considering others, too) and serve themselves more if they are still hungry.

Mealtimes are opportunities to practice grace and courtesy. We can model grace and courtesy at every mealtime by saying please when we ask someone to pass a plate and saying thank you when they do; eating with our mouth closed; waiting to finish our mouthful before talking; taking turns to talk; staying at the table and learning to excuse oneself; expressing gratitude for our meal; using cutlery; and asking people if they'd like any more of a dish before taking the last portion.

We can also respectfully remind our child of manners; for example, if they talk with their mouth full, we can say, "I didn't hear you so well. Do you mind repeating yourself once you've finished your mouthful?"

Children enjoy food they have helped prepare or prepared themselves. Junnifa's family has inspired many to cook their own omelets. Working by the stove requires adult supervision and lessons in how to use the stove safely, how to pick up a hot pan, how to chop vegetables, and which utensils to use to turn over the omelet. We can simplify the processes for younger children and allow older children to do more and more themselves, being available to offer help if needed.

Similarly, in Simone's home, Oliver was about 10 years old when he wanted to cook dinner for the family every Sunday night. He selected a recipe from a cookbook (an easy, tasty recipe with not too many ingredients), and together they made a shopping list and bought the ingredients. They read through the recipe together to see if there was anything he wasn't sure about, and Simone acted as sous-chef (although Oliver never needed much help at all). His cooking skills improved that year, and he was really proud of himself.

Cooking with friends can be a fun hobby for a 6- to 12-year-old child. They might enjoy going to a cooking class where they learn to cook or bake with friends; some learn this at scouts, and others learn from relatives—particularly if we don't enjoy cooking ourselves.

There are many learning opportunities around food. When we prepare and eat food together, there is so much our child can learn. In the Activities Appendix, which begins on page 232, we can find many ideas for learning vocabulary, fine-motor and gross-motor skills, practical life skills, how to grow food, sensorial experiences, as well as how their bodies work, how to make balanced food choices, and what helps bodies grow.

Food can provide cultural experiences. One of the most important parts of preparing food is learning about our family culture. There are recipes, traditional foods, ways of eating, and rituals around food from our culture that we can honor in our home. It could be making a braided challah bread for Shabbat, eating with chopsticks, or cooking paella to share with friends. In this way, we pass on our cultural heritage and traditions. We can also learn about other cultures by visiting restaurants run by people of that culture, visiting friends from different cultures, or, if means allow, traveling to other places around the world and tasting the food, from Berber pancakes in Morocco to roti canai (a typical flatbread) in Malaysia.

Our own attitudes and behavior around food are being absorbed. If we speak about being too fat or thin, are often on a diet, or have disordered eating, our children will be absorbing this—the 3- to 6-year-old child with their absorbent mind and even the 6- to 12-year-old through their intellect. We may need to do some internal work on healing our relationship with food for our children to develop healthy attitudes and behaviors around food.

Allow time and lower expectations. This can be easier said than done. Cooking with kids has many benefits, yet speed and cleanliness are not always among them. If we work full-time, we may wish to spend more time cooking with the children on the weekends at first so we can allow more time to make a family meal. We might like to make a special Sunday-night dinner of homemade pizzas, wraps with toppings for everyone to help themselves, or homemade sushi.

Problems at mealtimes

When we worry about what/how much they are eating

If we are worried about how much our child is eating, we can use an observation journal to note down every day for one week:

- What and when they eat and drink, including snacks and drinks while they're out and about.
- Where they eat. Are they sitting at a table to eat? Or playing at the same time?
- With whom they eat. Are they eating alone or with others?
- What eating time looks like. Is the table clear of other things? Is it set beautifully, maybe with flowers or candles? Is it free of screens, including our phones?

We can then see if they are filling up on snacks or drinks between meals, what their appetite is actually like over a whole week, what their favorite foods are, and what foods we would like to introduce.

Remember that we cannot make a child swallow their food. We can decide when mealtimes will be, what will be offered at mealtime, and where we will sit to eat. They decide how much they eat, and we are there to be their guide if needed. "It looks like you are all done. Would you like some help to take your plate to the kitchen?"

If they refuse to try a new food, we can keep offering it to them without any expectations and without too many words. Often when we want to encourage them to try something, we end up making it a big deal and we can make them wary. Children have a good sense of whether they are being manipulated. Instead, make the food look inviting, offer food with all the colors of the rainbow, invite them to help in the kitchen, and, above all, keep things relaxed at mealtimes.

If we have bigger concerns about our child's diet, we can seek help from a dietician or medical professional.

When we want to avoid using dessert as a bribe

If we want our child to eat more vegetables or we worry that they'll wake up hungry if they haven't eaten their dinner, we may end up bribing them: "If you eat your dinner, you can have dessert." However, this strategy does not allow our child to explore whether they are full. As Megan McNamee and Judy Delaware of Feeding Littles say, we are also unconsciously "ranking food," implying that dessert is more special. Instead, we can help our child learn that we eat lots of types of food—sometimes it's cookies, sometimes it's yogurt, sometimes it's fruit. Or we might ask them if they are all done: "Are you feeling satisfied? Do you have room for some yogurt or fruit?"

When our child refuses to eat what we have made and asks for something else

When our child demands something else for their meal, they may protest when we kindly and clearly say, "We are having this meal tonight. We can have that another day." We stay calm knowing that we have decided what to serve and they can decide how much of it they eat. As hard as it is for us, they may not eat anything. However, when we respond in a predictable way each time, they will learn that we aren't going to change our mind based on their demands. Some children like to be able to make a choice, and we can offer one when we are preparing the food: "Would you like peas or carrots tonight or both?" They might like to help us do some meal planning and assist us with the shopping. Or we might decide to have a small selection of food on the table that we are happy for them to choose from.

We can also see things from their perspective. "I hear you. It sounds like you really wanted that for dinner tonight. Maybe tomorrow." We can make a note so they see that we have heard them, and then we can make sure to prepare that meal when we can.

When they want to get up from the table as soon as they've finished eating

A 3-year-old may not want to stay at the table once they are finished. We might make an agreement with them that they may get down from the table and take their plate to the kitchen while others continue eating. Older children can learn to stay at the table until everyone is finished—although we may need to practice telling interesting stories and asking good questions to keep them engaged in the conversation.

Simone has a self-confessed bad habit of needing to get up to fetch things in the kitchen during mealtime. If our child is having a hard time staying at the table, we can observe how often we also get up during mealtime and work to have everything we need on the table so we can model staying seated at mealtimes.

When our child has a case of mealtime sillies

At the end of a long day, we want to relax and eat our meal in relative peace. Our children, on the other hand, can be a little tired and silly, and one child seems to wind up another until they are doing silly things with their food or just laughing uncontrollably and not eating.

Honestly, this is part of life with family. Junnifa will observe, and if they are happy and not being disrespectful, then she'll let it go. If we feel impatient, we might want to take ourselves out of the room to get ourselves a glass of water, breathe, and check in with ourselves about why we are feeling activated. Maybe we wait until most of the laughter has died down (as long as we know everyone is safe). Maybe we can find our sense of humor, come back, and laugh along. However, if the behavior is inappropriate or unkind, Junnifa reminds them that we respect ourselves, each other, and our food and asks them to compose themselves.

When we want to avoid screens and other distractions during mealtimes

In order to taste the food and enjoy all the social and sensorial aspects of mealtime, we leave toys, phones, and other screens away from the table. There may be some protests at first, but our children quickly learn to enjoy the connection and conversation. It might be the adults who have the most difficulty leaving our phones in silent mode in a basket or another room while we eat. Yet our children are watching, and we are an important example to them.

When our child still wants us to feed them

If our child is used to us feeding them, we could plan a conversation with them at a neutral time (not at mealtime itself) when we discuss with them that we did this for them when they were younger, and now they can learn to feed themselves. This may be a call for connection, so we can make sure there is some lively mealtime conversation that they can join in. They may eat less at first than they would if we fed them. They are learning to listen to their bodies. It can often go more easily than we expect when we stop feeding them. It may be that we were more attached to feeding them so we knew they'd had enough to eat rather than them needing us to feed them.

When they throw food

By showing our children how we respect food (see "We respect food," on page 121), we teach them to appreciate the meals we are able to make in our home. Children older than 3 years old can learn that food is not for throwing. If they have finished their meal, a 3-year-old can tell us they feel full and ask to leave the table to put their plate in the kitchen. We can let them know to leave anything they don't like on the edge of their plate (or to get a bowl to put it in if they can't stand it on their plate).

If they are having difficulty, we can support them through their feelings but set a limit kindly and clearly: "It looks like you are all done. Let me help you get down from the table so you can bring your plate to the kitchen."

FURTHER READING

- The Feeding Littles website (feedinglittles.com)
- *First Foods to Family Meals* by Sarah Moudry

SLEEPING

Montessori children are not allowed to stay up as late as they like. Our role is to help with the where, when, and how. But we cannot make our child's eyes close to fall asleep.

WHERE
- A calm sleeping environment.
- A consistent, cozy, and relaxing space for them to sleep.

WHEN
- A consistent bedtime for our 3- to 6-year-olds.
- An agreed-upon consistent bedtime for our 6- to 12-year-olds.

HOW
- By offering a predictable bedtime rhythm—including reading stories at bedtime, even for school-age children.
- By coming up with agreements with them—for example, about what to do if they wake in the middle of the night or early in the morning.
- By checking our attitudes about sleep and the energy we might be bringing to bedtime—for example, can we picture our children going happily to bed rather than expecting a battle? How can we be a calm and clear guide even at the end of the day when we are exhausted? Can we have a predictable bedtime so that we have some time to rest ourselves?
- By being clear about expectations—stepping in kindly and clearly if they are making a lot of noise or turning the lights on and off.

PROBLEMS AROUND BEDTIMES

If our child is getting up out of bed, having troubles falling asleep, refusing or stalling bedtime, waking up early, or experiencing any other sleep issues, we can observe:

- What the bedtime routine looks like

- What helps to relax them

- What winds them up or makes them overexcited

- How they fall asleep, and how they wake up

- What time they lie down in their bed and whether they talk or read once they're in bed and for how long

- What time they fall asleep

- What their sleeping environment looks like

We can problem-solve with our child and find a way that works for all of us. We might like to consider the following:

- **What are they digesting?** Not just the food they eat, but everything they take in: the music they listen to, the media they watch, the books they read, the friends they spend time with, and the atmosphere at home and at school. All these things can result in poor sleep, nightmares, or fear of the dark or monsters.

- **Are they getting enough time outdoors?** Fresh air can promote sleep.

- **Are there sustainable ways for them to get to sleep?** White noise helps some children. Listening to the same audiobook every night can give their brain something to focus on while being familiar enough to not overactivate their brain or keep them awake. Older children may be able to learn relaxation techniques or a meditation that we can do with them. Some children need a deep-pressure massage or a weighted blanket to help them decompress. Others find that wrestling before bedtime gets out the last of their energy.

- **Do they have breathing issues that could be affecting their sleep?** These can be assessed by a sleep specialist.

- **How do they process their day?** A bedtime conversation can help them let go of the day's events. Older children may enjoy writing or drawing in a journal.

- **Can we offer gratitude as part of our bedtime rhythm?** It can be calming to end the day by thinking about the things we appreciate—from something tasty they ate to something kind someone did for them.

- **Is there a cue to help them know when to get up in the morning?** A clock that lights up in the morning at a time you set (like Groclock) can be great for young children; a regular alarm clock works for older children.

- **What does the weekend rhythm look like?** From around 5 years old, children are generally happy to let us sleep longer while they get up to play and help themselves to a piece of fruit if they are hungry while waiting for the family breakfast. We could put a note on the door as a reminder not to wake us, "Please play quietly until 9 a.m. Help yourself to a piece of fruit if you are hungry."

- **Is the light making it difficult to sleep in summer months?** Closing the curtains in the living room after dinner is a helpful visual cue that we are starting to wind down for our bedtime rhythm, regardless of the light outside. Investing in blackout curtains will be useful too.

- **Is the darkness making it hard to wake up in the winter months?** An alarm with a wake-light may be of help, or our child might come up with their own solution.

Note: For preschoolers still using a pacifier at bedtime, look for other ways for them to relax their nervous system, like sucking yogurt through a straw, blowing bubbles, holding on to a book or soft toy, a brisk towel rub after bath, deep-pressure bear hugs, kneading dough, squeezing bath toys, or a slow and firm back rub. Agree to a time to say goodbye to the pacifier; for example, passing it on to a family with a new baby could be helpful. Then be patient and supportive as they make the transition. Mostly it goes more smoothly than expected, and we see that we were just as attached to the pacifier as they were.

TOILETING AND STAYING DRY AT NIGHT

Learning to use the toilet

If our child has not yet learned to use the toilet, we can support their transition. Here are some steps we can take to scaffold the skills they will need:

- Set up spaces for them to be able to reach their own underwear and clothing if they get wet; have cleaning cloths and spray at the ready for them to use in cleaning up if they wet their clothes; have a bucket available in the toileting area for their wet clothes.

- Have them practice pulling down their trousers or pulling up their skirt and pushing their underwear down, then repeating those actions in reverse.
- Choose clothes that are easy for them to manage themselves when toileting (avoid overalls, tight jeans, etc.).
- Offer the potty at each diaper change so they get used to sitting on the potty.
- Start offering the potty at regular times, like on waking, after meals, before leaving and after returning home, at bath time, and before bed.
- Teach them to flush the toilet and wash their hands.
- Let them choose some underwear they like at the store.
- Begin by having them wear underpants under the diaper so they start to feel wet when they pee or poop or use training pants (padded underwear).
- Let them choose a date on the calendar when they will stop using diapers.
- On the agreed-upon date, say thank you to the diapers, pass any that are left on to another family with a baby, and begin to use the underpants.
- Continue to offer the potty at regular times.
- Our child will eventually start to feel when they are peeing or pooping; then they will begin to transition to knowing when they need to go; and then they will make it to the potty or toilet by themselves without being reminded. This is a process and can take more time depending on the child.
- Show them how to fold the toilet paper and wipe from front to back. They can wipe themselves first, and we can offer to finish off the wiping for them. Then over time the child can manage this more and more for themselves.
- If they wet themselves, we don't need to shame them. We treat them with respect just as we would want to be treated in the same situation. We can wait until they finish what they are doing and say to them, "I see that your clothes are wet. You can change your clothes and come back to clean up." They can clean themselves up and then wipe the floor, at first perhaps with some support and then taking over the whole process. It may take them more than 15 minutes to do this. We don't need to rush them as this is valuable time learning to care for themselves, but we can offer help if we see they are having difficulty. It's no different from what we do if they break a plate—we show them how to make it right again and move on.
- It can be most difficult for them to stay dry when they are in the middle of working on something. There's a struggle for them between leaving what they are doing and needing to use the toilet/potty. This comes with maturity and being able to hold on longer, until they are able to choose to come back to what they are doing or complete what they are doing and get to the toilet/potty in time.

Staying dry at night

The child may be able to transition to using underwear at night at the same time as learning to use the toilet or potty. Here are some tips:

- We can set up their bed to have a protective cover on the mattress and can tuck in a towel across the bed or use a pad on the bed to absorb any wetness.
- They can learn to go to the toilet/potty before bed and immediately upon waking.
- We can show them how to clean up their sheets and open windows if they are wet during the night.
- If they wet the bed, we can make observations as to when and how often to notice any patterns. Again, we don't shame the child, and we equip them with the skills to deal with whatever is causing a problem and empowering them with solutions. These could be setting an alarm clock to wake themselves up during the night to use the toilet or limiting their water intake in the evening. Or if, for example, we notice that they wet the bed on cold nights, we can anticipate it and offer to wake them during the night to avoid this.

If we have concerns about our child's toileting or ability to stay dry at night, we can see a specialist.

FURTHER READING

- *Toilet Awareness* by Sarah Moudry

CARE OF TEETH

As children move into the second half of the first plane of development, at around 3 years old, they will be taking over more responsibility for their oral hygiene. Caring for their baby teeth helps build a foundation for caring for their adult teeth. We can be there to supervise and perhaps to finish off their brushing; the rest they can manage by themselves.

We can help them take on this responsibility by reading books about cleaning our teeth and why it is important to look after our teeth and gums. We might like to brush our teeth while they clean theirs. For reluctant brushers, we can sing a song while they brush

("This is the way we brush our teeth . . ."), or a sand timer or music box might give them a visual or aural cue while they brush.

Their first trip to the dentist can be very casual. They could come with us to our next dental appointment and watch while we have our teeth cleaned. The dentist might allow them to sit in the chair and make it go up and down. They could open their mouth while the dentist looks inside, and that can be enough to orient them to the idea for their first visit. Reading books about going to the dentist will also help them prepare themselves and understand the process.

If they often forget to brush their teeth, we can help them come up with ways to remind themselves, from a sticky note on the bathroom mirror to following the same sequence in the morning and evening to make it automatic.

When an older child refuses to brush their teeth, it can help to appeal to their reasoning mind by exploring the importance of tooth care. Then we can make a plan to research human teeth, teeth in different animals, how we care for them, and how animals take care of their teeth. We might go to the library to look up information about what happens when we don't brush. Information from the dentist at regular checkups will likely be more readily received than information from us as they are the expert. The dentist can also give the child extra tips on cleaning any hard-to-reach spots or what to do if there is any gum disease.

Regina Lulka, who was the head of a Montessori school in Toronto for many years, has a lovely suggestion for the early second-plane child who loses their first tooth: They can learn about different cultural traditions surrounding this event; for example, by reading *Throw Your Tooth on the Roof: Tooth Traditions from Around the World* by Selby B. Beeler and learning that children in Botswana throw their tooth on the roof, and in Afghanistan, they drop their tooth down a mousehole!

PART TWO

PRACTICAL QUESTIONS

WHEN TO HELP OUR CHILDREN . . . AND WHEN NOT TO

When to step in

Many people think that Montessori children can do whatever they like. However, Dr. Montessori was clear.

We will step in to stop them if:

- They are hurting themselves.
- They are hurting others.
- They are hurting the environment.

This could be if they are causing harm verbally or physically (whether intentionally or not) or creating a disturbance.

These situations need to be immediately addressed without shaming the child but showing them how they can do better; for example, by saying things like:

- "I can't let you bang your head. You look frustrated. Can you show me with this paper and pencil instead?"
- "I can't let you hit your friend. I'll help you calm down, and then we can come up with some words to tell them why you are angry."
- "Those flowers are fragile. This is how we care for them."

When to wait and observe

Then there are far more times when we can stand back to observe to allow our child to learn from the experience.

We can observe and wait a little longer if no one is in danger and the child:

- Will learn from the natural consequences
- Is trying to master something
- Is trying a different way to do something
- Is expressing themselves
- Is testing the limits of their body

In these moments, we try not to comment or react. As long as it is not an emergency, we can wait and show them at another time when they will be more receptive to learning from us.

A couple of examples:

1. With a child who is learning to write, we don't correct their spelling. We continue to model spelling and careful writing when we are writing something for them.
2. If a child slams a door in anger, we can make a mental note and later show them in a fun way how we close the door slowly and quietly. "Can we do it as quietly as possible? Did you hear it?"

When to help our child

Sometimes helping our child is giving them just the smallest amount of assistance so they can get further.

Help might look like:

- A verbal cue
- Asking if they'd like help
- Telling them they can ask us if they'd like help at any point
- Asking if we can have a turn to show them something, then stepping back to see if they can get further
- Setting up an activity to help them learn a skill they are missing

Imagine a 6-year-old is cutting out a model of a paper house. We can see that they are about to cut off a piece that they will need. Can we wait to see if they correct themselves? Can we wait to see if they cut it off and then work out how they will fix it? Or we might give the smallest verbal cue—"I can see that flap looks like it is about to be cut off"—and then wait to see what they do with that information.

As children get older, they can manage more and more themselves. These questions from Dr. Christine Carter, a sociologist, author, and speaker, can be helpful to assist them:

- What's your plan?
- You're going to do that later? What does that look like?
- How will you remind yourself?
- What would you like me to do if you ignore your alarm?

INSTEAD OF "GOOD JOB"

Many adults believe that if we praise our children ("Good job," "Good boy," "Good girl") or offer them rewards, it will motivate them to learn or behave. However, by praising them, we teach them to look outside themselves rather than fostering their own intrinsic motivation. For those wanting to find out more about the effect of praise, we recommend reading Alfie Kohn's article "Five Reasons to Stop Saying 'Good Job!'"

So what to say instead? We can instead give them feedback using objective language, to help them build a picture of themselves. Adele Faber and Elaine Mazlish's book *How to Talk So Kids Will Listen & Listen So Kids Will Talk* has some helpful suggestions:

- Describe what they did. "Look at that! You carried that bucket of water all the way up the hill to make the moat you are building." (Rather than saying "Good job!")

- Describe their effort. "You've worked every night on that report, and it's nearly done." (Rather than focusing on its not being complete yet.)

- Describe what they might be feeling. "You look really excited/pleased/proud of yourself." (Rather than saying, "I'm so proud of you.")

- Sum it up with a word: "You helped Grandma all the way up the stairs. That's what I call being thoughtful/kind/patient!" (Rather than saying, "Good girl.")

- Say how we feel. "I enjoy cooking dinner with you." (Rather than saying, "Good boy.")

For older children, Terrence Millie (an experienced Montessori elementary teacher and trainer) likes to engage the child in self-reflection by asking questions here, too, like: "I noticed you _____. How did that make you feel?"

HOW TO ENCOURAGE INDEPENDENCE

We have talked in this book about the benefits of our child's being able to care for and think for themselves. For the children who resist and want us to continue to do things for them, we can scaffold the skills of independence. It might be that they never clean up after themselves, or that they won't wipe their own bottom, or pull up their trousers. They might expect us to sit next to them while they play.

Remember, the more we force them, the more they will resist. Instead, here are some tips to encourage independence:

- **Inspire them.** Make the task interesting and engaging for them, follow their interests, get them involved.
- **Look for and remove obstacles.** Look for distractions and perhaps physical obstacles (ourselves included) and remove them.
- **Observe.** How long can they play by themselves? How close do we need to be? What self-care activities can they manage by themselves? Do we need to stay in the same room doing something else to keep them accountable?
- **For something difficult for them, do it together first.** Then the next time, we can help them get started with the first step, and then let them take over.
- **Build up slowly.** Let them get used to leading the play. Then step out to another room to do a job and come back. Build up the time they are playing independently.
- **Leave the problem with them.** Let's stop rescuing them. We can set up the environment, we can help them make a plan, and then we can let them feel the natural consequences.
- **Assess whether they have the skills.** How can we support them to learn them? Can we break the activity into smaller steps they can manage?
- **Make the task age appropriate and scaffold skills.** For example, we don't let a young child ride their bike through the city by themselves. First, they start in a park with us running alongside them. Then they might soon be riding on their own in a bike lane or on the sidewalk. As they acquire more skills, they learn to bike on the road with us on our bike at their side. Then we bike a lot through the city together over the years to give them more experience. By the time they start high school, they have enough experience to go alone, with a mobile phone in case of emergency.

When our child demands our help

Our child might shout at us, "I can't!" or demand, "You do it. I don't want to!" We can observe to see if there is an obstacle that could be removed. They may be seeking connection with us in this moment (we could offer a small amount of help and let them get further; e.g., by saying "I'll do this one, and you can do that one"). Or perhaps they are feeling rushed (we can look at how our mornings could be restructured to allow them more time), or that there is too much that's out of their control (how can we give them control over more parts of their day?).

We don't need to accept their shouting. We can calmly and clearly guide them to learn ways to request our help without demanding. We like the phrase in Jane Nelsen and Chip DeLorenzo's book, *Positive Discipline in the Montessori Classroom*: "How can you ask me in a way that I can hear and understand you?" We can reassure them that we are doing our best to support them and will be available if they get stuck (we might do some self-reflection here if we are indeed doing too much for them).

For more, refer back to page 47, "Fostering independence and responsibility."

STAYING HOME BY THEMSELVES

It will be some time before we leave our child at home by themselves. In many states in the US, there is a legislated age; in some states, from 12 years old. In the meantime, we can build skills they will need.

Here are some things to consider:

- **Safety.** What would they do in case of a fire, accident, or other emergency? Teach them how to contact emergency services. Have important contact numbers readily accessible.
- **Strangers.** What do they do if someone knocks on the door or if the phone rings?
- **Snacks.** What can they eat while we are out?
- **Security.** Keep any alcohol, cleaning materials, and lighters out of reach.
- **Distance.** How far away are we?
- **Contact information.** Are we reachable by phone?
- **Time.** How long are they okay by themselves?
- **Community.** What kind of community do we have around us? Do we know our neighbors? Can our neighbors look out for them? Do we live in a big city?

If our child has a friend who is allowed to be home alone and we don't feel comfortable with our child playing there, we can discuss it with the child's parent or invite their child to our home instead.

Children around 6 years old will want more independence and risk, so we can find ways for them to play with friends with less supervision. For example, we could take them to an adventure playground in our neighborhood and stay in the café area while they explore, climb, and take greater risks in a controlled environment. There may be community groups like scouting where they can practice more advanced activities like learning to start fires and sleeping under the stars.

TRAVELING WITH KIDS

If we are lucky enough to have the resources to travel with our children, Montessori principles can also be packed in the bag with us.

- **Get the children involved from the time we start planning.** They may not get to decide our final destination, but we could let them pick from a couple of places we have come up with or from two accommodation options. We can also go to the library together to do some research on the area, people, food, and culture of our destination before we go.

- **Have a physical map of the area.** It will be easier for them to concretely understand where we are staying and the places we are visiting, and the children can help us plan any public transportation we will be using with a transit map. They can also decorate the map with colored stickers to mark highlights from the trip or glue entrance and travel tickets onto special places from our stay.

- **Children like to have an idea of, and be involved in making, the plan.** We can give our child a heads-up the night before of the following day's plans and get their suggestions for things they might like to add in to make sure that everyone has a say in what's happening. We could also make a visual calendar of the days ahead if this helps them.

- **Make a travel journal.** It could be a combined family journal or a notebook with a lock for recording events and inspiration from their travels. We can add photos when we get back home.

- **Appreciate, don't appropriate.** To be mindful of how we spend our time and money, we can seek out tours from locals rather than large companies and avoid buying cheap trinkets from the markets and instead buy fewer but better-quality and more authentic items made by local or Indigenous people. We can teach our child that appropriation begins when people profit from what they saw, learned, or bought on their travels.

- **Plan some downtime.** Think about how we can bring unscheduled time to our travels. Likely one or more members of our family will need some time to decompress during the trip. Schedule a pajama morning or day off or some time each afternoon to read books and play, or visit a park or playground between museum tours to allow some big movement. We might pack our current favorite board game to play as a family.

- **Get packing.** Find child-sized luggage that they can manage themselves. A 3-year-old can pack and carry their own backpack, and a 10-year-old can lay out everything they need to take for us to check and give any feedback, then pack the items into their bag. Children might make their own checklists or ask how many sets of underwear, pairs of socks, and items of clothing they will need.

- **Think about food.** Finding accommodations with a kitchen can be useful. We can prepare some food for during the day to take with us or mark on a map some cafés near places we are visiting so that we don't have tired and hungry children on our hands.

- **Practice the language before arrival.** Learn some phrases to use in greeting people and saying thank you and goodbye. If we will be traveling abroad for a long stay, we could consider attending classes with our children or practicing with a friend or neighbor who speaks the language.

- **Provide alternatives to screens.** While we may choose to allow our children access to screens on travel days, as much as possible, look for hands-on activities that fit in their backpack or suitcase. If possible, include a notebook and pen, a secondhand camera, a pack of cards, a book to read, and maybe some travel watercolor paints. For some old-fashioned games to play on long trips, check out the Activities Appendix organized by interest online at workman.com/montessori.

- **And remember to look for ways to reduce our impact on the Earth as we travel.** Consider destinations that can be reached by shorter train travel over long-haul flights, make less frequent trips, find eco-friendly lodgings, take reusable bottles and cutlery, and avoid buying disposable souvenirs that will soon get dusty.

BILINGUALISM/MULTILINGUALISM

The child from 3 to 6 years old with their absorbent mind will absorb any language we use in our home. Common ways to introduce languages are one parent, one language (OPOL) or domains of use. In OPOL, each parent uses their native language with the child, and a family language is chosen to be used between parents. Applying domains of use means that we have consistent times (e.g., a day of the week or mealtime) and/or places (e.g., inside or outside the home) when and/or where each language is used.

About 30 percent of our child's waking hours need to be in a particular language for it to become a literacy language (meaning the child is proficient enough to study in this language). We can look for ways to increase exposure to a language like finding additional caregivers who speak the language, asking a neighbor who speaks it to read books with our child, or planning longer holiday visits to our country of origin.

A child from 6 to 12 years old can start to learn another language; however, they no longer have the assistance of an absorbent mind or sensitive period for language. Instead they will apply their conscious, logical, reasoning mind. We can make it useful and fun for them to learn a language—for example, we can use the new language to make films or write poetry, or read translated editions of their favorite books.

FURTHER READING

For more on this topic, read Eowyn Crisfield's book
Bilingual Families: A Practical Language Planning Guide.

MONTESSORI FOR CHILDREN WITH A DISABILITY OR NEURODIVERGENCE

As we touched on in the first chapter, Montessori is for every child. We meet each child where they are and make adjustments where needed. There are now Montessori courses for children with disabilities, and while it's beyond the scope of this book, here are some general examples to get you started:

- A child with a physical disability often has similar cognitive ability to that of other children their age. We can look at ourselves and the environment to adapt them so the child gets the opportunity to master the same skills as other children though they may need additional support in some areas. For example, a child with less muscle tone may not be able to carry a tray or to speak, so we can look for ways for them to be able to access the materials (e.g., having everything at floor height) or to express themselves (e.g., by using a computer program to assist).
- A child who is deaf has a need to communicate, and we want to give the child the opportunity to express themselves and to understand others. We can offer rich language experiences from sign language and spoken language from birth, get their attention first before communicating, use our body language and gestures to add more meaning, and be mindful of acoustics and lighting in our spaces.

- For a child who is blind, we can be intentional about how we set up the room and stay with the same arrangement. We can have braille books and tactile or braille labels where needed. Any siblings can be shown how to guide the blind child. And we can allow more time for them to navigate the room themselves.

- A child who is neurodivergent may need more practice in some areas of learning like motor skills, language, sensory processing, and emotional regulation. We can let them focus on their strengths and give them opportunities to practice the skills they find difficult as well as seek any necessary additional support from experts and therapists.

- A child with ADHD may benefit from an environment with fewer distractions and less clutter. We can look for those activities that help them self-regulate, including many of the practical life activities.

- An autistic child may have a strong need for order in their environment and their day, and we can make things as predictable as possible (and help them build skills around uncertainty and adjusting to changes as they grow). Some may benefit from additional support and learning in social situations and in communicating. We will observe the child and make adaptations accordingly based on their unique needs.

As the adult supporting them, we need to remember to support ourselves. It can take a lot of energy to advocate for our child, to help them as little as possible and as much as necessary, to get them to extra appointments and assessments, and to support their emotional journey. Look for community, and look for ways to get sufficient rest, to get a break, to exercise, and to eat well.

Every child's timeline will look different. There will be individual challenges to navigate. All children deserve to be treated as the beautiful human being they were put on Earth to be. Let's look at capability and help them build skills and adapt ourselves and the environment where necessary.

FURTHER READING

- For families with neurodivergent children, we recommend *Differently Wired* by Deborah Reber.
- Learn about the signing community from the website What Dad Did with Ashton Jean-Pierre (whatdaddid.com.au).

PART THREE

WHEN DIFFICULT SITUATIONS ARISE

Raising our children in a Montessori way doesn't mean there will never be any conflict; instead, our children are learning to work with others and to solve conflict in a respectful way. For us to be their guide during these difficult situations, we need to notice when we are activated by a situation and how we can regulate ourselves (see chapter 8 about preparing ourselves).

CULTIVATING COOPERATION

We might find ourselves saying, "They just won't listen to me!" They are tired, overscheduled, and want to do things in their own way, on their own time, and do not want us to nag them. In these moments, remember that this is often when the "good stuff" happens.

Let's see it as an opportunity:

- To cultivate cooperation in our family
- For our child to learn something new about themselves or others
- For us to help them build the skills to face difficult situations
- To maintain the relationship with our child that we have built

Know that it's not too late to learn new ways to cultivate cooperation. We can start today to be more respectful with our child. We can explain to them that we have been learning some new skills, that we want to be in a better relationship with them. It usually doesn't take long for our children to like this new approach. After all, we are now working together, on each other's side. Not against each other.

WHEN OUR CHILD DOESN'T COOPERATE

Let's learn to be a proactive guide, rather than a boss or servant. When we're trying to cultivate cooperation with our child, here are eight questions we can ask ourselves:

1. WHAT CAN WE OBSERVE/WHAT INFORMATION CAN WE OBJECTIVELY COLLECT?

We often feel that our child never listens to us or never tidies up or never goes to bed on time. What can we observe to see the situation more clearly?

For example:

- What time does it happen?
- How often does it happen?
- Is the child tired or hungry?
- Are there any changes in our family?

- What communication do they use?
- What are they doing when it happens?
- Is anyone else involved?

2. WHAT IS THEIR NEED/WHAT IS OUR NEED?

Nonviolent communication can be a very helpful tool in a Montessori home. We want to respect the child and solve problems with them, and we want to find solutions that work for everyone.

An important part of Montessori is to "follow the child," letting them develop in their unique way. Yet this can sometimes be misunderstood to mean that everything is about the child. We may have conversations with our friends or our partner constantly interrupted by our child; we may make plans only around the children without making time for our own interests and hobbies; and we might forget to look after and nourish ourselves. Instead, being a Montessori family means meeting the needs of our child while also having our own needs met. Below are some examples:

> "It sounds like you are really interested in going out with your friends. And it's my job to keep you safe. I wonder if we can come up with a plan that addresses my concerns about safety and still allows you to go. If not, I'll have to say no, but I'd really like to see if we can come up with something."

"It sounds like you want to sing loudly, and I have a headache. How can we solve the problem?" (They help us lie down on the couch with a cup of tea and go into their room to sing with headphones on.)

Even when they seem too young, we can ask them to be involved in coming up with a solution by asking, "How can we solve the problem?" It's amazing some of the creative ideas they come up with.

3. HOW CAN WE KEEP THEM SAFE WHILE THEY HAVE THEIR NEEDS MET, IF APPLICABLE?

We might stand at the entrance to the store while they make a purchase by themselves; we might encourage them to invite their friends to our home to hang out; or we might first review a game, book, or film so that we can guide them if needed through any possibly scary or adult parts.

4. HOW CAN WE FIND A WAY TO WORK WITH THEM IN THIS SITUATION (VS BRIBING, THREATENING, PUNISHING, OR LECTURING)?

In his book *Unconditional Parenting*, Alfie Kohn talks about getting children to help come up with ways to solve problems ("working with") rather than using extrinsic means that come from us like bribing, punishing, or threatening ("doing to"). When we work with our child, we acknowledge that we have something that needs to happen and that we want this to align with what our child wants to happen (see the Venn diagram below showing this sweet spot). When they are involved in the process, they feel empowered and capable.

WHAT OUR KID WANTS TO DO

WHAT WE WANT OUR KID TO DO

THE SWEET SPOT

Depending on the age of our child, this might be doing some brainstorming with them, writing down the ideas they come up with, or suggesting some ideas for them to choose from or as a springboard for their own ideas. For a 2.5-year-old, we may need to help them create a visual schedule to get ready for bed that they can follow. For a 10-year-old, we may need to gently remind them that it's 8:03 p.m. and we cannot hear the shower running.

5. ARE WE SUPPORTING THEIR DEVELOPMENT?

This is a useful question we learned from Alison Awes to reflect on. We can look at the direction our child is headed in and the skills they will need to move in this direction. We may need to scaffold skills, but let's not keep them in a stage of development that they have outgrown. Let's ask ourselves if we are keeping them in an earlier stage of development or if something they are doing (e.g., overreliance on technology) is not supporting their development.

6. HOW CAN I SET A KIND AND CLEAR LIMIT IF NEEDED?

We are the child's guide. We give them freedom within limits. We can remind them of agreements that we have made and help them follow through (see page 150 on setting kind and clear limits).

7. WHAT CAN THE CHILD (AND WHAT CAN WE) LEARN FROM THIS SITUATION?

Even though it can be difficult to see our child having a hard time, they are growing from these experiences. They may be learning to overcome their fears, to make plans and stick to them, to regulate themselves when they are anxious or worried, or to see that they can solve problems. We are likely to learn more about our child and ourselves too.

8. HOW CAN I MAINTAIN CONNECTION WITH MY CHILD IN THIS SITUATION?

Again, we come back to the importance of connection when getting their cooperation. We try not to get frustrated. We try to be a calm and clear guide. Yet if there are times when we get frustrated, we can apologize and try again. "What I should have done is _____." "What I should have said is _____." "Let's try it again."

If they won't listen

Instead of blaming them for not listening to us, we want to look for ways to communicate so we will be heard. What comes to mind is the Walter B. Barbe quote "If you've told a child a thousand times and he still doesn't understand, then it is not the child who is the slow learner."

Here are some ideas we use in our classrooms; many we have learned from the book *How to Talk So Kids Will Listen & Listen So Kids Will Talk* by Adele Faber and Elaine Mazlish. (Also, refer to page 117, "Talk in a way that helps them listen.")

Keep them involved in coming up with a solution. Offer questions to activate their brain, like "What could you do?" or "What could you try?" or "What is our family agreement about _____ ?"

Allow time for them to process our request. We all need some time to switch activities. So ideally, we can wait until they have finished what they are doing or allow them time to process our request ("tarry time"). It works well to count to 10 silently in our head (not out loud), allowing time for a child to respond. Try it. Often by the time we have counted to around 8 in our head, they are starting to finish up what they were doing and are ready to listen or respond.

Use positive language and tell them how to be helpful. When we use "no" or "don't," the child hears first what we don't want them to do. Then they have to work out what to do instead (if they work it out at all). Instead, there is always a way to say things in a positive way; telling them what we want them to do, not what we don't want them to do. For example, say, "Be gentle with the baby" rather than "Don't hit;" "Use two hands" instead of "Don't spill;" and "Let's sit to eat" rather than "Don't leave the table."

Instead of saying no, we can also use "yes, when . . ." For example, "Yes, you can have another cracker when you've finished the one you are eating." If there are no more crackers, we could say, "Yes, you can have another one when we've been to the store tomorrow."

We can say "Let me think about it." Sometimes we automatically say no to our child's request. Instead, we can say we'll think about it to see if we can make it work (as long as we remember to come back to them).

Actions speak louder than words. Children can tune out long explanations or instructions given from across the room. We can stand up and go over to them or show them where something goes by tapping a shelf and saying, "It goes here."

Give information. We might respectfully tell them, "Diego, the door is open," "I see a lunch box on the table," or "Milk goes bad if we leave it out of the fridge." Then we let them work out what needs to be done. We avoid using a patronizing or sarcastic tone, modeling respect for each other.

Provide age-appropriate choices. A 3- to 6-year-old can decide what they would like to have for lunch based on some healthy options, and a 6- to 12- year-old can decide if they would like to play first or do their homework first, as long as it gets completed.

Use one word. If we need to remind our child of something they already know well, often a lecture or constant nagging will be ignored. Instead, saying "lunch box" or "shoes" in a kind tone might prompt a child to check if they have forgotten something or remind them gently of the next step. Again, they are invited to think for themselves, rather than passively receive an instruction.

Talk about how we feel. We can model clear boundaries with our child (without giving a guilt trip). "When you hit me, it hurts me. I'm going to move over here. I'd like you to be gentle with me."

Write a note. When something is written down, it gives it some authority. Use this option sparingly, but do use it. "Please put me away" placed on an experiment left on the table; "Please let us sleep until 9:00 a.m." stuck on the bedroom door; "Please use tiptoes" along the hallway where the downstairs neighbors complain about noisy feet can all be effective. For children who can't read, we can add a picture or tell them what it says. "It says 'Fragile.' Let's be gentle with that glass cabinet." "It says 'Private.' I think your brother wants to be by himself. Let's do something together." Or "It's time to turn the oven on. Let's put a sign on it that says 'Hot' to remind us."

Use humor. A little humor can go a long way. With a young child who is resisting putting on their shoes, we can pretend to put their shoe on our foot and say, "Ah, it seems to be too small. What's going on here? Why doesn't it fit me?" Or we can use the wrong name/color and let them correct us. They'll delight in telling us, "Those shoes are not blue! They're purple." This can lighten the mood, and they may then be willing to put on the shoes. With an older child, we might substitute some silly lyrics for the usual ones in a favorite song or put on some music to clean up to together.

WHEN OUR CHILD IS UPSET

Allow all feelings

Our child's feelings help them (and us) understand what is important to them, judge situations, have empathy for others, and make sense of the world around them. When we hold space for our child's feelings, we are learning to see things from their perspective while not jumping in to solve things for them. It's not our role as parents to take away the hard stuff for our children. Our role is to be there to support them in the joy and the sorrow. We need to let them have their own experience.

When our child is feeling big emotions, we can help them by:

Guessing how they are feeling. By responding in this way, we are showing our child that we are available to help them even when they are having a hard time. We aren't telling them they are angry—the child will usually retort with an angry "I am *not* angry!" But when someone touches on a feeling we may be experiencing, we can feel seen and supported.

Here are some of our favorite stem sentences to use:

- "It sounds like you _____."

- "Are you maybe feeling _____?"

- "You really wish you could _____?"

- "I can understand if you were feeling _____ right now."

- "When _____ happened, it could be upsetting."

- "Of course you'd feel _____."

- "That's understandable. I can imagine that could have been _____?"

- "That makes sense. I can understand why you might feel _____."

Helping them process their emotions. When we try to distract a child or cheer them up quickly before they have processed everything, it's like we are putting on a Band-Aid. But as soon as the Band-Aid comes off (i.e., something else happens), the wound will still be there, and the emotions will resurface. In *The Whole Brain Child*, Daniel Siegel and Tina Payne Bryson talk about "naming it to tame it." We can help our child process their feelings (from the right brain) by talking about them (using the left brain); for example, helping them retell a story about something that happened. Similarly, if they have fears, we want to accept their concerns, not dismiss them; we seek to understand them and then help make them manageable for our child. (See page 157 for more on managing fears.)

Helping them regulate themselves. There are times when our child flips their lid and is no longer able to access their prefrontal cortex (the part of the brain used for rational decision-making, planning, self-control, and control over emotions). The reptilian brain (what Siegel and Payne Bryson refer to as the "downstairs part of the brain," which contains the brain stem, limbic region, and amygdala) has kicked in, and they become dysregulated. This might look like a tantrum or when they are completely out of control of their emotions. They won't be able to hear us until their lid is closed again and they are calm.

We first help our child come back to regulation and then, only once they are calm again, talk to them about what happened and help them take responsibility if needed.

Ideas for self-regulation:

- They choose to take themselves to their room when they are upset.
- They choose to go to their calm space (see page 149).
- They allow us to co-regulate (e.g., allow us to give them a cuddle, rub their back, breathe with them). When we are regulated, we can imagine "lending them" our nervous system.
- They rock or sway their body or hum.
- They move their body (e.g., by doing jumping jacks, running, or cleaning).
- They do a breathing exercise (e.g., breathe in, smell the flower, breathe out, blow out the candle, or breathe in for 3 seconds, hold for 3 seconds, breathe out for 6 seconds).
- An older child may be able to look for five things they can see, four things they can touch, three things they can hear, two things they can smell, and one thing they can taste.

FURTHER READING

- *Self-Reg: How to Help Your Child (and You) Break the Stress Cycle and Successfully Engage with Life* by Stuart Shanker

Staying calm. There may be times when our child looks like they are out of control, but this time they are using what Siegel and Payne Bryson refer to as the "upstairs part of their brain" (including the prefrontal cortex). We might, for example, see that they are able to stop crying to argue or talk. Then we can stand firm—we do not negotiate—while acknowledging that it can be hard to hear no. We are kind and clear.

All behavior is communication, and our child may be expressing a need for attention or affection or other. Again, we stand firm, we do not change our mind, but we will look for any underlying reasons to understand what is going on for them.

Creating a calm space. A calm space can be useful anytime they are upset (an idea from Dr. Jane Nelsen's Positive Discipline books). For children from around 2.5 to 3 years, we can create a space in our home with them (usually in a common area of the home) where they can go to calm down when they are upset. "What might make you feel nice at times when you're upset?" They may choose to have some books there, a favorite soft toy, some fairy lights, cushions, trains or cars; anything that makes them feel good. It's different from a time-out, when the child is sent away as punishment. Going to a calm space is sometimes referred to as a time-in. They can choose to go to self-regulate, and they can stay as long (or as briefly) as they like. If tempers are high and they don't want to go, we can always go to the space ourselves to calm down or go there with them. They are learning how to bring themselves back to calm.

Have a notebook available for each child. When they are having big feelings about something, another way for them to feel heard is to have us write down what they are upset about. When we write it down, it feels very important to them; they feel acknowledged. If a child wants to juice oranges but there are none left, we can write it down so we can let them know when there are oranges again. For older children, we can encourage them to write down any reminders for themselves in their own notebook. (This also works well if they are nagging us to buy something in a store. We can write it in our notebook as an option for a birthday or special occasion.)

Help them talk

Sometimes it's hard for them to talk to us. As we mentioned earlier, some of the most difficult conversations happen most easily while we are doing something else, doing a job around the house ("Come talk to me while we fold some laundry"), sitting side by side on the bus, building Legos together, or throwing a ball.

We can ask them what is going on for them and what they need (not what they want). Their ability to articulate their needs (e.g., reassurance, a hug, space, connection) will improve as we continue to practice this with them.

Amanda Morin, author of *What Is Empathy?*, talks about being a detective, gathering information, making sure we understand the situation correctly, listening, and affirming.

- "You looked kind of grumpy, and I wonder how you are feeling now."
- "What I hear you saying is _____? Did I get it right?"
- "Tell me what you need me to know/what you need to tell me."
- "Is there something I can help you with?"

If they lash out at us, Morin says we can be clear:

- "I don't feel good when you shout at me."
- "I can't fix this for you, but I can be that person that you can talk to about it."

Remember not to take it personally, especially with 6- to 12-year-olds, who notoriously talk back and are rude. They want mental independence and are showing us they can think for themselves. And we will let them know what language is okay and what is not okay for us, perhaps coming back to it at a later time when everyone is calm.

SETTING KIND AND CLEAR LIMITS WHEN NEEDED

In those moments when things have escalated or someone may get physically or emotionally hurt, as the adult, we need to be the child's prefrontal cortex. We can use the phrase we learned earlier: "It's my job to keep everyone safe." It's calm and clear and takes ownership of our responsibility as the parent/caregiver.

We might then refer to one of our agreements, "We agreed to no biting, hurting, or teasing in our home" or "We agreed to eat food at the table."

Sometimes the child will protest: "It's not fair. _____ is allowed to _____." We will not negotiate on one of the agreements in the moment, but we can add it to our list to discuss at another, neutral time or at the next family meeting so we can weigh the pros and cons and make a balanced decision. "It sounds like it's important to you that we review that agreement. Let's write it down to come back to on _____."

If needed, we can give them a respectful choice ("We agreed to no screens this weekend. Would you like to turn off the TV, or shall I do it?"), and if they don't respond, we follow through kindly and clearly.

"If you say it, mean it, and if you mean it, follow through."

—Jane Nelsen and Kelly Gfroerer, *Positive Discipline Tools for Teachers*

We need to be careful of our tone so it doesn't come across as a threat, and we also need to be careful not to be too weak. ("Shall we put these away?" we ask timidly.) Instead, we need to be kind and clear, and follow through. ("I expect the floor to be clear of muddy footprints by dinnertime.")

If they become upset when we set a limit, we can help them come back to calm as we learned earlier. We show them that we see their struggle and that we are not overwhelmed by their discomfort (nor do they need to be). They might shout at us for setting a limit. "I hate you!" They might go to their room and slam the door. We have to be okay with them not liking us in that moment and look for ways to regulate ourselves if needed.

When everyone has calmed down, we can make a repair (see "Making a Repair" on page 154).

The period from 6 to 12 years, as we've said earlier, is more stable. When setting limits for children in this age group, we can appeal to their rational mind and their moral and social development. If we don't want them to run inside, we need to give them a reason or two. "If you run inside, there is a chance you will bump into the table with the vase from Grandma, which is special to me, and it's noisy for your brother, who is studying for his exam tomorrow." They may not be happy about it, but they will respect it.

Additionally, if we have already been practicing Montessori in earlier years, then our children will already know that when we say yes, we mean yes; when we say no, we mean no; and when we say, "Let's see," we'll be sure to think about it some more.

Children in the Montessori approach aren't allowed to do everything they like. They have a lot of freedoms, but we are there to guide them, set clear limits if needed, and keep them safe.

PROBLEM-SOLVE TOGETHER

There are times when we'll need to make a time to sit down to resolve a problem that keeps coming up.

In a Montessori school, if a child keeps coming to school late, instead of being punished, they have a meeting with their teacher to work out the reason for the lateness. Is it because they are having trouble getting out of bed? Maybe there is something going on in the family? How can we help remind them so they'll be on time? The teacher is working with the child to find a way to get them to come to school, rather than punishing them and making the child not want to come to school at all.

We can use a similar idea at home if our child is having trouble waking up in the morning for school. We can have a meeting and brainstorm a list of ideas (even silly ones), for example:

- Setting an alarm
- Setting a series of alarms
- Putting the alarm clock across the room so they need to get out of bed to turn it off
- Not going to school at all
- A parent coming to check on them

Once we have a long list with everyone's suggestions, we can go through and remove the ones that definitely won't work ("Not going to school isn't an option, so let's cross that one off.") and then choose one to try.

After that, we can make a plan to review how it's going (usually around a week later) to see what's working and if anything needs to be changed.

RESOLVING CONFLICT BETWEEN TWO PARTIES

When our child experiences conflict with another person, we can allow them space to resolve it on their own, and we are there if they need support. In this case, experience is the best teacher. In *The Absorbent Mind*, Dr. Montessori wrote, "Apart from exceptional cases, we ought to leave such problems to the children. We can then study their behavior objectively. . . . It is through these daily experiences that a social order comes into being."

When our support is needed

In the article "Did You Say 'Sorry?': Seeing Through Montessori Eyes," Donna Bryant Goertz does not force a child to say sorry. Children are guided to listen to each other, understand what the other child didn't like that they did, and come up with a way that would work for both of them. The child causing the conflict is not seen as a problem, but supported to do the right thing and to feel like they belong.

When we see that our children are having a hard time, we can involve them in the problem-solving process. They listen to each other, we are there to act as a neutral guide if needed, and they come up with their own solution. They will feel supported, loved, and more engaged in following through with the solution. The process may need to be revisited, adjusted, or refined, but the children are involved and taking responsibility for the solution.

When there is a basis of trust, Bill Conway, head of Montessori East in Sydney, Australia, for many years, likes to ask older children, "What do you think you could have done differently in this situation?" They are often very aware of how they could have done better and what to do to make it up to anyone else involved.

Solving problems by themselves

As our children get practice in conflict resolution, we can remove the scaffold of our support. We can offer young children the opportunity to solve the problem for themselves: "One of you wants to play, and the other wants to be by themselves. I'm curious how you will work this out."

Older children will begin to solve more of their disputes and may want to tell us about it later. Or if we hear arguing, we can stand on the side in view so they see that an adult is watching; and if needed, we can offer our help: "You both sound angry right now. Let me know if you need any help."

MAKING A REPAIR

When a child breaks something or hurts someone, whether physically or with words, we can offer them an opportunity to *repair with dignity* (this is a phrase we learned from the Nautilus training with Montessori in Public Action). This teaches the child to think, *I know how to fix things that are broken*, and the other party receives the care they need. If the child doesn't take responsibility, the victim may continue to feel hurt and the child may continue to carry the guilt or shame too.

First, make sure all parties have calmed down. Then we can help them make the repair. It might be offering a tissue or wet cloth to a child that they pushed; fixing a toy that was broken; or making them a picture or card. These are more meaningful repairs than a hollow "Sorry."

For a child from 3 to 6 years old, it's best to make a repair right away while the incident is fresh in their mind. With a child from 6 to 12 years old, we could wait for a more neutral moment later in the day. We can say, "You know earlier, when you said _____ to me?" They will often respond with a spontaneous apology: "I'm sorry. I don't even know why I was so angry."

In Junnifa's family, she tries not to force her children to apologize. She suggests and encourages as needed but gives them time to think about it and come to it themselves, because only then will they be willing to give a genuine apology.

In Simone's family, in times of conflict, they would discuss together how they could make it up to the other person. One time, Oliver played a prank on Emma and her friend having a sleepover, setting their alarm for 4:00 a.m. To make it up to them, he agreed to cook them French toast for breakfast. They were happy, he was pleased with himself for making amends, and he also never pranked them again.

When there is not another child involved, our child may learn to take responsibility through natural or logical consequences. Natural consequences might be, for example, that if they don't want to put on their coat, they'll feel cold outside. If they eat their snack first thing in the morning, there will be no more snack for them to eat. If they don't remember their sports bag, they won't be able to participate in sports practice, or their teacher may not be happy with them.

Sometimes we may apply a logical consequence in a kind and clear way. If the child has borrowed our tools and left them out in the rain, they may find that the next time they come to use our tools, there is a lock on the box. If they are kicking a ball inside, the ball might be put away until we head to the park, and we can invite them to kick a punching bag or jump on an indoor trampoline instead. If children are fighting in the car, we might pull over until it's quiet so we can concentrate on driving. We can talk to them about what we could do next time so that they can eventually use our tools again, leave their ball somewhere inside, or keep themselves occupied in the car so the driver can concentrate.

These are not done in a shaming way ("See, I told you you would get cold") or by threatening them ("If you do that again, I'll _____"). Once they have learned the lesson, we need to drop it too. **They are learning to take responsibility, not to feel guilt.** If the same situation arises, we can remind them what happened last time so they can make a better choice this time.

One reason that a partner or family member might think that the Montessori approach is too soft or that children are allowed to do whatever they like is that people often miss this step. Do not skip this step. Help children make a repair and take responsibility—this is how they grow.

SOME COMMON PROBLEMS

When there is throwing, hitting, biting, or meanness

If our child is upset, we cannot allow them to hurt themselves or others, or act out on something in our home or the environment. If a child throws things, hits, bites, or is being mean:

- We connect with them and stop any dangerous behavior. If they are physically hurting someone, we can say, "I can't let you hurt them," and separate them. If they are hitting something, we can smile at them and say, "You're really giving that thing a hard time. Can you come inside for a minute for me to check something with you?"

- We seek to understand them and help support them to find ways for their needs to be met or build any lagging skills. For example:
  - ◦ Do they need some physical activity to get out some energy or frustration? Can we provide opportunities for them to exert this energy in acceptable ways, from a punching bag, to chopping wood, to going for a swim or run?
  - ◦ Are they having trouble expressing themselves with words? Can we ask them if they need help to talk to their friend or sibling? Or can we practice at neutral moments until they are integrated?
  - ◦ Do they feel seen and like they belong? If not, they may look for other ways to be seen or belong in the family or group.
  - ◦ If they are throwing their activities at home, are the activities meeting their needs? Are they too hard or too easy? What are they interested in right now?

- We help them make a repair if needed (see page 154).

When a child whines

A whining child is telling us something—we can be like a detective to uncover what is going on. As a child, Simone had the nickname Moany Macaroni because she would complain a lot. Her family owned a store, and one day she was so bored. Simone lay behind the cash register kicking her legs in defiance. She wanted out of there. Simone eventually learned to pack a bag of books and knitting to keep herself busy. Her parents also gave her jobs around the store, which made her feel like she was contributing.

We can observe our child: When do they whine, and why do they whine? Are they missing any skills? Can we teach them how to interrupt politely? (See page 102.) Can we see what needs are not being met? Are there moments when they are engaged and able to communicate calmly? Can they practice at neutral times how to ask for help? Can we find time for them to tell us about their woes?

A parent in Simone's classes allows her three children to have "grievance time" when they can talk about things that are bothering them, particularly with their siblings, which helps them get rid of their frustrations and sometimes even come up with solutions.

How to manage fears

A preschooler might have a fear of things like monsters under the bed, the dark, dogs, or learning to bike or swim. Children ages 6 to 12 may also begin to fear things like bad things happening to those they care about or not being liked by other children.

We may not be able to get rid of their fears, but we can help them begin to manage them by:

- Being a safe place for them to talk about it. We can allow all feelings and listen to them without enabling their fear (e.g., we don't play along by squirting water under the bed to keep the monsters away).
- Finding practical solutions with the child to help them manage the anxiety (e.g., by providing a night-light and leaving the door open for a child who is scared of the dark).
- Looking for any input that could be adding to their fears (e.g., television programs or books like fairy tales with witches or monsters).
- Assisting them in building up practical skills slowly. We could visit a dog park regularly for them to learn about dogs from a distance (for a child scared of dogs); they could sit on the side of the swimming pool to watch for a few weeks of classes (for a child frightened of water); and we could find a balance bike so they can touch their feet to the ground to move and slowly learn to glide when they are ready to release their feet (for a child scared of falling off their bike).
- Staying calm ourselves. If we scoop up our child at every loud noise or have some uncertainty ourselves, our child will feel it. We can model how we might approach a dog or tell them about a fear we learned to overcome.
- Offering a security object. They may wish to choose a soft toy or blanket to sleep with or keep with them if they are scared of the dark or monsters.
- Researching things together. If they are scared of storms, we can find out what they are and the safest things to do in a storm.
- Using the rainbow ritual to help them feel connected to us at night or if they have difficulty separating from us. We send the colors of the rainbow from our heart to their heart ("I'm sending the color red—the color of strawberries, tomatoes, roses, and fire engines—from my heart to your heart. Now the color orange . . ."). This rainbow ritual was developed by the Quest for Life Foundation to help children deal with sad or difficult news. Children feel connected to us by this rainbow, which can feel very concrete to a young child.

PART FOUR

DISCUSSING SENSITIVE TOPICS

Most people would say that they find honesty and telling the truth important. Yet children ask tricky questions, and at times we aren't sure what to say. Answering questions around sex and death can be some of the most difficult conversations—not for the children but for us. We may have shame around these topics, remember embarrassing experiences from our own childhood, or not know the right thing to say. Yet if we avoid answering our children's questions about sex, gender, race, and other sensitive subjects, then our children learn that we don't talk about these things or that there is some shame around them.

So what to do instead?

Be a model of honesty

Telling our children to tell the truth and telling the truth ourselves might sometimes be at odds. For example, do our children ever hear us telling a little white lie? Our example is being absorbed by our child. And what we do is more powerful than what we say.

Instead of saying, "Let's just tell them you are only 3 years old so you don't have to pay for a train ticket," we can be honest: "Now that you are 4, we'll need to buy you a children's ticket."

Give age-appropriate factual answers or look them up together

In Montessori, we like to answer children's questions with the correct facts. We don't have to give them all the information straightaway. It might be sufficient to answer a 3- or 4-year-old's question with one simple, clear sentence. In response to the question "Why don't they have a daddy in their house?" we could answer, "Some people have two mommies, some have two daddies, some have a mommy and a daddy, some have one parent, and there are many other types of families too." If they don't ask any further questions in the moment, we can follow up later to see if they have more questions.

Books can also be a great way to facilitate these discussions. If we don't have a book on hand, we can tell them we could have a look at the library for a book about their question and write ourselves a note so we don't forget.

Older children will likely have more detailed questions. Be open, be honest, and don't shame them or be embarrassed. We want them to learn to trust us with their questions so they will continue to come to us and not get their information from less reliable sources.

If it's not a good time to talk, plan a time to come back to their question

Similarly, if we don't have the time or answers right now, we can tell them we'd like to give their question some thought or do some research before answering. Even better, we can agree to seek out the answer together. Then be sure to make a time to come back to it so they see that we value their question and are not avoiding it.

Respond with curiosity if we hear something that does not sound kind or appropriate

If we hear something that sounds racist or is unkind about someone, we can respond first with curiosity. It may have been an innocent mistake, or we may need to tell them that it's not kind to exclude someone based on how they look.

Even though the situation may be uncomfortable, if we don't say anything, the children miss a learning opportunity. We can also empower children to stand up for themselves or for others: "It hurts me when you say _____" or "It's not kind to say that to _____."

We highly recommend Britt Hawthorne's book *Raising Antiracist Children* and the book *Anti-Bias Education for Young Children and Ourselves* by Louise Derman-Sparks and Julie Olsen Edwards, both of which have useful examples of how to have discussions with children about race, gender, class, and ability. For more on this, see chapter 6.

Similarly helpful is the important message shared by Lucy and James Catchpole (of the Catchpoles website) that disabled adults and children are not teachable moments; they deserve the same privacy and common courtesy as everyone else. So if our child says something like "What happened to you?" to a person in a wheelchair, we can mouth "Sorry" to the other person, tell our child we all look different, and remind them that we don't ask personal questions of people we don't know.

IS SANTA REAL?

Being radically honest with our children means that for those celebrating Christmas, some people are starting to talk about Santa as a cultural symbol but choosing not to lie about who brings the presents. Christmas can still be a cozy celebration full of surprise and wonder, just as birthday celebrations are magical occasions, too. For those who would like to keep their own childhood memories alive and continue the story of Santa, Simone heard a mother answer the question if fairies and Santa were real with "I haven't seen them myself. Have you?"

If one does have Santa in the home, be careful not to threaten the children to be good or Santa won't come. Or to use the Elf on the Shelf to keep an eye on them. These hollow threats and forms of bribery conflict with our goal in Montessori for our children to develop self-discipline, not to only behave so they get something.

Setting limits around sensitive topics

Parents and caregivers ask us about setting limits when there is a sensitive topic. As hard as it is, we use the same kind and clear approach in these areas too. When we do this, we don't bring any shame to the child, we give the information needed in an age-appropriate manner, and we respect and model our boundaries too.

As easily as we might say, "We eat at the table. I'll put your cracker here for you when you are done playing," we can set a kind and clear limit with sensitive topics. For example, "It's okay to touch yourself, but it's something you can do in a private place. Would you like to go in your bedroom or to the bathroom?"

FURTHER READING

- Little Parachutes books for children about sensitive topics like grief, divorce, and disabilities.

TALKING ABOUT DEATH

Losing a family member, a friend, or a pet is one of the hardest experiences we suffer as humans. Our children will see us sad and might have questions. The best thing we can do is give honest, accurate, and age-appropriate answers. Here are some suggestions:

- Instead of telling them that our deceased loved one is having a long sleep, we can use accurate language and say, "They died," or use terms that we use in our culture to express this, like "transitioned from the physical plane."

- When they ask us what happens when we die, we can answer, "Some people think _____ and other people think _____. What do you think might happen?"

- If a pet dies, we might want to cheer our child up by getting a new one straightaway. Yet sitting with sadness and grief will allow the child to reflect on their time with their pet and understand that life has a beginning, middle, and end. We can offer them compassion and understanding and allow them to have all their feelings.

We can make a photo album, book of memories, or video about the person or animal who has died to celebrate their life. We can honor their passing by preparing their favorite meal, playing their favorite songs, or taking photos of places they loved. Involve your child in these activities as much as they are interested. Children's books can be a good way for children to process what they are feeling.

If our child is talking a lot about death, they are likely seeking answers to the questions of life or trying to process their feelings. We can listen, we can share our own experience, and we can get them help if needed.

As young children live very much in the present moment, they may not talk about a loved one's death much at all. If one of their parents has died and we would like to keep their parent's memory alive, we can find ways to celebrate them so that the young child will build a strong memory of them. We can find natural ways to do this, like talking about their favorite food if we see it at the supermarket, and we can also do this in a more intentional way by visiting some of their favorite places, displaying photos of them, making a simple book about them that we can read at bedtime, and celebrating their birthday or other special days by making a card for them together.

TALKING ABOUT SEX

Talking about sex is not a one and done conversation. Through honest and open dialogue with our children, we can help them have a healthy relationship with their body, to respect others' bodies, and help break any taboos or trauma that we might have picked up in our own childhood. In addition to our Montessori training, the work of Melissa Pintor Carnagey of Sex Positive Families has been so helpful to us in framing these conversations with our children. Our culture and beliefs will also be a part of this conversation.

Children will learn about sex and relationships in many ways. Whether we like it or not, they are and will be receiving and exposed to information, images, and conversations about sex. If we can be the first point of contact or introduction for our children, then our children are more likely to check what they hear against what we have told them instead of vice versa. We also have the opportunity to frame it within our value system. Here are some things to consider:

How they will learn about consent. It starts in the first year, as we ask them before handling their bodies, saying, "I'm going to pick you up," then pausing to allow them time to process this and give us permission. We touch their bodies gently, with respect. We ask our child if they would like a hug or a kiss, modeling consent from the earliest ages. We use gentle hands when buckling them into their car seats. We guide them rather than pulling them by the hand.

When washing babies and children, we can also use the same gentle touch on all parts of their body, including their vulva, penis, or bottom. This helps them complete their body schema—how their body is made up.

Simone also had a rule in their house: "Rough play by mutual consent." If anyone wasn't having fun when roughhousing, the word to use was "Stop!" and then it was clear that the rough play was over. If Simone heard someone not enjoying rough play, she would ask, "Does someone need to say stop?" or she'd say, "I heard someone say stop," if needed.

Naming their body parts with accurate language. When we name our child's body parts, we can use the correct names; for example, "vulva" (for the external sex organs— clitoris, vaginal opening, urethra, labia minora and majora), "vagina" (for the canal that connects the vulva to the cervix and uterus), and "penis."

We are giving our children the tools to be able to communicate clearly to their adults (parent, doctor, caregiver) if there are any problems. And there won't be any shame as they get older, when they will already be using the correct terminology for their parts.

Babies don't grow in tummies. They grow in uteruses. We can use this language with our children, who we have already learned are capable language learners.

How we interact with our partners. Young children observe how we speak to each other, how we show love, how we touch each other, and how we resolve any conflicts that come up. They will learn to be in healthy relationships by seeing healthy relationships around them.

Following their interest in baby animals. On a farmyard, our children can see and feed baby animals and sometimes even witness animals being born. In Dutch schools, they talk about "lentekriebels" ("spring fever") in animals when children are around 5 or 6 years old. This is a natural way to talk about where babies come from. The 6- to 9-year-old child is already interested in reproduction and biology. We can introduce human reproduction in the same way as we would the reproductive patterns of insects, birds, rabbits, or farm animals.

Beginning the conversation well before puberty. It's best to talk with them earlier than later, because once a child enters puberty, they can become more self-conscious about their body and may be more embarrassed to talk with us.

Using gender-inclusive language and ideas. Gender encompasses a person's body, expression, and identity. While many of us grew up with the binary categories of male and female, there can be many different gender expressions, including gender-fluid, agender, and trans.

We want every child to feel that they are accepted as they are, however they present. No one can tell a child how they feel. Our child or their schoolmates may feel outside the gender binary. To make everyone feel most affirmed, we can consider:

- Keeping our language gender-inclusive; for example, by saying, "You're becoming an adult" (instead of "You're becoming a man/woman").
- Modeling using our pronouns when we introduce ourselves: "My name is Simone and my pronouns are she/her." This will show how we feel most affirmed and help others reflect on the pronouns they use to feel most affirmed.
- Questioning the idea that pink is for girls and blue is for boys, that toy stores have toys for girls or boys, and that clothing stores have girls' or boys' clothing.
- Allowing children of any gender to show emotion, dress up in their parent's clothing, wear clothing that they feel comfortable in or would like to experiment with, play sports or not, and consider any career path of their choosing.

Answering their questions or finding out the answers together. They may have questions about their body because they want to know if they are normal. They may ask questions about something they see. Simone remembers walking with her family through the red-light district in Amsterdam to a café. Oliver—then around 10—asked why there were women standing in the windows in their underwear. Simone didn't avoid the question and instead gave a simple answer about prostitution and what it was. He didn't ask anything further, and they continued on to the café.

If we ignore our child's questions or seem embarrassed, they will learn that this is something we don't talk about. If we feel embarrassed, we can be honest about it. "I'm noticing that I'm feeling embarrassed talking about this topic. I never had anyone to talk to about this stuff. But I want you to feel comfortable asking me anything. I'd like to find out some more before we talk about it. Can we make a plan to talk tomorrow after school?"

Teaching all children about menstruation. Some people feel comfortable having their children, regardless of gender, in the bathroom while they are menstruating—for example, while changing a pad, tampon, or menstrual cup—so that all children learn that menstruation is a natural cycle. Other families may mention that someone is having their period if they are needing more rest or feeling sensitive. We all live in community with people who menstruate, and our children will learn about this in a natural way.

Allowing them to learn from our stories. As our child gets older, we can be vulnerable and share our experiences. Even if these were not perfect, we can reflect on how we wish they had been better. Being open with our children will show them that we are comfortable with them coming to us to talk about sex, sexuality, or gender or when they have questions.

Offering them an understanding of a wide range of experiences. If we live in a cisgender, heteronormative family, the child will have absorbed this as normal in the first six years. Regardless of our family constellation, we can teach them to respect all types of families. We might choose to have books about different types of families, to examine our friendships to see if we have a wide range of families in our circle, or to consider finding ways to be in community with more diversity, such as through the activities our children do. Our child will also want to see their own family constellation represented in the books, media, and online resources we offer to feel most affirmed.

Bonus (for the older child). Sex is shared with someone we love and can be fun. Many of us learned that sex is to make babies. Sex education in the Netherlands also explores the idea that people have sex for pleasure, how to have safe sex, and methods of contraception. The rate of teen pregnancy in the Netherlands is one of the lowest in the world.

FURTHER READING

- The Sex Positive Families website (sexpositivefamilies.com)

Some books for children:
- *What Makes a Baby* by Cory Silverberg is inclusive and educational when it comes to explaining where babies come from to young children
- *Sex Is a Funny Word* by Cory Silverberg is for older kids, around ages 7 to 11, and discusses touch (of others, of oneself) and consent
- *Making a Baby* by Rachel Greener

TALKING ABOUT BODIES

In addition to teaching them about their changing bodies and sex, we also want to help our children accept their bodies and all bodies in their diversity. This includes hair texture, skin color, height, and shape. Children are looking to answer the question, "Am I okay as I am?"

Here are some ideas that Junnifa and Simone apply in their homes and classroom:

- With children from birth through 3–6 years old and into 6–12 years old, we work on building their self-identity. This involves their having an understanding of their culture (their race, ethnicity, family history, etc.) and seeing themselves represented in their surroundings, including in books, art, and media. (For more detail on building identity, see chapter 6.)
- Practicing self-care in the home and classroom—learning to care for our bodies.
- Being grateful for our bodies—wondering and learning about the role of every cell in our body.
- Being careful not to focus only on appearances; for example, when we meet a child, instead of saying, "That's such a pretty dress," we can say, "I'm so happy to meet you."
- Focusing on the person and their characteristics and/or efforts when we give feedback rather than on what people look like: "I saw you working really hard together today. I'm so curious what you learned."

- Being kind about our own bodies and eliminating negative self-talk or saying, "I shouldn't have had that cake today" or "I've got to go out for a run" when these come from a place of guilt or shame.
- Modeling intuitive eating—eating just what our bodies need; listening to our bodies after each bite to see if it still feels good (see more about eating on page 121).

In her book *Raising Antiracist Children*, Britt Hawthorne shares a powerful message about beauty from Trisha Moquino (a highly respected Indigenous Montessori educator): "You don't need to wear makeup to be beautiful. Our grandparents taught us not to rush into wearing makeup. They stated that our creator made me the way I was supposed to be and that I was fine that way, I was beautiful that way." This is one of the messages Trisha has shared with her girls when talking about self-love in their family over the years.

The same book also has us think critically with our children:

- About corporations selling products to make us look "right."
- About the use of Photoshopped images and the messaging in advertisements.
- About setting boundaries around body-shaming—that no one is allowed to make fun of someone's body size or shape. We can say, "Bodies are just bodies. All bodies are worthy bodies. It's not okay to comment on someone's body."
- About valuing all bodies, including bodies of all colors, abilities, sexualities, and genders.
- About saying, "I love my body; it belongs to me" if someone comments on our body.
- About how everyone is allowed to choose what they wear.
- About learning to have respect for disabled bodies and to recognize where we have privileges and immunity and how we can advocate for others in the community.
- About how disability can be both visible and invisible.
- About learning more about body positivity from *The Body Is Not an Apology* by Sonya Renee Taylor.

We are living in a world of commercialization, and it can feel like we have little control. In an interview on the *Tilt Parenting* podcast, Zoë Bisbing and Leslie Bloch of the Full Bloom Project, which promotes body positivity, said that we can create an environment in our homes to buffer the effect. We can take away the morality around food, diet culture, healthy food, and junk food. And it is never too late to make adjustments in our home. We can talk with our child, tell them we've learned something new and what we are going to try instead.

All that said, our children live in society, and we can help them build the skills to feel safe in their body. If they feel under someone's gaze, they may choose to put on a jacket over what they are wearing; if someone puts down what they are wearing, they can practice saying, "It's not your business what I wear. My clothes make me feel like me."

TALKING ABOUT MONEY

One part of raising children is teaching them about money.

The 3- to 6-year-old child is beginning to understand abstract concepts; for example, that a note or coin is a representation of a sum of money that we give in exchange for an item or service. As so much money is now exchanged digitally via a card at checkout or online, it is more difficult for them to see concretely. It can be nice for us to have cash available for them to see us pay for groceries and receive change. They also enjoy handing over the money and receiving the change, and we can do simple grace and courtesy lessons to practice this.

Like any skill they learn, much of what our children will learn about how to manage money starts with our own example. The 3- to 6-year-old child with their absorbent mind will absorb our attitudes to money in our daily life: when we are at the grocery store, how we react when we receive bills, how we talk about finances and taxes.

We can look at our own attitude to money. How do we feel about money? Do we have an abundance or scarcity mindset? Do we spend a lot? Are we careful with money? Do we put money aside for savings? How do we model charity in our family? How do we redistribute wealth to under-resourced communities? None of these questions have a right or wrong answer, but they help us to consider what values we want our children to associate with money.

The 6- to 12-year-old child may start to become more interested in the idea of money, and they can learn about the origins and history of money, different types of currency around the world, physical cash, and electronic money. They may have questions for us about how we earn money, how other people earn money, where money is kept, and how we manage our budget.

One way of learning about money is through practice—both earning and spending money. We can open a bank account with them so they learn how to keep track of their money. Some young children can be quite entrepreneurial and want to set up a lemonade stand, do jobs for neighbors to earn money, or do jobs for us to earn extra allowance. However, an interest in earning money and having some economic independence is mostly seen in the following plane of development, from ages 12 to 18.

Some people like giving children an allowance so the child learns how to save, spend, invest, and donate money. Traditionally, an allowance is given if a child does chores at home. However, in a Montessori home, we have the child take part in doing things around the home to contribute to and be part of the family. Giving an allowance in return for chores then is at odds with the Montessori approach.

Educators like Michael Grose (not a Montessori educator but an Australian parenting expert very aligned with the Montessori approach) advocate for giving an allowance as a right, not tied to any behavior or chores. The amount could be nominal, to use in purchasing an occasional ice cream or to save up for a toy. Or the child may receive as much as they would need to buy their own clothing, gifts for friends, and any additional snacks that they want. This can be quite a significant amount, and if they spend too much at the beginning of the week or month, they will naturally experience that there is not enough for the end of the month.

Simone's children didn't receive an allowance at all before they were 12 years old, with the idea that if there was something they needed, it would be purchased by the family. If someone needed a new pair of shoes, these would be bought with the family budget in mind. There was not a lot of spare money, so the children understood the value of what was bought and were not always asking for more stuff. They sometimes received some money for their birthday and had the opportunity to practice saving and spending. With regard to giving money to causes, the family had discussions about current causes they wanted to support and would make a family donation.

When her children were 12, they were given €5 a week each to buy lunch at school if they wanted. Quickly, Oliver and Emma realized that they could make their lunch at home and save the money. Around the age of 15, they were given a clothing allowance every 3 months. They also obtained part-time jobs, Oliver at the cinema and Emma helping out Simone from time to time with administrative tasks as well as briefly working at a store.

Now, at university, they receive a student loan and manage their budget independently. When Simone asks if they need any money or help, they ask for advice occasionally but otherwise refuse any help and want to manage by themselves. True characteristics of Montessori children.

If an allowance is given, guidelines can be agreed upon with the child about what money can be spent on as well as putting some aside for saving, giving (e.g., making a charitable donation), and investing. It can be very frustrating to have them save up for plastic toys that don't align with our values of being mindful of consumption and the environment.

TALKING ABOUT STEALING

Stealing provides a thrill, the risk of being caught; or stealing can be about a child wanting something they aren't allowed. There may be a friend inviting them to take part. They may be the ringleader themselves. We are not going to get the truth by being angry or asking direct questions. We need to understand that they must be very dysregulated to think that stealing is okay.

As difficult as it may be, we want them to know we are on their side. That everything can be worked out. We don't need to rush into a conversation. "I'm concerned about what has happened, but I need some time to calm myself down and prepare myself for this conversation. Can we come back together tonight to talk about it?"

We will want to understand what their needs are and if we can find other thrill-seeking ways for them to meet them. If they are getting into trouble with a particular friend or friend group, we can't stop them from seeing each other, but we could have limits on the number of sleepovers per month or time they spend together during the week. We can use this time to reconnect with our child and help them come back to their path. If it's about not being allowed things, we can review if we are being too top-down about certain things and how we can hand back control over parts of their lives.

We also must make sure that the child takes responsibility for their actions, owning up to what they have done, apologizing for their mistake, and returning the item to the store/owner or paying for it.

We can also use opportunities when they arise to discuss this with our child to prevent such situations occurring. For example, if we read an article about shoplifting, this could open a conversation with our child. We can talk about why some children feel they need to steal. We could discuss with them what they could say to a friend who might encourage them to steal. We also might cover what they could do if they hear someone else they know has been stealing.

TALKING ABOUT TECHNOLOGY

Technology has become part of our lives. We want to use it in our homes as a tool rather than an obstacle to our child's development.

Here are some things to consider when it comes to technology:

Some ideas for technology by age. As sensorial learners, 3- to 6-year-olds will still learn and understand best through hands-on exploration of concrete materials.

At home consider:

- Limiting the use of technology to video calls with family; for example, when a loved one might read a book with them
- Instead of using the internet to look up their favorite construction vehicle, going to the library to find a book about one or watching one at a building site
- Rather than asking an AI chatbot the answer to a question, choosing a concrete way to find the answer (using a set of encyclopedias or writing the question on a Post-it Note to make a "wonder wall" of things to investigate further)
- Instead of using a screen to entertain them at a café, taking a notebook to draw in or a book to read, having a family conversation, or playing "I spy"
- Allowing them to use our camera or phone to take photos and edit them
- Using concrete materials to learn about patterns and sequencing, which later could be used as building blocks for coding and programming if they show interest
- If the child is exposed to screens, consciously choosing the programming: shorter programming, slower edits, and, as much as possible, based in reality rather than fantasy (avoiding wicked witches, dragons, pirates, etc. for children under 6 years); having an adult available to support their understanding and answer any questions that come up; and referencing websites like Common Sense Media when making media choices

For 6- to 12-year-olds, who are seeking to understand the universe, we can talk to them about using technology actively as a tool rather than passively to consume content or to copy information. Some examples:

- Using computers for research—we can guide the child how to evaluate the information found as well as assess what information is the most reliable; our favorite websites can be saved as bookmarks on the toolbar for easy access; and we can encourage the child to think about media literacy, such as by visiting the News Literacy Project website

- Learning how to make a summary of information found, how to note their sources, and how not to simply copy and paste text into their work
- Encouraging them not to rely only on online search information but also to seek out books in the public library or find experts to interview
- Using specialized software like 3D modeling and architecture programs, or learning coding basics, how to create a presentation or video, or how to build a website
- Connecting with an expert overseas or possibly other (Montessori) schools in different parts of the world

- Making a difference in the world like raising money for a cause
- If they are interested in social media, having a shared family account, maybe about our family pet or our cooking experiments, to try out social media together
- Making a family film night a social occasion by inviting friends over, hanging up an old sheet, and projecting a film onto it. It will make for a memorable evening.

In his article "Technology and Montessori," Montessori educator Mark Powell adds:

- Taking photos with a digital camera.
- Making stop-motion films.
- Creating digital stories (recording a voice-over and images and then cutting them together with movie editing software).
- Recording digital audiobooks for younger children.
- Using technology like a ProScope (a lighted handset held over an animal/object to project it onto a computer screen) to make photos, videos, and time-lapse recordings, for instance, of a plant growing).
- Watching well-produced educational videos (e.g., about volcanoes) or listening to inspirational historical speeches, such as by Dr. Martin Luther King Jr.

> "We want the playground experience whereby children learn to think creatively, reason, and collaborate. We want the emphasis to be on collecting, analyzing, evaluating, and presenting information."
>
> —Alison Awes (an elementary AMI Montessori trainer)
> "On Building Character: The Elementary Child's
> Moral Development in the Digital Age"

The needs of the child. The child needs to move, to be social, to be creative, and to get good sleep. We can ensure:

- The child has enough movement (3 hours a day according to the World Health Organization)
- Screens in our lives are not affecting face-to-face communication with our child
- The child has lots of unstructured time to explore the real world, play with friends in person, and come up with their own ideas (rather than passively watching television or playing a computer game or spending time on social media)
- Screens are not affecting their sleep (no screens in the bedroom or within an hour or two of bedtime)

Agreements. There is interesting research by the Royal College of Pediatrics and Child Health in the UK showing that children themselves recognize that technology can be both useful and harmful. So we can invite them to help develop agreements for their tech use and and give them credit for sticking to them. For the 3- to 6-year-old child, the family agreements are likely to be made by the adults. For 6- to 12-year-olds, these agreements become more collaborative. The agreements would cover:

- Whom they can communicate with and for how long.
- Where they can engage with screens—ideally, any computers and other devices will be kept in the living area so an adult can see the screen to supervise if needed.
- What technology options/apps/games are considered okay—do they align with our family values? Do they require the child to be active in coming up with solutions? Are there opportunities for the child to move their body?
- Any safety considerations (see "Safety" below).
- Avoiding snacking during screen time.
- Whether they need a cell phone to catch public transportation.
- Whether there are different rules when the family is traveling on longer trips.

If the agreements are broken, the child is showing us that they do not yet have the skills or enough practice to master abiding by them. We can come back to see how we can help them follow the agreements, or review them if necessary at the next family meeting. We can involve the child in reading the latest research on screens and ask them what they think should happen. Sometimes they are harder on themselves than we would be.

Note: If there is an older sibling in the home with more access to screens, we can discuss what is appropriate for any younger sibling to see. We can make family arrangements; for example, that they watch a film in the evening after the younger child is asleep.

Grace and courtesy. We want our children to learn how to communicate online respectfully, use technology wisely, and recognize any suspicious behavior online. We call this digital grace and courtesy. For example: How do we interpret emojis? How do we read someone's tone? What is the etiquette around communicating on different channels like email, text, and social media? How do we make space and take space in conversations online? Would we say this to the person directly?

Research by data journalist Alexandra Samuel showed that children who were mentored by adults when learning to navigate the digital social environment got into less trouble in digital spaces than children who had no guidance.

Safety. Ericka Sóuter, author of *How to Have a Kid and a Life: A Survival Guide*, has some useful questions around digital safety. Does our child know who to trust? Do we know who they are talking to? What does spam look like? What do scams look like? How can they protect their digital footprint? What are they sharing? Has the child gotten permission from an adult to make an online purchase? What to do if we see inappropriate content? What are the guidelines if we allow the child to play online games with friends? How do we manage passwords?

We also need to think about safety issues with location services and people being able to know where our children are at any moment.

Be an example. Our children observe how we interact with technology. We can use our phones and devices purposely; for example, telling them what we are doing when we pick up our phone or are on our computer: "I'm going to send a message to let them know we are here." And when we use it as a break: "I'm going to go online for 10 minutes to check my social media." We can also get their permission before posting any photos of them or information about them.

Other considerations. In her article "On Building Character," Alison Awes also mentions:

- Questioning with our children stereotypes found in online media, especially idealized images.
- Letting them explore the history of technology. How was it developed? By whom? How did we listen to music before computers?
- Talking about setting boundaries, including with friends, on text and social media.
- Inappropriate content. If a child sees pornography, Awes writes, "Parents will want to discuss how that is different from real sex in a loving relationship, explaining why they feel the content is demeaning or promotes a narrow view of sexuality." Or if they come across some disturbing news while watching a weather video, "The adult can apologize that the child found something that was not meant for children."

Artificial intelligence. We can raise our children to use AI as an additional tool in the same way we teach them to use the internet. We want to help them become critical users of AI (for example, questioning the ethics around AI-generated art) and to discuss when it's appropriate to use it (and when it's not). We (Junnifa and Simone) suspect that AI will mean that many schools will move towards a Montessori approach to learning in the classroom—where children are learning by doing, not generating their answers via a chatbot.

Making changes. If we have not been intentional with the use of technology in our family, we can start a conversation with our child. In her course Montessori Homeschool by Design, Jana Morgan Herman suggests adding things rather than taking things away. For example, thinking of other activities to do in the evening instead of being on screens, like playing a game together or going for a walk after dinner. It will take some time to change habits, and we can move step-by-step toward making new agreements.

FURTHER READING

- "On Building Character: The Elementary Child's Moral Development in the Digital Age" by Alison Awes
- "Technology & the Elementary Student," www.creoschool.org/blog/kidsandtechnology
- *Screenwise: Helping Kids Thrive (and Survive) in Their Digital World* by Devorah Heitner

TALKING ABOUT GUN PLAY

The most helpful Montessori perspectives on gun play are offered by Donna Bryant Goertz and the late John Snyder of Austin Montessori School. Snyder spoke of children trying out power in their play, from throwing rocks, snowballs, and dirt to pretending to use guns or spears. When children use sticks, their finger, or Legos to "shoot" at people, the adult offers the phrase, "We don't pretend to shoot people."

As Montessori families, we want to instill an attitude of solving problems with others in nonviolent ways and not have guns in our home. We can redirect our child's play toward other ways to try out power with activities that involve noise and (possibly) shiny objects. These could include making a "volcano" with vinegar, dishwashing liquid, and baking soda and watching it "erupt"; banging pots and pans with a hammer; playing with water balloons (yet not throwing them at people or animals); making a go-kart; or launching their own DIY rockets to the moon.

We can also look at where their need to explore guns is coming from. Is it from books, television, video games, and other stories with "good guys" and "bad guys"? From other children at preschool and school? Wouldn't it be nice if we could move away from these types of stories as a society? We can be the ones to start.

There is also an opportunity to have discussions with our children around war, fighting, and international diplomacy between people, groups, or nations having opposing views. Speak often of peace, and compassion, and foster finding solutions in our homes so that everyone's needs are met.

TALKING ABOUT WAR AND CLIMATE CHANGE

In March 2022, following the outbreak of war in Ukraine, Lead Montessori hosted a conversation called "How to Talk to Children about What Is Happening?" with three AMI Montessori trainers—Madlena Ulrich, Tiina Suominen, and Carla Foster—and Dinny Rebild, a longtime Montessori educator who worked for 5 years at the Red Cross asylum center Kongelunden in Denmark. The information shared can be applied to any difficult world events, from war to the climate crisis to natural disasters to a school shooting. Harrowing events happen around us, and we can help our children process them even when we ourselves may find it difficult to comprehend them.

The first thing to say is that we have to take care of ourselves before we take care of the children. It helps to have a safe person or circle we can talk to so that, as much as possible, we can show up for our families. We don't have to pretend to be happy. We can be authentic. We can tell the children that this is upsetting for us, too. When we have done some of our work already to process the event, we will find it easier to stay grounded to hold space for, and help, our children. We don't want to burden them with our problems.

With children younger than 3 years old, we do our best not to expose them to information that can harm them or their minds. We need to be their guardians and be careful about the information coming in around them to protect them as much as possible. We want to provide them with physical and psychological security so they know they can trust us. We can keep our routines as stable and normal as possible, including with predictable mealtimes and bedtimes. We want to be careful not to pass on our own feelings of doubt or fear to the children.

The 3- to 6-year-old child may hear something from our conversations, at preschool, or school, or they might see a newspaper or the news on television. We can start by observing whether they show signs of unusual behavior. We can say, "You don't look yourself. Is there anything worrying you?" We can let them know that it's okay to feel sad or worried, we can ask them what they know, and we can answer any questions that come up for them. Remember that if they see a newsclip played again and again on the news, they may think that it is happening over and over rather than being replayed, and they may also feel like it is happening nearby or could happen to them or our families.

We could model and involve them in doing something to help. They might do some fundraising, offer help to an affected neighbor, or assist us with anything we are doing to help, from making a donation, to baking for a bake sale, to knitting blankets being collected. We can also let them know of things that are being done to help in the international community and any peacekeeping talks being held to find solutions and restore peace.

For the 6- to 12-year-old child, Carla Foster mentions Dr. Montessori's call for the united nations of humanity, not individual countries. Foster says, "Pride in our culture is not nationalism." We can share how humans' hearts, minds, and hands have been able to solve problems over the course of history. We respond to a threat by coming to action together in community, not aggression. Where they may want to stamp "good" or "evil" onto any party involved, we can help them instead explore the question of how humans can deal with the dilemmas that we come up against and find better solutions. They can help alleviate suffering by finding ways to offer support, such as via an NGO or international organization.

Most of all, we can be available. We can again start by asking what they have heard and answering questions they have. Keep information factual, find information from different perspectives, and look critically at information to find out what is reliable. We can correct any misunderstandings they might have and look on a map to see where the conflict is happening. They might like to process what is going on through making art or music.

We can remind our children that these things are rare. We don't have to lie to our children and say that everything is going to be okay. But we can assure them that everyone is doing their best to make things as safe as possible. As Mister Rogers would say, "Look for the helpers. You will always find people who are helping."

When we are directly affected by events, we do our best to cope, to tell our children in an age-appropriate way what is going on, and to make things in their daily routine as predictable as possible. Again, we don't want to make any promises we can't keep, but we can offer them reassurance that we are doing our best, that others are helping to make sure that we will be safe and secure, and that we are doing it together.

The same principles can be applied to conversations about the climate crisis. We can acknowledge the facts, let them know what is being done, tell them we also sometimes feel worried about it, and make a plan for what we would like to do as a family to combat climate change. (For more, see p. 266, "Connecting with and feeding Earth.")

TALKING ABOUT FAITH

Our beliefs and faith are personal to ourselves and our families. Children younger than 6 years old will absorb the beliefs we share with them. From 6 to 12 years old, they will become interested in what their friends believe in and how this is similar to or different from our own family.

For some of us, this is an important part of our culture, and we will include our child in our rituals and ceremonies. Or we may not be religious but still be spiritual. Regardless of our faith, we can pass on to our children in their early years a love for all humanity and the concept that every living thing has a cosmic purpose. We can show respect for others' beliefs: "Some people believe _____ and other people believe _____. In our family, we believe _____." Or "I believe _____. What do you believe?"

For those interested in a Montessori-based approach to religious education, there is the Catechesis of the Good Shepherd. This program was developed in 1954 by Dr. Sofia Cavalletti and professor Gianna Gobbi based on Dr. Montessori's pedagogy. In this approach, the Atrium is a prepared mixed-age learning environment where the child can ask, "Help me come closer to God by myself." The principles are based in Catholicism but have also been used in other Christian denominations, Islam, and other religions to share their faith with children.

FURTHER READING

- *The Child in the Church* by Dr. Maria Montessori
- *The Religious Potential of the Child* by Sofia Cavalletti

PART FIVE

WORKING WITH OTHERS

There's an African saying that it takes a village to raise a child. We can't raise our children in isolation. We work with others, including immediate family members like our partner (if we have one) and other children; extended family members like our siblings, parents, in-laws, uncles, and aunts; our chosen family, those friends and neighbors in our trusted circle; and other caregivers who help us care for our children and teach them, such as nannies, au pairs, schoolteachers, enrichment program teachers, and religious guides. We also work with the parents and caregivers of our children's friends, other neighbors, and sometimes even people whom we've met in parks or shops.

Many times we will be working with people who do not share our philosophy. They may not know what Montessori is, or some of them may know of it but not necessarily have a positive opinion of it or agree with us. How do we interact with these people and communicate our beliefs to them? How do we get them to buy in to or at least respect our opinions with regard to how we want our children to be raised?

General principles for working with others

Inform. Be clear about our beliefs. Communicate our limits and nonnegotiables clearly and respectfully. If others are open, we might go into detail about the whys. With some people, it might actually be better to focus on the principle and not even mention Montessori. For example, Junnifa's children are not exposed to screens during their early years. This stems from Montessori recommendations for more sensorial experiences for young children. We also know that research and most medical bodies agree, so she tells people that her children are not allowed to watch TV or use phones, and when they ask why, she refers to research or WHO recommendations because she has found that people are more open to that source than to Montessori.

Educate. It is especially important to educate those with whom our child will have a long relationship or spend a lot of time with about the core Montessori principles. People are more likely to buy in to what they understand. We can help them understand topics like:

- What Montessori is.
- Key principles: respect, independence, freedom with limits, cooperation with our child
- The outcomes: short- and long-term goals we have for our child
- Our values

- How to support independence
- The importance of talking to and listening to children

We can also share practical information like:

- "What to say instead of"
- Why we don't praise or say "Good boy/girl" or "Good job"
- What to do when the child is upset or throwing a tantrum
- Activities to keep the children busy or what to do instead of watching TV
- How to set limits

Some of the ways that we can educate others:

- Sharing what we know in conversation or writing it down.
- Sharing information: articles or text images, podcasts, memes, reels, or social media posts with small pieces of relevant messages.
- Sharing books. We can read the same book and discuss if they are open to it.
- If we are connected to a Montessori school or community, we might invite them to adult education sessions.
- We can gift them Montessori e-courses or invite them to webinars. Both Junnifa and Simone have enjoyed having partners, grandparents, and other caregivers on their e-courses.
- Modeling and explaining later why we did what we did.

Model. We can model what we want to see. We can model how to interact with our children, how to talk to them, treating them with respect, not interrupting them, allowing and supporting their independence, listening to them when they speak. We can also model teaching instead of correcting, Instead of "Why are you always making a mess?" say, "It's time to clean up your room. What would you like to pick up first?" We can model positive discipline principles, limit setting, collaboration in the kitchen and bathroom, slowing down and being present with our children, patience, and any interaction we want to see with our children.

We can also model respect in our interactions with others, not just our children. So treating our partner (if we have one), caregivers, other children, and others that we interact with respectfully will make people even more likely to treat our own children with respect.

Share joy. When we see ways that Montessori made a difference, we can share them, but not gloatingly. Notice when the child shows independence or reflects values that our beliefs nurtured because of our Montessori choices. "They look so happy to be folding their own clothes from the basket." Gabriel Salomão of Lar Montessori talks about sharing joy when he is at the playground with extended family. He doesn't mention the word *Montessori*; instead he points out what the child has mastered and is enjoying. We can also share experiences from Montessori families in our community who have older children who reflect the values we aspire to.

Offer alternatives. We could also discuss their challenges with maintaining the freedoms or limits we have set and find ways to help them be successful. For example, we can send activities with our children when they are visiting a place where they are usually offered screens for entertainment.

Be patient and give them time. It often takes time for people to first digest and understand Montessori. It is important to give grace and be patient. Acknowledge small efforts and continue to model, guide, and encourage as much as possible.

Have regular check-in meetings with caregivers. It is reasonable if they are looking after our children a lot that we try as much as possible to have a similar approach. We can set aside time each week or month to discuss any problems they are having and come up with solutions together.

Look for their strengths. Our children benefit, too, from different perspectives and skills. We could invite others to take our children to the community garden, play sports together, visit an animal shelter, or bake together, depending on what the friend, relative, or caregiver also loves to do.

SOME SPECIFIC RELATIONSHIPS

Our partner

Ideally, our partner (if we have one) would be on the same page with us, and we would have a plan together of how our children are being raised based on the Montessori philosophy. We can set goals and dream together about the kind of home environment we want for our children and the future we envision for them. However, many times this is not the case. So how do we proceed knowing that we would ideally present a united front to our child?

At a comfortable, happy, neutral time, have conversations about our hopes for our child's future and what kind of humans we want to raise. Ensure that we listen to our partner's views as we share ours. Also identify what we don't like or want, and how we don't want to be. Hopefully, we can find some alignment. Perhaps we both want happy children who grow up to be confident, independent, creative, responsible, kind, respectful, and good stewards of the world. Point out how the Montessori principles can take our child to that desired future. The great thing about Montessori is that its outcomes are long-term and are usually tied to many of our hopes for our child's life as an adult. Focus on the big picture and why we would choose it as a family. We might also talk about the application. What are some of the differences that this choice will make for how we already raise our child, or for the ideas that our partner may have previously held about raising children? This will probably not be a onetime discussion; it can be revisited often as we go on our journey together.

What do we do when our partner wants us to be stricter or maybe our partner corrects our child harshly, yells at them, or even punishes or spanks them? How do we react?

First, remember that they are probably doing what they think is best. It is important to remind ourselves of this so that we can respond logically.

Next, remember that it is best not to argue or disagree with our partner in front of our children. This can be hard, so it might be better to leave the room when something we don't feel comfortable with is happening (unless our child is in danger). This minimizes the chance of a confrontation. We can then have a conversation later, making sure not to come across as an expert or as judgmental. We can mention what we felt did not go well, offer alternatives for how it might have been handled differently as respectfully as we can, and then let it go. We might be able to convince them, or not, but often we have sown a seed, and seeds take time to grow. We will have opportunities to water these seeds and plant more, and over time, our partner will hopefully start to shift.

They can also have their concerns heard in the moment. Let's say we go to the park and our child wants to climb a tree, and our partner immediately says, "It's not safe; you can't climb it." But the child has done it before and we know they can, so what do we do? We might say, "It *can* be unsafe to climb trees," acknowledging our partner's point of view. "What if I stand close by and help make sure they are safe?" That way the child gets a chance, and the partner's concerns are not ignored. If the partner still says no, we could redirect the child to another activity and then have the conversation with our partner later to better understand and allay their concerns.

Sometimes a disagreement may happen in front of the child. Then it is best to show our children how we resolve conflict. So often we do this part when the child is not around. They need to see us making repairs with each other, too, when they see a conflict.

As mentioned in the general principles, we can do our best to educate our partner. It's great to find courses that we take together, discuss, and implement together. It is fun to try out our learnings, to observe and celebrate wins together.

Build community. Identify families whose values align with ours so that we can do things together and grow together. We could find them to be models for ourselves and our partner. Junnifa has found this to be very helpful for her family. Oftentimes, hangouts with family friends open doors to conversations about raising our children. If we belong to a Montessori school, building connections with other families in the community provides our child with friends from families who share the same values.

Reinforce what they are doing well. It is tempting to only have a discussion with our partner when they do something out of line, but we have to remember that what we water is what grows so we can try to highlight what they are doing right. We can excitedly share the effect of something they did right and encourage even small efforts or changes.

Again, it is a process, and we want to be patient. Everyone is on their own journey, doing the best they can, developing on their own timeline just as the child is.

Extended family

With our extended family, it helps to first remember that they usually mean well and also to remind ourselves that our child will benefit from a relationship with their loved ones. This helps us put things in perspective when things don't go as we wish.

It is helpful to make our beliefs clear and set limits from the very beginning. We can do this respectfully and kindly but also firmly, especially when it comes to the big things that mean a lot to us. For some it might be respect or punishment, for others it might be screen exposure, and for another it might be processed foods or sugar. Whatever our big things are, we can communicate them. We can also educate, but what we have found to be the most effective tool for extended family members like grandparents is modeling. It might take a while, and that's okay. Remember, we want to be patient. Seeds take time to grow. People often come around when they start to see the difference in the children. Ana-Kay of Pickneys at Play shared that her family came on board when her family witnessed her twins doing practical life activities. They could not believe how capable they were at such a young age.

We can also advocate for our children in situations where it is necessary. For example, if we are visiting family and our child is expected to hug or kiss their relatives and they don't want to, we can explain that we do not force our children to hug or be touched by people. We ask our child's permission and respect their choices about their body. In this way, we are teaching our child body autonomy and consent and that it's okay to say no, even to another adult. And we are teaching our family members about an important boundary.

It can be especially challenging to get grandparents on board because often they feel like they successfully raised their own children and may not then want to be told what to do. Some may also feel like our new choices are a challenge to or judgment of their own methods. There are several areas that may represent challenges:

- Discipline
- Allowing things we would rather not allow, like TV, sweets, plastic noisy toys, phones, and digital devices
- Encouraging dependence and hampering independence
- Being overprotective and not allowing exploration
- Being laissez-faire and not supervising the child

Sometimes we need to reach a compromise with grandparents because, many times, they will do what they want to do. But by reaching a compromise, we let them do what they want within the limits that we have set. It might be that instead of not being allowed to watch any TV, our child can watch TV for up to 1 hour. We can involve our child in holding to this limit also when we are not present. We can discuss the value of integrity and doing what is right even when we are not there and letting them know our expectations.

If issues arise with grandparents, we can focus on what we appreciate about them and the value they bring to our children. We can prioritize the issues, address the big things, and let go of the small things.

Caregivers

We can ensure that we go through a thorough process when selecting caregivers, and once they've been hired, we can educate and train them.

We can be explicit in how we want them to interact with our children and what our expectations are. Let them know what we want our children exposed to and how we would prefer for them to speak to our children. In addition to telling them, we can show them and outline it in a document for reference. We could arrange for them to follow a Montessori course or pass on this book to them to read. We can also check with our children if our caregivers align to our values when we are not present.

To encourage respect from our child, avoid correcting the caregiver in front of the child and speak respectfully. Also avoid speaking negatively about the caregiver in front of the child.

An alternative offered by Trina of DIY Corporate Mom is to give very little instruction to a caregiver except to say, as Dr. Montessori said to her first assistants, "Do not interrupt." She adds, "Relax and observe my child . . . just relax and observe." Then Trina also prepares their home environment with things like knives and glasses accessible to the children, so any caregiver would soon be on board with the Montessori approach in their home.

Our child's teachers

We view our child's teachers as partners in supporting our child's development. In every partnership, communication and trust are keys to success, so we ensure that there is open, honest, and respectful communication. We can discuss preferred means and times of communication. Most teachers would prefer a scheduled meeting or conversation over a spontaneous one. We also work toward building trust. Take time to reflect on what would help us trust our child's teacher and communicate this to them. Engage with them for both positive and challenging reasons so that we are not coming to them with only complaints or challenges. Express genuine care for them. Before jumping into a conversation about our child, we ask how they're doing. Acknowledge their efforts and appreciate them. Share examples of how we see their work reflected in our child at home.

We can attend parent-teacher conferences and other school events. Teachers often put a lot of work into these gatherings, and attending is a way of showing appreciation. We show interest in the child's work in school, ask questions, give feedback, offer our time, help, and expertise when possible.

It can also be respectful to include the child in any meetings at the school. They can express for themselves what they enjoy and what they find difficult, and when there are problems, they can be involved in finding solutions.

Other teachers (enrichment, religious)

We can work to ensure that the enrichment options we choose for our children are in line with our values and that, as much as possible, the other children and families also share our values. This is of course not always possible, so we can supervise and communicate any preferences, limits, and considerations to the teacher from the beginning. Our children should also know these and be empowered to speak up when necessary. We can also have conversations with our children about their experiences and give feedback to the teacher respectfully.

Friends' parents or caregivers

If our child has a friend whose parents or caregivers offer options that are not in line with our preferences, we can make our homes the safe place where our children and their friends gather, and we can be on-site during these gatherings so that we can observe, supervise, and provide guidance as necessary. The advantage of this is that we get to know our children's friends, and our children get an opportunity to positively influence others. We can also follow the general principles discussed earlier.

In a situation where our child has a disagreement with another child and their parent or caregiver confronts us, we can calmly address the complaint and suggest that our children work it out themselves where possible. If not, we can offer to be an impartial mediator, mostly to ensure that each side is being heard. For example, at the park or a party, another adult might expect our child to share a special toy or do something that is not in line with our beliefs. We can help our child advocate for themselves, giving them words to say if they are stuck, or if needed, we can explain to the adult respectfully.

JASMINE, ANDREW & THEIR 3 CHILDREN AGED 1, 9, 10

Three-Minute Montessori
Singapore & UK

"Montessori is less about the physical materials and more about the attitude to life and learning. It looks like setting high expectations while providing enough freedom for them to manage their home responsibilities (e.g., washing dishes and tidying their own bedroom) and school responsibilities (e.g., homework and test prep). It looks like providing enough unstructured downtime to balance out the rigor of a school day, so children can still be children. They love Legos, collecting gemstones, reading, and exercising."

"I used to dread helping them with their homework. Now I've developed a respectful, Montessori approach to provide enough homework guidance, but also enough freedom for them to plan how and when they will complete their homework, make mistakes, and correct their own mistakes."

"During Lunar New Year, watching lion dances is a favorite activity. When younger, children may need earplugs, and we warn them in advance that there will be loud drums and huge crowds, so they do not get overstimulated. When older, this yearly activity becomes firmly cemented as part of their childhood memories around Lunar New Year. It may also spark curiosity about the origins or variations of the lion dance, which serves as a springboard to further research and reading."

"Having done Montessori parenting for a number of years, the payoff becomes more evident in the long term. The children are quietly confident in their abilities. It is not a false confidence built on external rewards or people's praises, but on experiencing for themselves that they are capable."

PREPARATION
OF THE ADULT

8

As we start our Montessori journey, our focus is usually on our child and how to support their development. We soon realize that to do this we, the adult, need to work on preparing ourselves. Dr. Montessori talked about our preparation as not just intellectual (learning more about child development) but also emotional (understanding ourselves) and spiritual (seeing our role in the bigger picture).

Preparing ourselves to bring Montessori into the home inspires significant transformation in us and in our relationship with our child, and will likely extend to how we show up with others in our lives, from members of our community to coworkers. In this chapter, we will explore the work needed to prepare ourselves as we embrace Montessori.

> "Now, if the child is to receive a different treatment from what it receives today, in order to save it from conflicts endangering its psychic life, there is a first, fundamental, essential step to be taken, from which all will depend— the modification of the adult."
>
> Dr. Maria Montessori, *The Secret of Childhood*

HOW WE SHOW UP FOR OUR CHILD

As the adult, we have a responsibility to be on our child's side and to see things from their perspective. This may come naturally to us, or it may take some work.

Understanding, trusting, and guiding our child

Every child is capable and unique. We can learn to see our child with fresh eyes every day, from an objective point of view, so that we can understand their needs and support them. Much like the idea of *unconditional positive regard* in psychology, we see our child as doing their best given their life experience, and we seek to understand them rather than judge them, and allow them to be whoever they wish to be.

Even while our child is still a mystery to us, their full potential still unknown, we honor their way of viewing the world, as well as their rhythm, pace, intellect, emotions, and spirit.

We see them, accept them, and seek to understand them (without unloading on them our expectations, dreams, or unlived childhoods). When we do this, we become guardians of our children and help them flourish and grow.

In Montessori, our role is to trust that with their natural desire to learn, our unconditional love and support, and a prepared environment, our child will have the opportunity to develop to their full potential. We don't need to force them to learn. We don't need to worry ourselves over their meeting every developmental milestone or skill according to a standardized timeline. We need only be their guide on their unique path.

Those of us who like to control everything may need to practice letting go, being more flexible, and improvising when needed. When raising children, things are not always going to go as expected, but we can resist our instinct to control the situation by thinking of a time in our lives when we were flexible (perhaps while traveling as a young adult, unsure how plans would unfold) and applying the same skills with our children.

Looking for the joy

By viewing the world through our child's eyes and being next to them as their guide, we can find so much joy. The joy of:

- Watching our child making a discovery for themselves
- Their delight as they look up to the pine trees or out to the ocean or down at the crunchy leaves
- Their hugs and tears and pain and love that we will experience together
- Seeing them offer a tissue to a friend who is sad
- A homemade cake that is not perfect but made by our child's hands
- Being engaged in rich discussion and debate around a kitchen table
- Winter nights cozied up under blankets and summer nights looking up to the clear starry sky
- Adventuring in our own city or exploring new lands
- Critical minds that seek to make a change in the world toward social and environmental justice
- Reading books together because we are never too old for someone to read to us
- And so much more

Wondering together

One of our favorite things to do with the children we work with and our own children is to wonder with them. We can set aside our expertise and look at things with a childlike curiosity so we can make discoveries and imagine together with our child.

Tammy Oesting, a Montessori educator of nearly 20 years who has a passion for studying awe and wonder, suggests activities like going outside, asking exploratory questions, studying morally inspiring people, dancing or making music together, or going to an art museum, all of which support sparking a sense of awe that leads to the state of wonder.

> "The laws governing the universe can be made interesting and wonderful to the child, more interesting even than things in themselves, and he begins to ask: What am I? What is the task of man in this wonderful universe? Do we merely live here for ourselves, or is there something more for us to do? Why do we struggle and fight? What is good and evil? Where will it all end?"
>
> —Dr. Maria Montessori, *To Educate the Human Potential*

Always learning and modeling curiosity

One thing we can continue to model for our children is our role as a lifelong learner. We can learn more about raising children (reading this book is part of that education) and finding what matches our family values. We can listen to podcasts, attend workshops, follow Montessori training, find inspiration on social media (and stop following accounts that make us feel inadequate), or join an online learning community.

We can also inspire our children by pursuing our own interests. Whether it be ceramics, religion, permaculture, activism, sports, playing guitar, or skydiving, we can model taking lessons, practicing, and sometimes failing. Even if we are not good at something, we can show that we are having fun learning, regardless of our ability or the outcome.

The practice of discernment is also integral to continued learning. Do not follow any philosophy, guidance, or text (even this book!) blindly. Don't yield to the latest toy or activity trending online. We need to make sure that what we adopt suits our family by considering our child, the activity, and our values.

HOW WE SHOW UP FOR OURSELVES

As parents and caregivers, we must remember that our children want to see us happy. No one wants to hang out with someone who does not want to be there. Therefore, let's consider how we can meet our own needs and receive care from others, so that we can bring joy to our role as our child's caregiver.

Filling our own cup

To be able to show up for our child and our family, we need to have a full cup. If we are tired, or haven't eaten a nutritious meal, or haven't taken time for ourselves, it is hard to be patient and kind. Looking after and caring for ourselves might look like:

- Drinking a cup of coffee or tea before the children wake up
- Meditating, perhaps while lying in bed in the morning
- Getting into nature, such as at the park or in the woods
- Soaking in a bath in the evening with the door locked
- Going away for a weekend
- Watching a film, reading a book or newspaper, or listening to a podcast or audiobook
- Gardening, woodworking, or crafting
- Sleeping

We can be creative in our pursuit of our favorite activities: Find a friend who can do a babysitting swap; if we have a parenting partner, schedule time alone and time together each week; or hire a teenager in the neighborhood to read books or play games with our child while we work on filling our cup.

Those of us who put others before ourselves may need to put these moments to look after ourselves as can't-miss appointments on our calendars. We show up for appointments with others; now it's time to show up for ourselves.

We don't have to wait for time off to fill our cup, especially when life is full. We can light a candle at mealtime, put on some essential oil to relax us, sit down to have a cup of tea and reconnect with the family at the end of our day, play music as we get some chores around the house done, have moments of silence when we gaze out the window at the passing clouds or droplets of rain on the window, or take a pause as we transition from one activity to the next, even if this is just sitting in the car for a minute or two before getting out.

Making intentional decisions about our time

By intentionally (re)assessing how we spend our time and what we find important, we can examine whether our family is honoring our values and priorities. If nature is on the list, make time to be out in nature on a daily, weekly, or monthly basis. If we want to spend less time in the car, we can research our options and find a local school, grocery store, or yoga class within walking distance.

When we pare down our schedules and focus more deeply on what is left, our children benefit. This gives them time to focus on their favorite interests and people, as well as unscheduled time for exploration, conversation, connection, boredom, and creativity.

When circumstances do not allow

Some people are not in a position to make big life changes. We see you. We hope that you can find small conscious and intentional ways to bring joy to your days at times when some things in your life are difficult.

> "Grant me the serenity to accept the things I cannot change, courage to change the things I can, and the wisdom to know the difference."
>
> —Reinhold Niebuhr

Cultivating calm

From a place of calm, we can be the best guide to our children. We can do things to help ourselves stay calm (preventative) and things to help us come back to calm when needed (restorative). Some things might do both. Below are lists of some of our favorite ways to cultivate calm to use as inspiration.

Preventative. Be prepared. Wake up before the rest of the family. Meditate. Practice yoga. Go for a run. Spend time with a friend. Light a candle at mealtime. Put on some music. Eat nourishing food. Take a nap. Have a bath. Dance. Drink water. Burn some incense or put on some essential oil. Keep a gratitude journal. Go to bed early. Stay up late.

Restorative. Step away. Make a cup of tea. Go to the bathroom. Ask someone for help. Put on music to dance or shake it out. Rock or sway from side to side. Do some primal screaming with our child or with our friends. Find pillows to hit. Laugh at ourselves.

Finding a community where we feel at home

We live in a time when we often no longer reside under the same roof as our extended family, and may, in fact, live far from any loved ones. Contact with our family or friends may be occasional or rare. But we do not raise children alone. We need support from elders and friends who can listen, hold us in hard times, and offer advice if we seek it. We need people to share in the ferrying of children to school, to sports, and to other activities. We need others who can inspire our children with their craft, their wisdom, their grace, or their music. We need people around us who can feed our child if we are held up in traffic or needing a night off from cooking.

Can we find like-minded families in our school or in the wider community? Is our community diverse and a source of different experiences and perspectives to our children? Are there online communities where we can find folks to inspire us and be inspired by us? Can we reconnect with the land and support the Indigenous people? Can we volunteer in our community in a way that we find fun?

If what we are looking for does not yet exist, we can create it and invite others to join us. We have friends who have moved to find their community. Others have moved back to their hometowns to be closer to family. Junnifa and Simone both built schools to create Montessori communities that didn't previously exist near them.

Communities hold us, and we hold them. Communities challenge us, and we challenge them. Communities celebrate with us, and we celebrate with them.

Aiming for connection, instead of perfection

We might feel that the goal of Montessori is perfection—the perfect response, the perfect space, and so on. While we do strive to be more intentional, to be constantly evolving to be better, and to be present with our family, we do not have to be perfect. It's about supporting our children, having fun with them, and remembering to smile when we take it all too seriously. We are doing our best.

Simone knows that she has a tendency to get excited in a conversation and cut people off; she still moves faster than she would like in the classroom; she catches herself talking while showing a young child an activity when it's easier for them to absorb if she shows them slowly and clearly without words; and there are always gray areas in knowing whether to step in to help or not. Yet despite these imperfections, the children know that she is a safe place and that she accepts them for who they are.

We are real. The Japanese concept "wabi-sabi" (roughly translated as perfectly imperfect) describes it well. If we are only perfect or demand perfection from our children, they may become scared of trying or of doing something wrong. We can model acceptance, trying again, and seeking forgiveness when we've made mistakes, because mistakes are not failures. Can we offer ourselves the same grace we are trying to offer to our child?

Taking care of our mental and physical health

Raising our children and thriving ourselves can be in opposition if we are not careful. Let's avoid burnout: Take care of our mental health; nourish our bodies, minds, and souls; and model true self-care for our children.

Let's sit down to eat. Find exercise we love. Look at what we are taking in, including media, people we spend time with, and any chemicals in our home. Cultivate moments of silence.

Let's do less in order to be more; the lure of having it all is slowly making us exhausted parents and caregivers. Both Junnifa and Simone have had to prioritize more time for family and themselves in their week. They still work, care for others, and do their best, but they do enough, not always more.

It is also important to receive care from others. To allow others to look after us—by cooking for us, making space to listen to us, or holding us. We can also visit a specialist like an osteopath, chiropractor, acupuncturist, reflexologist, or massage therapist. And get help from a mental health professional when we know it shouldn't be this hard.

HOW WE GROW

Being the adult requires us to go on our own personal internal journey. According to Dr. Shefali Tsabary in *The Conscious Parent*, raising children can be a spiritual journey. Similar to peeling away the layers of an onion, once we master one aspect, there is always more to unpack.

Being open to understanding and healing ourselves

We have all been there. Our child says or does something, and we find ourselves being activated. It could be because of our mood that day, because there is a lot going on, or because it touches on the memory of an old wound from our past. If we notice when we're being activated, we can work out what the root issue is—there is room for us to hold it gently, mourn it, and heal it.

For example, when we feel like our child isn't respecting us, it may remind us of times when we weren't respected in the past or when we weren't respecting ourselves or others. We might then be able to apologize (including sometimes to a younger version of ourselves), do over a situation, or write a letter to someone about how they made us feel, a letter that we may never send but that helps us own our emotions and move toward healing.

We can also be activated when our child hands us their problem. Let's say they are always late for school. Instead of getting upset about it and trying to solve the problem for them, we can hand it back to our child. A mother in Simone's workshop did just that. The mother made a plan with her 5-year-old daughter so that she could get to school on time, and the daughter then took responsibility for getting ready herself. The mother was no longer activated, the daughter didn't have her mother nagging her, and everyone was a lot calmer.

What activates us? What are we ready to unpack? Is there a problem we need to hand back to our child?

Exploring ways to heal

By healing ourselves, we can be free to guide our children without our past interfering. Some people like talk therapy, others like to process things with friends. We might choose to move our body by cleaning the house or going for a run, or we might take some space to be alone. Meditation and yoga can help us regulate our nervous system and connect to our body, and they can be practiced either on a daily basis or when things come up.

More and more research shows that trauma and past experiences are held in the body, and there are techniques aimed at accessing and soothing these "old wounds." Eye movement desensitization and reprocessing (EMDR), hypnosis and self-hypnosis, Rapid Transformational Therapy (RTT), tapping, kinesiology, breathwork, and somatic work can all help.

Simone uses a technique called "bean bag releasing," which she learned from Bella Lively, a modern-day spiritual guide. It uses our pure awareness to clear past activations from our body. It eliminates the charge of the active emotion so we can respond rather than react. While this is by no means an expert explanation, these are the basic steps:

1. Recognize when we are activated (whether by a recurring thought, an ongoing issue, or a pushed button).

2. Feel where we are activated in our body (e.g., our neck, our heart, our arm).

3. Describe how big the feeling is in our body and what it feels like (e.g., the size of an orange, spongy inside).

4. Observe the feeling, hold it gently, and acknowledge it ("Of course I'd feel that way").

5. Keep observing in awareness (not judgment or analysis) until it becomes smaller or completely melts away.

FURTHER READING

- *The Body Keeps the Score* by Bessel van der Kolk

Helping others understand our needs with healthy boundaries

When we are clear on what is important to us and let others know if something is bothering us in a kind and respectful way, it's amazing how much peace it can bring to our lives and our family. Boundaries help others understand our needs. And they allow our children to see healthy boundaries in action. When we feel resentment, it's a sure sign that our boundaries are being crossed. Those of us who didn't grow up with adults who were able to set kind and clear boundaries with us or others may need to start from scratch and learn.

> "Boundaries are expectations and needs that help you feel safe and comfortable in your relationships."
>
> —Nedra Glover Tawwab, *Set Boundaries, Find Peace*

Using "I" language and stating how we ourselves feel helps our message be heard, particularly if someone is feeling defensive. "When you walked away, the way I took it was _____" or "When you shouted, I felt scared." Avoid language like "You made me feel _____" or "When you attacked me, _____."

We might choose to delay the conversation too: "Let's make a time to talk about it when we are both feeling calm" or "It's important for me that we stick to our house agreements. We can discuss any changes at our next family meeting." We need to remember that people may not immediately respect the boundaries we are communicating or may forget them. We can remind them of a boundary by restating it kindly and clearly.

Once we learn about boundaries, we might find ourselves going from having *porous* boundaries (when we are unclear or do not act in accordance with what we say) to having *rigid* boundaries (where we show no flexibility and can put up a wall between ourselves and others). Instead, therapist and relationship expert Nedra Glover Tawwab encourages having *healthy* boundaries, which allows us to consider the current circumstances and our values, know our limits, and be able to say no and to hear no without taking it personally. For example, a healthy boundary might be allowing our child a moderate serving of cake at a fiftieth wedding anniversary celebration for their grandparents, rather than never allowing sweets (rigid) or giving in to their demands for sweets instead of a balanced dinner (porous).

FURTHER READING

- *Set Boundaries, Find Peace* by Nedra Glover Tawwab.

Addressing our biases

In her article "Understanding Implicit Bias: What Educators Should Know," Cheryl Staats tells us that everyone—regardless of our race, ethnicity, gender, or age—has implicit biases, "the attitudes or stereotypes that affect our understanding, actions, and decisions in an unconscious manner." Our unconscious mind will operate faster and contribute to decisions we make before our conscious mind is even aware.

The good news is that we can do something about our implicit biases. First, we can identify where our conscious ideals differ from our automatic implicit reactions, and bring them into closer alignment. Second, we can increase our contact with people of different religions and ethnicities, as well as people who identify in ways other than we do. When we don't encounter these people in our community, we might follow people on social media with different beliefs, backgrounds, and experiences to ensure that our perspective remains as broad as possible. Last, we can seek exposure to folks who show up in nonstereotypical ways, including those who break occupational gender norms and those with lived experiences that are different from our own.

Our aim is to eventually reduce the difference between our implicit and conscious understanding of the world. This is important work to reduce our biases and allow our children and any child in society to reach their full potential.

Digging deeper

As Montessori adults, we aim to cultivate more patience, more compassion, more empathy, and more forgiveness for the child. Less anger and pride. More love and acceptance.

Remember that the teachings of Dr. Montessori encourage us to dig deeper by being constant in our willingness to learn and grow as individuals, families, and communities. In her article "Grace and Courtesy and the Adult," Catherine McTamaney of *Montessori Daoshi* challenges us as adults to aspire to the same social cohesion that happens in a Montessori classroom—respecting others; understanding that when we take something (materials, resources, or time), there is less for another; practicing our own grace and courtesies; offering to be of service to others; and being conscious of and caring for our environment.

HOW WE CULTIVATE A PRACTICE OF SELF-REFLECTION

We have learned so much from Andy Lulka and Pamela Green, two of the most experienced Montessori educators in North America, about the important practice of self-observation and self-reflection in our preparation as the adult. We have talked a lot about observation in this book. It also plays a critical role in this chapter as we work on ourselves.

Self-observation

It's easiest to practice self-observation in calm moments. Then we can build up our skills to manage in moments where we are activated. It's like going on a meditation retreat. It may be easier to find peace and calm when in a quiet place up in the mountains. Then we build up to maintaining that peace and calm back in the haste of our busy lives.

Here are some ideas for observing ourselves. We can make a column on the side of our paper as we observe our child to note anything coming up for us. Or we can do an observation with the focus being solely on ourselves.

- What are our hands doing?

- What are we thinking?

- What are we feeling?

- What comes up for us as we observe?

- Can we stay in our body? Or are we only in our mind?

- Is our view of the world changing?

- Are we present?

- Do we need support?

- Are we listening to our bodies?

- What do we need to care for ourselves?

- How do we react when our child does something we wouldn't expect them to be ready for?

- How do we react when our child does something we expect they would already know?

Reflection

After observing comes reflection:
- What things are going well?
- What could be improved?
- What is one thing that could be changed that would make everything else easier or unnecessary?

Reflecting on our childhood

Part of our self-reflection will be on our own childhood. We carry this experience into our role as parents and caregivers. The memories of laughter and joy, sadness and pain.

Some questions to ponder. Did we feel seen? Did we feel trusted? Were we raised with a lot of freedom or very strictly? What happened when we made mistakes? What was important to our caregivers: creativity, school marks, independence? What qualities did our caregivers pass on to us: a love of travel, artistic talent and expression, a sense of humor, stubbornness? From these reflections, we can make intentional decisions about which lessons and values we choose to pass on to our children.

Reflecting on our childhood allows us to be gentler with ourselves. We might say to ourselves: "Of course I would find it hard to let go," "I understand why I don't like change," or "No wonder I find it hard to trust my child." Recognizing these things in ourselves is the first step in making a change. Reflection also allows us to understand our children better. Mister Rogers wisely said, "I think that the best thing we can do is to think about what it was like for us and know what our children are going through."

Accepting our journey

Perhaps reading this book brings up feelings like "I wish I'd known about this earlier" or "Why wasn't I raised this way?" Our story is our journey. Everything that we have experienced, the good and the bad, has made us the person we are today. Simone considers having had children in her twenties a very positive experience as she felt like she grew up right alongside them. There are things she could have done differently, but instead of wanting to change them, she is grateful for the mistakes she made along the way and accepts them as part of the journey.

We may have had a difficult relationship with our parents or not known them at all. This experience then often shows us how we would like to show up for our own child and break generational cycles if necessary.

Being a safe adult to whom our child can turn

Through self-reflection, we can examine what would make our children feel safe to come to us with a problem. We can practice acceptance, vulnerability, and being friendly with mistakes. Being predictable and responding, not reacting, are helpful to becoming a safe adult. If this doesn't come easily to us, another option is making sure there's an adult in our child's life whom they can turn to without fear of judgment or punishment.

Seeking guidance

Self-reflection reminds us not to forget ourselves. It means looking at ourselves to see where we can do better. Just as we help children build skills in lagging areas, we can identify our own difficulties and get help to build these skills. We can look for a mentor, attend a workshop, ask a friend to give us feedback, or seek advice from those in our community who support us.

Connecting to self and nature

Self-reflection reminds us not to forget ourselves. It requires us to get quiet, connect with ourselves, and listen to what we are feeling. We might put a hand over our heart, put our feet on the ground, and find a place in our body that is calm (toes are usually a good place to try if we feel discombobulated).

Taking a moment to drink a cup of coffee on the front steps, listen to the birds, and watch the clouds; taking the family on a hike; going to the beach and putting our feet in the sand; breathing some mountain air; or otherwise getting into nature can be restorative ways for us to turn inward.

HOW WE LET THEM FLY

Being our child's guide also means knowing when to give them space to spread their wings. The key here is knowing when to be together and when to give distance, when to fill our cup and when to fill our child's.

Enjoying every age and every stage

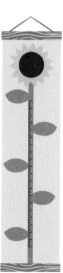

When Simone's children each turned 18, she reflected back on their years as children. People said to her, "It goes so fast." Instead, Simone felt like she was really able to enjoy every age and every stage of her children as they grew up by showing up and being as present as she could along the way.

It's easy to want to rush through moments and milestones: We may feel eager to put our child in school so we'll have more time to ourselves, or we might roll our eyes when driving our child to an early-morning sports practice. Honestly, it's impossible to be in the mood to act as the adult every day. But when Simone looks back, she is glad for every chance she had to connect with her children and witness their growth and development, as well as for the stray Lego bricks and rained-out sports days.

We also want to be having fun; our children know when we aren't enjoying being with them. Simone made a list of things she loved to do with her children—things like baking, playing board games, building Legos—and had it on the fridge; if they wanted to do something together, they'd choose something off the list rather than a game Simone was not able to enjoy. Everyone's needs can be met at every age and stage.

For Junnifa, enjoying every stage is embracing the understanding that her children will continue to change. Accepting each of them, their needs, and unique behaviors at each stage helps her enjoy every age. Knowing that while her toddler might want to pick up and put everything in order, her 6- to 12-year-old seems to enjoy making more of a mess, and that's expected.

Being their rock

When our child is having a hard time, the best thing we can do is to stay grounded while we support them. If we were on a boat in a storm, a captain's calmness and confidence would help moderate our feelings of panic. Similarly, we can be our child's rock, strong and steady when their world is shaking.

As hard as it is, when they attack us, we try to not take it personally. Instead, we can see that they feel safe with us, knowing we will keep loving them even if they lash out. If need be, we can also tell them (perhaps at a later moment) that their words hurt us.

When our child has these big feelings, it can be helpful to practice equanimity. Someone once described equanimity to Simone like this: *Imagine you are sitting in traffic. Instead of getting worked up about it, you imagine yourself in a large marshmallow. The marshmallow acts as a buffer between you and what is going on outside of your car. You don't get stressed by the traffic. You are in your marshmallow.* We can imagine being in our own marshmallow when our child is having a hard time. Not only is it likely to make us smile, it might help us stop reacting to what they are saying so we can stay solid and offer empathy and support.

Attaching and then letting go

By planting roots, we help our child unfurl their wings. But letting go is not easy for some of us. We can be gentle with ourselves, have people to support us (not our children), and let our children shed another layer as they get closer to becoming their beautiful butterfly.

Letting go is . . .

. . . having other people in their lives. This means selecting people we trust to teach, model, and care for our children. Their world gets richer by having others in it from whom to learn. At preschool, grade school, sports, clubs, and friends' homes, they can trust in others as much as their own family.

. . . letting them climb a little higher. By letting them take some risks, go further, or simply do things for themselves, we encourage our child to listen to their own body and make judgments about their capabilities. We stand ready if they need us but allow them to explore their limits.

. . . supervising, not abandoning. We can give them a lot of independence (when possible) and access to the things they need, but we'll be available to guide them.

. . . observing when they're ready. We can help our children scaffold skills so that over time they become more independent. Then remove the scaffold when ready.

. . . showing our child that we have confidence in them or in a new situation. If our child can see and feel that we are comfortable in a situation, they will trust our judgment and feel safer.

. . . constantly discovering who our child is. We see them for who they are, right now, and in every moment, without trying to change them. We let them become themselves.

. . . allowing them to make mistakes and learn from them. We try not to fix things for them but provide guidance and support. They are working out how to solve problems and taking responsibility if they get it wrong.

. . . standing on our own two feet so that our child can have wings. We are better caregivers when we fill our own cup. When we are happy in our own right, we are ready to support our child and be their guide.

Practicing simplicity, patience, and compassion

> "If we build our classrooms on simplicity, they are free to find our common soil. If we build our classrooms on patience, they are free to grow at their own pace. If we build our classrooms on compassion, they are free to wind together, climbing higher for the support we offer each other."
>
> —Catherine McTamaney, *The Tao of Montessori*

These words from Catherine McTamaney can be a guide in our homes too:

- Let our homes be simple and invite calmness, exploration, conversation, and connection. Let them be host to our unconditional love.
- Let us develop patience so we can let our children unfold on their own timeline. May we practice pausing to respond rather than react. May we take time to look at things from their perspective. May we allow a moment more for them to manage by themselves.
- Let us practice compassion so that our children feel supported and learn how to support others. May our home be open and accepting to all, and a place where our children feel safe to express their ideas, hopes, and dreams. May we be a shoulder to cry on.

SVETA, JOHANN, MAYA, NINA

It's a practical life
USA

"We try to balance developing the girls' skills and interests (piano, art, and tennis are their favorites) and finding lots of time to just be. If anyone complains of boredom, we say, 'You're welcome!' We prioritize having dinner together every night and don't schedule extracurricular activities that interfere with the flow of the evening. This is getting increasingly challenging for our 15-year-old, but thus far, we've been successful."

"I contend that Montessori environments are microcosms of society—they represent the 'real world' better than traditional environments—so that when children leave their Montessori schools, they are better equipped to be purposeful and responsible citizens of the world. I notice in Maya and other adolescents who have graduated from Montessori schools a love of learning, resilience, self-assuredness, and a genuine desire to figure out who they are called to be in this world."

"One of the biggest challenges when sending your children to a Montessori school or following the philosophy at home is having to explain yourself to family and friends with a more traditional mindset."

WHAT'S NEXT

9

In this chapter, we look ahead to the third and fourth planes to see what to expect in the coming years. We can be reassured that through every plane, many things remain the same for raising our Montessori children—connection, joy, respect, love, understanding, trust, and acceptance. Hold these values close, and the rest we can work out alongside our children.

It's fascinating that Dr. Montessori stated that childhood ends toward 24 years old, at the end of the fourth plane of development. Most people believe that childhood ends at around age 18. But brain science now confirms that the prefrontal cortex—the area of our brain that helps us make rational decisions—is still developing until the early twenties, supporting Dr. Montessori's observations on childhood.

TRANSITIONING TO THE THIRD PLANE OF DEVELOPMENT

The first time Simone's children rolled their eyes at her, she feared the teenage years were not far ahead and bought books like *How to Talk So Teens Will Listen & Listen So Teens Will Talk* and *Positive Discipline for Teenagers*. She started reading and immediately felt relieved. The approach recommended in these books was much the same as the Montessori approach she had already been using in raising her children. She built that strong base over the first two planes. This is the foundation we have helped lay as our child moves into the third plane.

We want to assure you that you don't have to fight with your teenagers, that they are great company, and that your parenting job doesn't end when they enter middle school and high school. Yet they are changing and now need support in a different way.

There are questions about when adolescence starts these days, as some children experience early puberty. Jenny Marie Höglund, one of the most experienced AMI trainers for 12- to 18-year-olds, views the characteristics and ideals aligning with the third-plane adolescent still becoming evident in children closer to 12 years old. The child is leaving childhood and entering adulthood. They are now asking, "What will my role be?" and "How can I contribute?" In practice, it's a gradual transition to be aware of. Sometimes the child will exhibit characteristics of the second plane, and other times those of the third plane.

WHO IS THE THIRD-PLANE CHILD, THE ADOLESCENT?

Teenagers, like toddlers, are largely misunderstood. Society paints them as difficult, self-absorbed, temperamental, and selfish. They stay up late, they sleep in, they lay about, they are out with friends, or they hide in their room.

In Montessori, we view adolescents in a different light. Teenagers are working out who they are—they might put on a brave face, but really, they are very vulnerable, doubting and questioning themselves and others. They can be enormously capable given the right environment, guidance, opportunities, and challenges. They can also be fun to be around, with their especially interesting conversations about how they would change the world.

If you've ever thought that toddlers and teenagers are alike, Dr. Montessori would agree. Remember how the first plane and the third plane are seen as parallel planes? (See the orange triangle in both of these planes in the diagram on page 24.) Both present enormous physical changes; both are very volatile periods of development; and in both, children are seeking independence (moving away from their parents in the first plane, and preparing to move into society in the third plane). We can also see this in The Bulb diagram, below. See the large orange area during the adolescent years, smaller yet still enlarged as in the first plane.

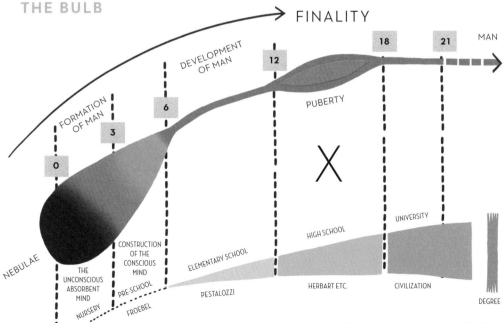

THE BULB   → FINALITY

Source: Association Montessori Internationale (AMI)

Let's take a closer look at how we view adolescents in Montessori.

Adolescents are as fragile as newborns. This is a vulnerable time. They are very self-critical about their appearance and abilities, they can be irrational, and they can isolate themselves in their room. They are working out "Who am I?" and "What is expected of me?" Rather than criticizing them, we can "hold" them as gently as a baby, being a safe person with whom they can explore these big questions.

Adolescents are going through an enormous amount of change. During the first 2 years of adolescence, their bodies are preparing; during the second 2 years, their bodies are blossoming; and during the final 2 years, their bodies are perfecting themselves. There are huge hormonal changes, making it an emotional period. With so much growth and change, adolescents are more fragile and get sick more easily. It is also a time of fatigue, when they like to stay up late and will eat whatever and whenever food is available. It is ideal for them to do physical work or exercise outdoors to strengthen their body and mind and challenge themselves physically.

Adolescents appear not to be studious. An adolescent's brain is in so much flux, which makes it seem like they have less academic capacity. Psychologist David Elkind calls this "pseudostupidity." They are actually still very capable and are now able to see a problem from different perspectives. But instead of making life easier, it makes it more complicated for them, as there is often no longer one simple answer. Their brains are wired for metacognition—learning about how they learn—like wanting to be involved in deciding what they are learning and how. They also enjoy studies that are meaningful to them and being able to practically apply things they learned in the earlier years.

Adolescents need protection. As their prefrontal cortex continues to develop, we need to provide an environment that feels secure and safe, that they can rely on. However, the adolescent does not want to be controlled. We need to show them we trust them, set up agreements and systems with them, and discuss options and solutions together, so that they can have their freedom with the accompanying responsibilities. All that said, sometimes we as their caring adults will need to make a decision they are not happy with to keep them safe. When they know we have explored all the options, they may not be happy but will understand that it's our job to keep them safe.

Adolescents need to understand society. We can have higher expectations for our adolescents and give them the opportunity to prepare themselves as young adults. Rather than just doing schoolwork, hanging out with friends, or having us take them to sports practices or drama or dance classes, adolescents need to have experiences of being in society. Whereas from ages 6 to 12, the child was interested in exploring the whole universe with their imagination, the place of exploration for the adolescent is getting hands-on experiences in their home, their school setting, and the wider community as practice for entering adult life. Practice in a prepared environment before they go out into the unprepared environment in the following fourth plane.

Adolescents seek economic and social independence. More than being given pocket money, adolescents want to take part in society to earn their own money. We think, "They should just be kids; they don't need to get a job yet." Yet there is a fire in their belly that is less about making a lot of money than about exploring how to function in this time and place in society. They begin to be financially independent and have an impact in the world. They also want to make decisions about how to spend the money they earn, with some guidance from us.

Adolescents need to belong and be part of a bigger purpose. At such a vulnerable age, they seek to be like others, want to work out how they can contribute to their group, and often have high ideals. As such, they can be part of self-organizing groups of like-minded adolescents who are working toward a bigger goal—it might be setting up a permaculture farm for their neighborhood, fundraising for a cause or community, making music as part of an orchestra or band, or visiting the elderly in nursing homes. This gives them a cause to support while working with others.

Adolescents need to differentiate themselves. At the same time as wanting to belong, they are also figuring out how they want to be different. They are navigating how to be themselves and how they'd like to fit into the group.

Adolescents say, "Help us to do it by ourselves." The first-plane child says, "Help me to do it myself." The second-plane child says, "Help me to think by myself." The third-plane child says, "Help us to do it ourselves." The adolescent, placing importance now on their community, wants to work with their peers and manage for themselves. This empowers them, gives them confidence, and provides them with real-life experiences.

Adolescents have a sensitive period for justice. They are developing their moral compass further. The adolescent continues to explore the morality that they began to acquire in the second plane, but it's no longer about things being only equal. They can see people's strengths and needs and consider what is right. They are also ready to think about systems and if they are fair or systems of oppression and power. This combined with their growing self-awareness and love for being in community makes them ready to be activists for change.

Adolescents have a sensitive period for dignity. They experience personal dignity when they make a contribution and feel like they matter. Dr. Montessori referred to this as *valorization*, how the adolescent finds their place in the world. Both dignity and justice are things that cannot be taught but must be lived. For the adolescent, this is by being in community.

Adolescents are drawn to risky behavior. *Valorization* also refers to valor's second meaning: to be brave. Research shows that the adolescent's brain seeks risk and reward and that they need to experience risk to experience valorization, that feeling of bravery. We need to help them manage the risk, though, as they are not yet able to assess risk very accurately. Instead we can guide them toward relatively safe activities like rock climbing and riding roller coasters where they can still experience a feeling of risk.

> "It is the 'valorisation' of the personality, to become aware of ones [*sic*] own value. Without this, as many psychologists say, the child only feels his own value if he is loved. This is another 'valorisation'—he is independent, he is sure of his own actions and knows how to act."
>
> —Dr. Maria Montessori, *Citizen of the World*

WHAT DID DR. MONTESSORI ENVISION FOR ADOLESCENTS?

Dr. Montessori proposed that adolescents from 12 to 15 years old attend a farm school, an "Erdkinder." It's hard to imagine our adolescents living away from us, but in this way, they are able to begin the application of knowledge learned to real-life situations with real-life consequences. To take responsibility with the other students to look after the animals and the farmhouse, to have a store and a guesthouse. All this in a prepared environment with a few prepared adults to support them.

The goal is not "success" or to prepare them for a career as a farmer or to get a good job. It's for every child at the end of this plane to be prepared to do something meaningful to them. We are, again, not filling them with facts or focused only on their intellectual development; we also want to help them meet their social, emotional, and spiritual needs, offering them experiences that show them what adult life could be like.

The prepared environment plays an important role in this plane of development, as it did in earlier planes. Both indoor and outdoor environments—the store, the guesthouse, the land—are essential. The young adolescents are practicing in this carefully prepared environment, which is safe and predictable, before they will move into the unprepared

environment as a young adult. This time away from home offers them the opportunity to do great things and to learn to live in a social group in an environment where they feel confident and secure, where they can find inner ease and balance while learning to adapt to not only their group but also the wider environment and groups.

The farm belongs to the adolescents. They work hard as a community to maintain the farm, learn to live with others, and see that everyone has a role to play. When they love their work, they care for their environment and become responsible for it. They take responsibility for their lives, from shopping to cooking and cleaning. They also experience the consequences of self-management; for example, that they will not have light if no one changes a bulb that's gone out or that they will run out of money at the end of the month if they do not budget well for their meals and other expenses.

In addition to doing farmwork, they study topics that are relevant to their life on the farm. They are applying what they learn in the classroom (theoretical) to real-life situations (practical). Their work and study cover self-expression (music, art, language); psychic development (moral development, mathematics, and language); and the study of Earth and life (human development, civilizations, and the history of humanity).

Alongside the "farm school" models, there has been a lot of work done—including by Mario Montessori and Mario Montessori Jr. (Dr. Montessori's son and grandson)—to develop Montessori adolescent programs in urban settings. They will involve a lot of community work, with the students working collaboratively.

A fun example is Embark Education in Denver, Colorado, a micro-school applying Montessori principles in a bike store and café. Some schools run a CSA (community-supported agriculture) project, growing and selling produce, and holding fundraising events for the school or charities. Other schools encourage their students to look at their gifts and skills to come up with and run their own micro-businesses. At the middle school program at Montessori Jewish Day School in Toronto, Canada, the money earned goes toward a two-week trip to Israel prior to graduation and to a charity carefully selected by the students.

The best of these programs offer meaningful work, incorporate outdoor communal work, are led and staffed by adults prepared to guide the adolescents, and take an interdisciplinary approach to their studies (i.e., by exploring the intersection of math, history, geography, and other subjects). The students are not just following a textbook at their own pace.

For more on life at an Erdkinder, refer to the case study "The Montessori Adolescent at the Montessori Centre for Work and Study, Rydet, Sweden" found in the online appendix. It is incredible to learn about all that adolescents are capable of there.

HUMAN TENDENCIES OF THE ADOLESCENT

Remember the human tendencies from chapter 2? These are still present in the adolescent, but they'll show up in different ways.

The adolescent's **orientation** is now to the larger society outside their family and to their peers. They explore not just the physical space but also their role in their family, their friend group, and school as well as who they are, including their gifts, their passions, their sexuality, and their values. And they observe adults and peers to see if we behave in line with our values.

Abstraction can be seen when they begin to look at things from others' perspectives. They are now aware of their thought processes and begin to understand the patterns behind them. They have a more global perspective, and they want to solve big problems, at first with big ideas and then later in the plane with more precise and realistic plans.

They use their **imagination** to look for ways they could make life better, from how a subject is taught at school, to what the future could look like, to how to improve their environment or make life on the planet sustainable for us all. Sometimes they'll feel small and insignificant; other times they'll feel powerful and that they can effect change.

Their **work** still requires their head and their hands to work together, this time with academic studies alongside practical experience (like working on the farm or being involved in a community project). They are working no longer just for themselves but also for their community and trying out different roles through their work. Through making or growing goods and selling them, they are connecting with the adult world, taking part in both the social aspects and commerce. They still strive for maximum effort, taking on work that is challenging and with a definite purpose as long as it is related to them and makes sense to them. The results of their work are not instant—for example, the time for vegetables to grow from seeds—and they learn to work not only with their preferred partner or group but with anyone in the community as practice for their adult life.

There are many opportunities for them to **calculate** now in real-life situations, such as when buying groceries or determining how much paint to buy if they are decorating their room. When making decisions, they are capable of assessing possible outcomes or consequences for themselves, others, and possibly their environment.

The human tendencies to **perfect**, to **be exact**, and to **repeat** are observed in adolescents as they aim to understand everything they do. They perfect what they are good at and refine these skills. Rather than allow them to be only outwardly focused on what others think of them, we can help them explore what they find important and be okay with who they are. We do this by helping them recognize their strengths and build skills in weaker areas. If we ask an adolescent to do a self-assessment around a task, they are often more critical of themselves than we are of them.

Communication is hard work for an adolescent. They are learning to express their ideas, try them out on others, and participate in discussions with peers and adults. They continue to learn how to collaborate with others, live peacefully in a social group, make decisions, and try out different perspectives. They can have some big emotions to let out, and communicating makes them feel alive.

THE MONTESSORI ADOLESCENT AT HOME

In some ways, we could say that our expectations of teenagers are too low. Or that we are asking too much from them in areas that are not important to them. Rarely are we offering them opportunities for adult work, thinking that it is too hard for them or that we don't want to weigh them down with the responsibilities too soon.

Yet when we see all they are capable of in the Erdkinder environment (see the case study in the online appendix), we can think about what prepared environment we can offer our adolescents, what their needs are, the atmosphere we want to create, as well as the experiences they will benefit from.

In *From Childhood to Adolescence*, Dr. Montessori wrote about adolescents having two needs: "If puberty is on the physical side a transition from an infantile to an adult state, there is also, on the psychological side, a transition from the child who has to live in a family, to the adult who has to live in society. These two needs of the adolescent: for protection during the time of the difficult physical transition, and for an understanding of the society which he is about to enter to play his part as an adult, give rise to two problems that are of equal importance concerning education at this age."

From this we see that our task is to be their safe space (giving them physical and psychological safety) and to support them as they transition in society from child to adult.

The prepared environment

The prepared home environment for adolescents is less about Montessori shelves with activities and more about the idea of their having a place to practice being a citizen in the safety of their family and wider community.

Here are some thoughts about the physical space:

- The adult helps them set up the environment with order, and the adolescent is then responsible for maintaining it. They may still need some assistance from time to time, like a prompt to do a seasonal inventory of their closets for clothing that can be sold, donated, or passed down to a younger sibling, or to make space to study by storing or recycling work that is no longer needed.

- The adolescent often expresses their need for privacy, and we'll want to create spaces where they can be by themselves, also during waking hours. If our home does not allow for them to have their own room, we can provide privacy with a room divider or curtain or half wall. Some people may be able to build a studio in their garden if they have one.

- "A place for everything and everything in its place" can still be helpful at this age when they are less organized; we can help them put it into practice by designating a storage area near the front door for sports gear or musical instruments.

- We can create a reading nook with an armchair, a lamp, and a table with books on it so they are drawn to sit down with a book rather than scroll on their phone.

- We can make board games accessible so they can play with family or friends. It can be fun to have a chess set, a mini-pool table, ice hockey table, or Ping-Pong table in a common area to create an opportunity for them to socialize in a way that is not centered around screens.

- Consider having a space in our home where they can gather with their friends. If we make it inviting for their friends to come over, we will be able to meet their friends and observe the group dynamics. We may be limited by space, but even having a table in the kitchen where they can eat snacks or play games means they always feel welcome.

- The environment can also be adjusted based on their interests. If possible, we can dedicate a corner of the home to encourage these interests, such as by setting up an easel for painting; a lightbox area for photographing items to sell online; an area for practicing piano, drums, or guitar; a woodworking area; or a table at which to make stop-motion films.

- As mentioned earlier in the discussion of the Erdkinder, adolescents have a need for physical work. They may be able to help mow the lawns of neighbors; have a paper route; help paint the house, sand the floors, and do practical repairs around the home; or help out in a community garden or a family garden. Look for opportunities that align with their interests. We can also hang a punching bag, ropes, or rings from the ceiling for them to use in channeling excess or emotional energy.

- They are busy with social relationships, and practical matters like locking the front door or turning out the lights are low on their list of priorities. Look for easy ways for them to remember these things, like a sign on the front door that says "Lights and lock" so they remember to turn off the lights and lock the door if they are the last to leave the house.

- Don't forget the outdoors. We can offer them opportunities to be outdoors and out in nature. If it doesn't happen daily, we can make time to go hiking on the weekends or camping on vacation, or make a vegetable patch in raised beds that they can help with. If we have an outside space, we can hang a hammock that they can lie in to watch the clouds and contemplate life.

The prepared environment is also their safe psychological space. Things we can do to create this space include:

- Helping them navigate their studies—not doing their homework for them but checking in as often as needed (daily or weekly) to make sure they have enough time to complete their tasks.
- Holding space for them emotionally as they navigate relationships with themselves and others.
- Observing when they are mentally overloaded and helping them assess their schedule and modify it if needed.
- Creating agreements around practical tasks like laundry, cooking, and cleaning—how much they do themselves, how much will be done collectively.
- Giving guidance when requested around logistical arrangements for things like making health appointments or getting to places further afield.

Developing agreements

Just as we did with the second-plane child, we establish with our adolescent a code of conduct. What is expected, how we do things safely, with respect for each other, and in a way that is predictable and consistent.

Our job as their parent or caregiver is to keep them safe. Their job as the adolescent is to keep stretching themselves, which may look like seeing how far they can push us. Instead of this being a battle, it can be done in collaboration.

They are not going to be told the rules. These agreements need to be developed with them. One family may opt for weekly family meetings. Others might have more casual conversations at mealtimes.

When we have made a new agreement, such as around use of screens in our family (including for the adults), the last step is to make a time to come back to review how it's going and see what could be improved. (More on screens on page 223.)

The agreements may need to be adjusted over time. But never when the adolescent is wound up and wants to change the rules on the spot. We can calmly say, "It sounds like you aren't happy with the current agreement that we have. Let's write it down to review when we are all calm."

Freedom and limits

The adolescent has an enormous amount of freedom based on trust built up over the years. They may have their own cell phone, be able to choose the subjects they study at school, and get themselves to where they need to go (depending on where you live, the safety of the area, and accessibility to transportation).

They also have the freedom to be themselves, as they have in previous planes. It can be easier for us to accept them for who they are when they are toddlers and preschoolers and the stakes are lower. Adolescents will remind us that they want to express themselves, not blindly follow what we might choose for them. This could be what they study, the sports they play, the hobbies they pursue, the clothes they wear, the music they listen to, their religious beliefs, their gender identity, or whom they are attracted to. With their freedom also comes our acceptance.

Having more freedom does not mean they have license to do whatever they like. They also have responsibilities arising from this freedom; for example, to let us know if there is a change to the plan, to do their part in contributing to the family, and to use their phones in a way that is safe and responsible.

If the trust gets broken, then there will need to be a repair. It might be that there is less freedom for a while until we can trust each other again.

Most of the time, we'll be able to collaborate with them to find a solution that works for the whole family. For example, when 14-year-old Emma wanted to go to a concert alone with a school friend, Simone said something like, "You want to go to that concert, and it's my job to keep you safe. How can we find a way that you can go to the concert and I know that we've done as much as we can to keep you safe?" The agreement they came up with was that the girls would eat pizza at Simone's house before the concert (so Simone could meet Emma's friend), that Simone would cycle with them to the venue and make sure they got in okay, that they understood the risks inside the venue with alcohol and drugs, and that Simone would cycle to meet them after the concert—she wasn't the only adult there—and the girls were able to attend the concert.

At times, we as the adult might need to set a limit and say no and, if so, there will be a good reason. Our children have learned over the years that if we say no, we have given their request a lot of thought, we have discussed it with them to try to find a way that would work for us both, and we have been unable to come up with one. They may not be happy about it and may rage against us, but sometimes we will see that they are relieved and can blame us while not losing face with their friends.

It's okay to have boundaries, and it's helpful for them to see us model boundary setting. If they say something rude to us, we can say, "I don't like it when you speak to me like that" or "Let's talk about this tomorrow when we are all feeling calm."

Do you see how the principles of working together (rather than threatening and bribing) and setting limits when needed are the same with younger children and teenagers? We are being their guide.

Handling big emotions

We've talked about helping our children process their emotions as babies, toddlers, preschoolers, and 6- to 12-year-olds. We can build on that foundation and continue to guide our adolescents through their big feelings. They are subject to hormones and changes they do not understand.

We can have compassion for them, remember to not take it personally if they lash out at us, and understand that they are actually going through a vulnerable transition in their life. It can be a good idea to remember that Dr. Montessori considered adolescents to be as "fragile as a newborn."

Hormonal adolescent outbursts are not so dissimilar to toddler tantrums. In the moment:

- We might be able to rub their back and ask what they need.
- We can offer them a glass of water and be there if they want to talk.
- We can offer to hold space while they let out their emotions. Some adolescents will be able to name the emotion and let us know where they feel it in their body. When they center their awareness on that place, they can help the emotion move through them, maybe assisted by their shaking their body, sighing, exhaling deeply, rocking back and forth, or crying.
- Some of them may want to move their bodies by going for a run or hitting a punching bag.
- Some will want to take some space and retreat to their room to calm down.

Unlike with toddlers, who need us to close the circle in the moment, with adolescents, we have the luxury of time. We can come back later in the day to ask about what happened, or to ask them to make amends if they said something unkind or hurt someone. As uncomfortable as these moments are, there is growth here. Our connection is made stronger. They learn that we love them even at their worst.

Contributing to others

In a Montessori Erdkinder, the adolescents get a lot of meaning out of being an important part of farm life. They work so as not to let the group down. They begin to make choices for the group, not just themselves.

Even if they are not living in an Erdkinder, they can look for ways to contribute to their community. For example, by being of service in their school community. They might visit the younger children's classes to read books or do planting with them, make materials for the younger children's classes, help fix things around the school, work in the school kitchen if there is one, or help with maintenance jobs like mowing the lawn. The younger students admire the adolescents, and the adolescents provide an example of what will come next to both the young children and their families.

They also need to feel part of something bigger than themselves. Outside of school and home, they can find a cause that aligns with their passions and join a group to help raise awareness or funds. The cause might be animal welfare, human rights, climate change, or peace for war-torn areas. Imagine them meeting each week with like-minded adolescents to plan a bake sale or festival to raise money. It means they'll need to work with others; everyone has a role, and they'll need to problem-solve, be financially responsibile, and give back to society. There are local councils that will give funds to youth groups who want to create a community project. They could come together to write an application to get their group some funding, and the parents and caregivers could offer to come to share their expertise as needed.

In vacation periods, there are opportunities to volunteer in other communities, look after the neighbors' children or pets, or take part in a community garden project.

Earning money

> "Productive work and a wage that gives economic independence, or rather constitutes a first real attempt to achieve economic independence, could be made . . . a general principle of social education for adolescents and young people."
>
> —Dr. Maria Montessori, *From Childhood to Adolescence*

Where the preschooler sought functional independence and the school-age child mental independence, the adolescent seeks economic independence. They want to experience at least a "real attempt" at working for money, earning money, and spending money. Earning money is a way they can practice being in society in these adolescent years.

Work involves learning new systems, following instructions, working as a team member, interacting with customers and colleagues, and asking for help when needed. They will be practicing time management by fitting in work around school, homework, sports, family and social commitments. There is also self-organization around reading rosters, being on time, and making arrangements during vacations.

If they work at a cinema, they'll be trained to perform various tasks like cleaning the screening rooms, selling tickets, checking tickets and ages for entry to certain films, and selling snacks at the concession stand. They'll need to make visitors feel welcome, as well as turn away someone who's underage or help calm a volatile situation. A manager would also have the additional responsibilities of building and organizing the team.

In exchange for their time, they receive money—money they can spend on things they save for. If they spend all their money on food and going out with friends, there may not be enough for an item of clothing they would like to purchase. If they want a video game, rather than asking us for it, they learn to save up for it. It is all an experience in earning, spending, and saving money, including having their own bank account.

As part of their financial education, we can introduce them to the idea of saving and investing money, including where we can put our money to save it, the concept of compound interest, and the risks of investing, all while modeling our own investment choices. Some families will be living paycheck to paycheck. Our children will then be learning how to manage the family budget to meet our immediate needs. When they begin to earn money, we can ensure that they put some aside to contribute to people, organizations, or causes they believe in. They are learning to be part of the financial ecosystem and a member of society.

As mentioned earlier, with money now being mostly digital, it's less concrete to understand than cash. We can observe our child to see if they understand the idea behind digital money or if we need to scaffold these skills with them by using cash to demonstrate how amounts are transferred between parties. Rather than labeling a child "bad with money," we can keep teaching them.

There are different approaches to pocket money. Some families cover the costs of everything the child needs, and the child saves money for more discretionary purchases. Other families opt for a monthly or quarterly allowance. In a Montessori home, an allowance is not generally tied to jobs they need to do around the home. This is how they have always contributed to, and continue to contribute to, the family. However, when they do a job that we would otherwise have to pay someone for, like doing the bookkeeping for the family business or helping paint the living room, then they could earn some extra money on top of their allowance.

For a younger adolescent, an allowance could be a smaller amount for them to buy lunch at school (they quickly learn that if they make their lunch at home, they can save their money for other things) or a larger amount for a clothing allowance to buy the clothing they will need (some children will choose to save up for a higher-priced item; others will go to thrift stores to stretch their money further).

Stay connected with them

It's easy for our adolescents to be pulled away from our guidance by the attraction of their peer group. In his book *Hold On to Your Kids*, Gordon Neufeld calls this *peer orientation*. Peers are great for helping adolescents find out who they are, have meaningful connections, and share interests. Yet left in the hands of their peers, adolescents are in danger of developing themselves only to please others and be liked in a superficial way, rather than to fulfill their human potential. Neufeld encourages us not to let our children slip away amid the power of peers and instead to keep our connection with them strong throughout these years.

We want to stay connected with them during these adolescent years so that we can continue to be a positive influence and someone they look to for feedback, counsel, and support. If we have little connection, our attempts to provide guidance will be ignored or be responded to with resistance and/or defiance. In these years, it's less about attempting to shape and correct their behavior and more about building our relationship.

How we now connect with our children will depend a lot on their unique interests and the relationship we have built over the years. Some examples from families we know include:

- Asking them to keep us up to date with the football results and how their favorite team is doing.
- Planning annual family visits to nostalgic places like an amusement park or a hiking trail.
- Making time to connect at the beginning and end of the day.
- Listening to music they like or music they play, or having a ritual of Sunday-night music evenings with the family and an old record collection.
- Hanging around the kitchen when they get in from school or we get home from work to have a cup of tea and debrief their day.
- Knowing their friends' favorite foods so their friends feel welcome and enjoy spending time in our home.
- Reading a longer book about a shared interest together at night—one of Simone's friends calls home while he's on business trips so he and his child can still read together.

- Having a tradition of Sunday-night dinners that they can invite friends to join.

- Doing ongoing larger art and crafts projects together like knitting, sewing, origami, or painting.

- Watching a series or film on television—where once we wanted to be screen-free, a show once a week can be time to connect, to cozy up on the couch together and build a shared interest.

- Traveling during school holidays to make special memories—adolescents can help research places to visit or spots they want to photograph; they can pack for themselves; and they can walk for miles when fueled with water and gelato.

- Having fun together rather than only giving out instructions all day.

- Eating meals together—food continues to be a perfect space for open conversation and connection. Eat breakfast and dinner together as often as possible; eat at the kitchen or dining table, rather than in front of the TV; switch off the phones; and offer simple, nutritious, home-cooked food. On the weekends, Simone would have a second breakfast with her adolescents when they woke up or a cup of tea to join them. On those days when they are happy to hang out chatting after a meal, we make sure not to rush off to do another job but stay and enjoy all the company we can get.

- Continuing the family rituals established in earlier planes, like special Sunday breakfasts or cake for family birthday celebrations.

- Attending any drama, music, or school performances or sports events—being there in the audience or on the sidelines to show support.

- Listening when they talk, even when we don't agree.

- Having them cook one or two nights a week—they can pick up any ingredients they need and delight us with new recipes they are trying.

- Showing interest in their passions, whether they be computer games, football, marine biology, designing fonts, or making short films. Ask them questions about it, remember to follow up on conversations, and perhaps do something together around their interests.

- Asking, "Do you want company or would you rather be alone right now?" if they are feeling moody.

We also build connection when, just as in earlier years, we show up to support them in hard times. Having a continued secure attachment provides space where they can make mistakes, practice, try out different identities, and learn. We can grow alongside them, sharing our own ups and downs. They observe how we navigate life, relationships, and challenges while we also model how to be vulnerable. In this way, they can find out for themselves what is the right or wrong thing to do, and how to build their own safe and healthy relationships.

We continue to trust them. We will not know everything they are up to. We can give them information to keep them safe, educate them about alcohol, drugs, sex, and being streetwise. Tell them to be with sensible friends if they want to try anything unsafe. Let them know they can call us at any hour to help them. Then trust and send a guardian angel to keep watch over them.

Timing is everything

Even though connection is important, adolescents may not appreciate being bombarded with questions the minute they walk in the door. They need a lot of alone time. They need time to transition from school to home. They need to open up to us when they are ready.

Junnifa compares being the parent of an adolescent to being like a potted plant. We hang around a lot in common areas of the home (like the kitchen and living room) to show we are available. We are careful to give our children their space, while making our presence known. Then when our adolescent comes in and wants to talk, to ask us a question, or to simply flop down next to us, we are available to them. We may have a busy work life during this period of their lives, so, we can let them know when we get home from work. We might make it a habit to have a cup of tea together or to prepare dinner together or wash up together after our meal, connecting at the end of the day side by side.

The social newborn

In Montessori, we describe the adolescent as a social newborn. They are learning how to step over the threshold from their family into society. We can help this transition by including them in the social life of the family and giving them responsibilities (instead of allowing them to retreat to their room). They can greet visitors, offer beverages, ask and answer questions, and learn the social graces of our culture.

Offer them opportunities to meet a variety of people with different backgrounds, jobs, ethnicities, and religions. They will learn about different experiences and may get inspiration about a profession they might like to pursue in the future.

Allow them to get themselves around the city or area by bike or public transportation so they can begin to discover how society works. They will run into problems, go the wrong way, run out of money, get a flat tire. They will find ways to solve these problems and see what it takes to live in a social group and eventually find their place in it.

So often when our adolescent is having a difficult time, we want to take away their pain, jump in and solve their problem for them, empathize for a hot second and then get into ways they can make it better, or share what we have learned in our extra decades on the planet so they don't have to go through it.

"It's hard to see you having a hard time." This is something that Simone says a lot and that is particularly useful during the adolescent years. Because one of the wisest things Simone learned in these years was, as painful as it is to bear witness, to let them have their experience.

Instead of jumping in, we can be there as their anchor to hold space for all their emotions as they suffer, wallow, grieve, ache, hurt, laugh, cry, learn, and grow.

Teach lagging skills

Sometimes we think, "They should know better!" They leave the back door open, forget their sports clothes, or leave some food in their room to grow moldy. Instead of being activated, we can recognize that they would do better if they could do better. Or as Ross Greene says in *The Explosive Child*: "Behaviorally challenging kids are challenging because they're lacking the skills to not be challenging."

Our teenagers need us to see that they are not trying to give us a hard time. They either don't yet have a certain skill or need more practice. We can think to ourselves, *What is the skill they are missing? What is getting in the way?*

Then we take the time to build these skills with them. It might be coming up with a system for unpacking their bag as soon as they arrive home. Or recognizing that they flop when they get home and would do better if they unpacked their school bag at dinnertime. We don't decide for them but work out a way with them to help them do better.

Technology and teenagers

Technology is a tool. It is not all bad—it is a matter of how we use it.

Where we might have once chatted with our friends on the phone for hours, this generation is connecting in group chats, on social media, and while gaming with friends, and most of this is happening and available to them in their pocket no matter where they are. Many hobbies might be online, from drawing tutorials to learning to play an instrument.

In the second plane, we helped introduce how to use screens safely, where to find accurate information, and how to have a limited but balanced approach to screens. In the third plane, the adolescent is ready to take on more responsibility in this area, as in other areas of their lives. They have reached a certain level of maturity where they are capable of using technology in a way that supports their development rather than undermining their self-esteem or using it to disconnect. This will not happen overnight, but we are available along the way to guide them.

We can apply the same principles of making agreements with them and preparing the environment (both physically and emotionally) to help them manage using screens. Here are some things we can do:

- Establish agreements about when there are no screens—for example, at mealtimes, when we have visitors, during important discussions.

- Educate them about digital safety—ensure that they know not to meet strangers via the internet and to get our permission before joining a new social network; agree for us to have their passwords, not to spy on them but for ad hoc checks if required.

- Discuss what information to keep private online—their real name, school, current location—and remind them of the responsibility and possible consequences of having a permanent digital profile for any text or email sent or social media post.

- Inform them about the power of words—discuss online bullying and unkind comments; make it clear that they are to alert us if they are a victim of online bullying or if something online makes them uncomfortable or is inappropriate.

- Make a space in the common area for screens to sleep at night, ideally stopping screen use an hour or two before bed.

- Model ourselves how we would like them to use screens—rather than scrolling aimlessly, we can say, "I'm going to have a 15-minute social media break" or "I'm going to look up the train times for tomorrow" or "I'm sorry. I don't usually check my phone during family time, but I received an urgent text. Let me step out to handle this and I'll be back in 5 minutes."

- Discuss what apps they use and how they can use them safely.

- If they are falling behind with schoolwork or not contributing to the home or fulfilling other responsibilities, have a meeting to help them come up with a plan to manage their screen time.

- Invite them to look up information at the library, arrange a face-to-face conversation with an expert, or attend a seminar on a topic they are interested in rather than using the internet as a first resource.

- Help them be critical thinkers about the information they find on the internet, even from reliable sources. We can ask them questions like "Who created this information?" and "For what purpose?"

- Familiarize ourselves with the social media they are using so we can assess risks, show them how to use it safely, and understand the input they are taking in.

- Encourage the use of timers for gaming sessions.

They are learning to navigate technology the same way adults do—turning off notifications so they can get their homework done, practicing communicating clearly with friends so that they can make plans to meet up, and finding the balance between online and offline life. We are there to help them navigate it, and we can step in to guide them if they need some limits.

If they are comparing themselves to others or getting lost in negative conversation threads and their mental health is being affected, set a time to discuss it with them and make a plan. Be sure to review the plan regularly to see if it is helping.

In *From Childhood to Adolescence*, Dr. Montessori wrote, "Children should learn to use machines habitually as part of their education. The machine is like an extra adaptable limb. . . . But beware." Let's help our children prepare for the world they live in. Provide plenty of time for real face-to-face social interactions, make sure they are joining for (screen-free) family meals, provide opportunities for concrete learning experiences, make sure they get exercise (cycling to school is great where possible), and they can supplement with technology when they are able to manage the associated responsibility appropriately.

THE ADOLESCENT AND SCHOOLWORK

It can be hard to motivate adolescents to do their homework if the work is not meaningful to them or is not challenging.

Tony Evans, the director of Dundas Valley Montessori School in Canada, sums it up succinctly: "Give them dignity, give them deadlines, and give them work that needs them to be working at a high level. You don't teach the adolescent maths. You reverse engineer: How can they care about learning maths?"

The adolescent needs to feel purposeful, to feel challenged, and needs goals to work toward. It might be preparing food for forty-five people in a soup kitchen or going on a canoe trip with their class. They need to be doing real work, not just receiving lessons.

The transition from middle school to high school is an enormous adjustment for many adolescents. We can prepare them by discussing what the expectations are at the new school, like being on time, completing homework assignments, and studying for tests. Many adjust quite easily. Others may take more time.

If we are not able to access a Montessori school for adolescents, we can still support them in their schooling in a Montessori way. Here are some ideas:

- We can help give meaning to their work by talking with them about the practical application of the skills they are learning in class.
- If they have tests at their school, they can learn to see these as an opportunity to find out which areas of a given subject they still haven't completely mastered or fully understood.
- If our child needs help with planning, we can sit with them once a week while they map out their timetable, sport commitments, assignments due, and rest time; we can check in with them to see if they are on track or if they are feeling overwhelmed.
- We can show interest in their studies—ask how they felt about their test, check that they have enough time to do their homework—but, unless they need help, leave it up to them to study for their tests and work on their projects. We can still apply the philosophy of giving as little help as possible and as much as necessary.
- If they are feeling overwhelmed, we can help them break down what needs to be done into manageable steps.
- Rather than our getting in the habit of nagging them, let them take responsibility for their studies and experience the consequence of not studying for a test or arriving late for class.
- When our child is having a hard time getting to school on time or is relying on us to be their personal alarm clock and rouse them from bed, we can sit down with them to make a plan. The idea is not to punish them (likely making them resent us and school) but to work with them to identify the obstacle and help them remove it.

THE ADOLESCENT IN A FAST-CHANGING WORLD

One thing about our adolescents today is that they have access to any information they would like and likely know more about some topics than we do. Here are some ways to address this:

- Stay connected with them. Have conversations; use television programs, social media, memes, etc., as jumping-off points to discuss topics like teen pregnancy, drugs and alcohol, pornography, and mental health.
- Listen to their ideas more than we talk—conversations are not lectures.
- Continue to talk about consent with adolescents of any gender. We build on the relationship established in the first and second planes.

- If we see signs of depression and anxiety, seek out information both for ourselves and for ways to support them.
- Establish emotional and sleep hygiene in our homes. Maybe have a time once a week when they can process what is going on for them emotionally. Have mobile phones out of the bedroom at night. Allow enough time on weekends for them to follow their natural sleep rhythms.
- Let them know that practical life at home still matters, too. Cooking for the family. Taking care of their space and the communal spaces. Washing the car. Taking care of pets. Babysitting younger children in the family. Being in charge of the family vegetable patch. All of these tasks help our adolescents be part of the family and take on responsibilities, and they counter the rise in self-centeredness, the effects of the digital age and a competitive world, and the adolescent's feeling that they cannot make a difference.
- Support valorization. Even in a fast-changing world, our adolescents need to feel like they belong, they add meaning, and they matter.

Valorization may not be able to prevent all mental health issues arising at this volatile time. But if adolescents feel like they belong and have their needs met (as much as possible), they can thrive and prepare themselves for adulthood. If we implement the suggestions above, we are doing as much for their mental health as we can. We need to be vigilant for indicators, as it's best to get help as soon as possible. We can seek out the help and support we need (including for ourselves) and continue to focus on our relationship with our adolescent.

The most delightful part is seeing these adolescents grow into themselves. They are exploring who they are, and they want to talk about big issues and to make a difference in the world. The conversations are fascinating. Their goals for the future are not often about money. They want to love what they do.

Toward the end of high school, they start to explore what they might like to do next. Rather than taking over this exploration, we continue to be their guide, allowing them the space to do the research, complete the application forms, and prepare any essays or portfolios, miss the deadlines, ask for an extension, take a gap year. We could have a weekly meeting with them to keep them on track, yet we can also step back, removing the training wheels one more time.

Then, before we know it, our adolescent finishes high school, turns 18, and possibly prepares to leave home.

We have a fourth-plane child.

MATURITY:
THE FOURTH PLANE OF DEVELOPMENT

The fourth plane goes from ages 18 to 24, and Dr. Montessori referred to this plane's work as developing spiritual and moral independence.

Similar to the second plane of development, this is a more stable period, and the young adult uses their reasoning, logical mind. They are busy exploring areas of interest in work and study at a deep level. Their brains are nearly completely formed.

They know largely who they are and can be their own person. They will see if the values they received from their family are also their values. They may reject them now and readopt them later.

Dr. Montessori said that "the adult is a result of a child," meaning that if everything necessary has been done in the first three planes of development, the fourth plane takes care of itself. We come full circle and see before us everything that was sown in the preceding years.

Young adults primarily want to give back to society, for example, through volunteer work or the Peace Corps. They may enter university and/or join the workforce.

In *From Childhood to Adolescence*, Dr. Montessori outlined her views on higher education. She was discouraged that many universities were, and still are, offering top-down education to their students, unlike in the Middle Ages, when philosophical and political debate was encouraged. Universities are an opportunity to take a deep dive into a field of interest and learn how to study. We want to keep the student active and engaged. Yet debate is also not enough.

According to Dr. Montessori, we want the young adult to get beyond the four walls of the university (just as we encouraged the child from 6 to 12 years old to go out into the community to find answers to their questions). She advised there's no rush to complete the studies as quickly as possible; it is also important to take a job (e.g., as a tutor, an artist, a waiter, or as an intern in broadcasting, journalism, or diplomacy), learn to be in society with people of different ages, and master economic independence. This also helps them to adapt to the culture of their society.

FURTHER READING

About the third plane:

- Appendixes A and B in *From Childhood to Adolescence* by Dr. Maria Montessori

About the fourth plane:

- Appendix C in *From Childhood to Adolescence* by Dr. Maria Montessori

Our role in the fourth plane

The young adult is now completely independent of us. They will still call us for help, and we will still give them our care and attention, but they are now discovering how to be a part of society in an unprepared environment. The scaffold has been removed.

Remember that Dr. Montessori said that childhood goes up to 24 years old. The prefrontal cortex is nearly fully developed, but there are likely to still be moments in this period when they will lack judgment and rational thought in their decision-making.

To help them in this fourth plane:

- Set up their finances so they are independent. They may be able to get a student loan, they may work, or we may choose to give them a monthly allowance. They will be responsible for ensuring that there is enough money each month to buy their groceries, pay their rent and bills, and have money for going out with their friends.
- Support their decision to move out of home where possible. They will be more independent when they are away from us. Some may even need to be a few hours away so we cannot drop by to rescue them.
- Be a facilitator. Check in on them; arrange visits where possible; sit next to them or be available when they are setting up bank accounts, completing application forms, arranging for mobile phones, or signing rental contracts. We can be their guide, but they make the phone calls, do the research, and complete any paperwork, just like a second-plane child arranges an outing.

If they still live at home:

- Discuss how they can contribute as an adult member of the household.
- Make a roster together to show who will be responsible for buying the groceries, cooking the family meals, and washing up during the week.

- Look for ways to replicate the experience of being responsible for arranging their whole week. If they weren't living at home, they would be learning to live with other students, interacting with others in a community of different ages, as well as cooking, washing their clothes, and cleaning for themselves.
- Encourage them to arrange their own financial responsibilities for things like mobile phones, insurance, and student loans.

We will want to hold on to them. This is another time for letting go. It's not called "empty-nest syndrome" for nothing. We have loved being their guide. Now we release them to the world to see where they fly.

May they fly far and wide. And know that our door is always open to them.

THE PATH TO PEACE

Our hope is that these young adults embrace the principles and values we have offered them. May their upbringing serve them in unfolding into their full potential.

May they be capable, have creative minds and compassionate hearts, with a strong sense of who they are and a desire to serve.

We as the adult are not untouched. We have learned to see through another's eyes, we have acquired infinite patience, and we now know the power of unconditional love.

Where once we may have interfered, now we hold back. Where once we may have ignored, now we reach forward to connect.

Let's keep spreading this promise for peace and humankind. Be gentle with ourselves, with our fellow Earth travelers, and with our environment.

> "I beg the dear all-powerful children to unite with me for the building of peace in Man and in the World."
>
> —inscription on Dr. Montessori's grave in Noordwijk aan Zee, the Netherlands

APPENDICES

ACTIVITIES APPENDIX

Any ages given are only suggestions. Follow your child's unique development and interests. Refer to the online appendix "Starter Kits" for a useful list of items to use for these activities. As much as possible, they will be things we already have in our home. Montessori is not about buying more things but using what we have, buying secondhand, or—where possible—repurposing something else.

	PRACTICAL LIFE ACTIVITIES
	Practical life activities are a wonderful way to support our child's innate drive to function independently as a person of their time, place, and culture. Activities around care of self and our home and environment introduce our child to lots of vocabulary, involve gross- and fine-motor movements, and help our child build discipline and their executive functioning skills. They provide opportunities for our child to notice, create, maintain, and restore order; to master tasks through repetition as many of these tasks are done on a regular basis; and to involve our child in real, purposeful work.
Care of self	**This involves the child's activities around caring for themselves, maintaining hygiene, and caring for their belongings. Many self-care skills require the use of their hands and develop the child's fine-motor skills. They also contribute significantly to the child's sense of self. Children want to be shown and helped to care for themselves.**
Dressing and undressing	Our child dresses and undresses multiple times a day, putting on and taking off sweaters and jackets, shirts, trousers, dresses, underpants, socks, and shoes. Each of these involves different movements and requires different skills. Some items need to be pulled, others need to be pushed; our child might need to shrug out of one item or sit to take their legs out of the other. Different items have different closures or fastenings like zippers, buttons, buckles, and laces. We can help our child learn how to dress and undress by focusing on one skill at a time. If our child is learning how to button, we can offer more clothes that provide opportunities to practice. As they master each skill, we can add another.
Brushing teeth	We can show them how to unscrew and replace the cap of the toothpaste tube, how to squeeze the tube, the quantity of toothpaste to put on their toothbrush, how to wet the toothbrush and turn off the tap, how to brush their teeth, how to brush their tongue (if we do that in our culture), and how to rinse their mouth and their toothbrush.
Taking a shower or bath	We can emphasize the key areas to wash. We can show them how much soap to apply, how much to scrub, and how to rinse. We can show them how to run a bath and how much bubble bath to add, how to dry their body, and where to hang their wet towel.
Caring for hair	We can isolate, demonstrate, and help our children with the specific steps of hair care, such as detangling, combing, brushing, braiding, unbraiding, moisturizing, oiling, packing, and styling.
Washing hands	We can show them how to scrub their fingers, in between the fingers, the palms, the backs of the hands, under the fingernails. We can show them how much soap to apply, how to rinse, how long to scrub. We can teach our values around preserving water while washing our hands. We can show them how to apply hand lotion. We can share key times for washing hands, like when we come in from outside, before and after meals, after using the restroom, after blowing or picking our nose, after touching an animal or a dirty item.
Caring for fingernails	From around age 4, our children might be interested in cutting their nails. We can show them how to use nail clippers and how to dispose of the nail trimmings. We can show them how to apply nail polish if they are interested, and an older child may wish to learn to give a manicure and pedicure.
Blowing their nose	We can show them the quantity of tissue to use, how much force to blow with, how to dispose of the tissue when done, and to wash their hands when finished. We can demonstrate by blowing our own nose while facing the child or in front of a mirror and then let the child blow their own nose.

Wiping or washing after peeing or pooping	We can demonstrate how much paper to use, how to wipe from front to back, wiping until the tissue is clean, and washing our hands afterward. Some religions restrict the use of a specific hand, and we can share this with our child if it applies.
Caring for clothes	We can show them how to check their clothing when they take it off to decide if it is dirty or can be reworn. They can learn to sort their laundry by color, texture, category, and fabric type and how to handwash clothes, load the washing machine, and run it. They also can learn to fold their clothes, put them on a hanger, and iron them. We can show them how to iron in a safe way, on a low temperature. As they get older, they can be shown any special care for specific fabrics or colors like the selection of water temperature and the amount of soap or bleach to use. They can also be shown how to sew on a button or mend a tear. (For more on sewing, see page 259.)
Caring for shoes	Children can be shown how to brush off sand and dirt from their shoes, how to scrub flip-flops or sneakers, how to polish and care for leather shoes, and how to air their shoes.
Caring for minor injuries	Children can be shown how to wash or clean a minor injury and apply a Band-Aid.
Personal hygiene	As the child moves toward puberty, we can show them how to care for themselves. How to shave; how to use sanitary pads, period panties, or tampons; how to use deodorant; how to wash and clean themselves; how to wash stains. This preparation can empower our children as they make the transition to adolescence.
Preparing things for school	We can show them how to organize their things, fill up their water bottle, make their own lunch, arrange clothes for the next day, and gather any additional items for sports or music lessons. Older children can make lists. We can also show them how to pack for a trip.
Caring for others	They can learn how to assist others with their self-care activities.
Caring for pets	Our child can learn to brush fur, wash the water bowl and food dish, put out food and fresh water, change kitty litter, bathe the pet, and take the pet for walks.
Going out/ returning home	Children can be shown how to climb into and out of the car, buckle their seat belt, take things out of the car, and put away their shoes and jacket (if their shoes are dirty, they can brush the dirt off).
Care of Self Starter Kit	*Find this online at workman.com/montessori*
Care of the environment	**These are activities to maintain our surroundings, and this can include the indoors and the outdoors. The tools used and the ways that we care for our environment will differ from place to place and culture to culture. These activities support the development of gross-motor skills and the child's sense of order, invite deep concentration, and help the child develop a sense of responsibility and stewardship for their environment/their community/the world.**
Maintaining our spaces	• Arranging—closets, shoes, belongings, bookshelves, table surfaces, rooms, play spaces, and toys. • Beautifying the environment—they can learn how to cut and arrange flowers, open and close curtains or windows to let in light and air, and make decorations to beautify the space. • Caring for plants—watering plants, dusting or washing leaves, cutting off dry leaves, and, for older children, transplanting. • Working outside—raking leaves; working in the garden planting flowers, vegetables, and herbs; composting; clearing snow. • Picking up the mail from the mailbox. • Woodworking—hammering nails, cutting wood, and sanding or planing wood.

Cleaning our spaces	• Dusting—surfaces and shelves using a cloth or duster; removing cobwebs. • Wiping—spills and surfaces. • Sweeping and vacuuming—we can show them how to sweep or vacuum different floors or surfaces. One simple activity used to give practice in sweeping is having dry petals or pieces of torn paper in a box or basket. The child can sprinkle them over a space and be shown how to sweep them together into a pile. A spot can be marked with tape or chalk to indicate where to make a pile. They can then sweep it into a dustpan and pour it back into the box or basket and repeat. • Mopping—we can show them how to handle and rinse the mop. • Polishing—wood, mirrors, and metal surfaces. • Scrubbing/washing—windows, cars, tables, furniture, walls, toilets, sinks, bathtubs/showers, surfaces, containers, toys, clothes, napkins, and rags. Children can also be shown how to hang fabric items to dry. An older child can be shown how to take down curtains for washing and how to put them back up.
Care of the Environment Starter Kit	*Find this online at workman.com/montessori*
Preparing food	Activities in the kitchen build our child's independence while helping them develop gross- and fine-motor skills, language, and confidence, and learn concepts in the areas of mathematics, geography, science, agriculture, and history. We can explore states of matter and different ways of combining ingredients, and we can follow our food from garden to table, all while connecting with our children. We can share stories about the source of an ingredient or recipe and travel around the world with our taste buds. We can introduce our child to our own family's cultural food traditions.
Beginner-level activities	• Rinsing—fruits and vegetables, nuts and grains, utensils. • Drying—fruits and vegetables, dishes, utensils. • Arranging—setting the table, arranging utensils and ingredients in preparation for cooking or baking. • Sorting—groceries, grains, fruits, vegetables. These can be transferred into bags or containers for storage. • Helping at the grocery store—making a shopping list, pushing the cart, fetching items, greeting the cashier, helping to pay. • Handing us things as we prepare food—ingredients, utensils. • Tearing and plucking—salad greens, herbs, the stalk from a fruit or vegetable, perhaps feathers from a chicken if doing that ourselves is part of our culture. • Peeling/shelling using their hands—fruits like bananas or tangerines, nuts, eggs. • Chopping—fruits, vegetables. • Slicing soft items using (butter) knives and slicers—eggs, bananas, strawberries, cheese, kiwis. • Measuring and pouring—grains, flour, oil, water. For example, from a bigger container to a smaller one; from a pitcher to a cup; into multiple containers when we want the amounts to be equal; using a funnel when pouring from a container with a bigger opening into one with a smaller opening. Our child can also measure using cups, teaspoons, and tablespoons. • Scooping and transferring—using their hands, tongs, spoons, forks, or a small scoop to transfer ingredients from containers to mixing bowls and using a special tool to scoop melon balls. • Spreading and brushing—butter, peanut butter, and jam on bread; tomato sauce on pizza dough; an egg wash on pastry dough. • Squeezing and juicing using a hand juicer—oranges, lemons. • Sieving and draining. • Mashing—bananas, avocados. • Stirring and mixing.

Intermediate activities	• Washing vegetables. We can show them what to use in washing and how to wash. Some people use water, some salt and water, some vinegar and water. For an older child, this can lead to conversations about disinfectants, combining a solid and a liquid vs. combining liquids, and the effect of a solution.
	• Peeling/shelling using tools, such as a vegetable peeler for carrots, cucumbers, and potatoes and a nutcracker for nuts.
	• Slicing, chopping, and cutting softer vegetables like tomatoes, okra, peppers, and leafy vegetables using a knife.
	• Measuring by weight using scales and by volume using a calibrated container or pitcher and also setting temperatures for baking.
	• Washing grains and beans.
	• Serving meals, including placing serving plates on the table.
	• Drying dishes. A younger child may need a surface to lay the dish towel on at first and can then move on to being able to hold a dish in one hand and dry it with the other.
	• Arranging salads, pizza toppings, and food platters.
	• Sorting. This can involve more fine-motor skills like picking out sand/small stones from rice or beans.
	• Grating carrots, zucchini, apples, cheese, coconut, okras, nutmeg, and cinnamon.
	• Smelling and tasting as they cook or prepare dishes.
	• Pounding yams with salt crystals, garlic, ginger, and spices.
	• Juicing using an electric juicer; extracting juices or milk from leaves, seeds, and nuts.
	• Churning cream into butter.
	• Lighting a match, lighting a burner, turning off a burner.
	• Using a microwave if our family uses one.
	• Pitting and deseeding fruits—pitting cherries, tweezing pomegranates, hulling strawberries.
	• Cracking eggs, walnuts, and coconuts.
	• Reading and following advanced recipes.
Snack preparation ideas	• *Sandwiches.* Children can choose the meat, vegetables, and/or spreads and cut the sandwiches into halves, quarters, or a fun shape. An older child can make wraps. We may want to have a shelf in the fridge where sandwich fixings are in easy reach.
	• *Crackers, bagels, chips, breads, fruits, or vegetables with spreads or dips, such as peanut butter, jam, or hummus.* Nonperishables can be stored in airtight, easy-to-open containers where the child can get them. An older child can learn how to make their own spreads— by grinding roasted peanuts to make peanut butter, churning cream to make butter, or caramelizing fruits to make jam—or dips like guacamole.
	• *Salads.* Vegetables and fruits can be chopped and combined in different ways to make salads. An older child might explore salads from different geographical locations and also different salad dressings, such as those made with oil, lemon juice or vinegar, and salt, and yogurt-based dressings.
	• *Cereal.* The child can scoop cereal into a bowl/cup and pour milk from a pitcher over the top. They can scoop yogurt into a bowl and garnish it with granola and fruit. Older children could layer and arrange cereal and yogurt in different ways in a glass bowl/cup and pour directly from a larger milk carton/container.
	• *Eggs, boiled and sliced or quartered.* An older child might enjoy making stuffed eggs. They can also fry eggs or make French toast. Pancake batter can be prepared by the child and cooked on an electric skillet.
	• *Juices, lemonade, and smoothies.* Juice citrus, chop up fruit for the blender or juicer. They can experiment with different flavor combinations.

Cooking meals	Introduce any meals we cook in our home to our child. One-pot meals, soups, and stews can be good places to start.
Cooking on the stovetop	We can start with items that are relatively easy and can cook on low heat, such as scrambled eggs, omelets, pancakes, or French toast. We can orient the child by showing them the ideal distance from the pan to stand and how to handle the pan when it's hot. We can gradually move to cooking over medium heat—sautéing things like onions, tomatoes, and minced meat. When we can trust the child and know they can handle more, we can then introduce more complex cooking tasks. An adult should be present or close by when a child under 12 is cooking on a stove.
Lighting a match	Lighting a match can be isolated as an activity using tea light candles. We can teach the child to strike away from themselves, hold the match horizontally, and blow it out as soon as possible. We can have a small jar of sand to place the used matches into. We can build up to using a match to light a stove.
Cleaning up	• Clearing and washing up after preparing food • Clearing and cleaning the table after meals • Scraping dishes • Washing and wiping dishes, containers, and utensils • Loading and running a dishwasher • Arranging ingredients and other items on a rack or shelf after use or cleaning • Sweeping and mopping the floor • Sweeping, wiping, or scrubbing the work surface/table • Wiping the stove or oven
Baking	Baking invites the child to be precise with measurements and ingredients, and to read and follow a recipe's specific sequence. It requires that our child concentrate over an extended period of time. Baking can also introduce a variety of sensorial experiences: tastes, shapes, textures, temperatures, scents, and colors. Reading the recipe provides practice in reading and enriches the child's vocabulary. The measurements involve math and introduce the child to fractions, counting, volume, and equivalence. Older children can be challenged to halve, double, or triple a recipe, thus requiring them to use division or multiplication and making their operation skills more practical. Baking also allows the child to experience the science of combining. They can explore time and temperature. Baking naturally encourages discipline and exactness. An extra spoonful of salt can make a significant difference to a batch of cookies. These experiences hold important lessons for the child. Baking, like other food preparation activities, also provides an opportunity to develop self-control. Perhaps baked goods can be had at the next mealtime, or we can sometimes bake for others.
Some baking skills to build	• Measuring and pouring ingredients • Sifting dry ingredients • Breaking eggs, whisking eggs, separating the white from the yolk • Mixing dough, making pastry dough, rolling out dough • Using cutters—cookie cutters, pizza cutter, pastry cutter • Brushing pastry dough with an egg wash • Crimping pastry and piecrust edges • Decorating cookies and cakes • Putting baked goods into the oven and taking them out

Baking ideas	Cookies, bread, pastries, muffins, pies, granola, falafel, pizza, crackers, etc.
Baking Starter Kit	*Find this online at workman.com/montessori*
Considerations for cooking and baking	• Prepare the environment. Decide whether the child will sit or stand to cook/bake. • Think about each step of the process and what is needed: Where will the whisk go when the child is done whisking? Where will the banana peels go? Set up a place for everything so that the child experiences order and the process does not get messier than necessary. • For a younger child, the ingredients can all be premeasured and arranged in order of use. • We can prepare a visual recipe for a child who is not able to read. This does not have to be fancy and can be hand drawn. There are also commercially available visual recipe books. A child who is able to read can tell us each step of the recipe while we do the actions and they assist us; then we build up to them doing more themselves. • We can show the child how to set the oven temperature as well as how to put things into and take things out of the oven. • We can tell them the name of the dish we are making and introduce them to the ingredients and utensils we will be using. • We can describe our actions and give the names for the processes, like marinating, boiling, frying, grilling, mixing, grinding, and blending. With older children, we can get even more specific: simmering, sautéing, shallow frying, or deep-frying instead of just frying. • They can help us measure, and we can give them the vocabulary for the measurements: cup, tablespoon, teaspoon, half, quarter. They can add the ingredients. We can mention the names as they do to reinforce the vocabulary and include the names of utensils being used. • They can taste the food, and we can talk about the taste—sweet, salty, savory, spicy, peppery. We can introduce them to different spices, textures, temperatures. • They can scoop, spoon, pour, and stir. • Over time, they can take on more responsibility until they are able to complete the entire cooking process independently. • We can take the opportunity to share how to store or preserve the food, then how to warm it up.
Food Preparation Starter Kit	*Find this online at workman.com/montessori*
Safety in the kitchen	We talk to our child about safety in the kitchen before we begin. When demonstrating how we use tools, we can talk about the risks—germs, cuts, burns, fires—as well as what to do in case of an accident. We can talk about washing our hands before meals; being careful not to dip utensils back into mixing bowls or pots after tasting; putting up our hair; keeping surfaces, utensils, and ingredients clean; keeping food at the right temperature; keeping raw food away from prepared food; keeping paper and fabric away from stove burners; concentrating when working with sharp objects or heat; and turning off the burner before leaving the room. We can assess our environment to determine potential risks and remove them.
Botany in the kitchen	Planting and harvesting are ways that we can enrich our cooking and food preparation with our children. We can have a full vegetable garden or some pots growing herbs and spices on a window ledge. If we do have a garden, herbs like curry, basil, and parsley; alliums like chives, garlic, and onions; and vegetables like carrots, tomatoes, peppers, radishes, lettuce, spinach, and native vegetables in season are great to grow with children. Tubers like potatoes and ginger can be grown in buckets or sacks. Research how to grow fruits and vegetables from food scraps. The children can care for the plants as they grow, weed them, harvest them, and explore different ways to prepare them, both locally and around the world. Herbs can be dried and ground for storage. They can be used to make scent pouches and be given as gifts to neighbors.

Numbers and literacy in the kitchen	When setting the table, the child figures out how many people will be eating, placing a plate and cutlery for each person. This is an activity around one-to-one correspondence—"one plate for me, one plate for Grandma"—an important step for number sense and numeracy. They can fold and place napkins for each person—an unconscious lesson in geometry. A square can be folded into a rectangle or triangle or smaller square, or it can even be rolled into a cylinder. They can place name cards for each person, an opportunity to read and maybe write and design each card. A child who is unable to write for themselves can sound out the names while an older child or adult writes it for them.

Science in the kitchen	• States of matter, such as liquid (water, milk) and solid (grains, fruits). • Ice water vs. room-temperature water vs. boiled water. When watching water boil, we can draw our child's attention to the changes—the rising temperature, the gases forming, and the condensation that occurs when the lid is on the pot. • Raw eggs vs. boiled eggs vs. fried eggs. • Raw rice vs. boiled rice and other grains. • Batter vs. cake. • The effect of yeast on dough. • The difference in rising when the dough is left in a warm place vs. when it's left in a cold place. • Mold and fungus on old food. • The consequences of handling bread with dirty hands. • How different items like fruits and utensils float or sink. • Volume when measuring and pouring using different containers. • The different reactions possible with milk—curdled milk or yogurt, ghee, buttermilk, cream, butter. • How different ingredients dissolve in water or over heat. • The different types of nutrients—protein, carbohydrates, fat—and what they do for the body. • Balanced meals. • Food sources for essential minerals/elements. • Body systems like digestive and muscular. • Vertebrates and invertebrates—fish and chicken vs. snails and calamari. • Alternative lifestyles like vegetarian and vegan. • Where animals live, parts of their bodies, unique characteristics (like ruminants having a four-compartment stomach and being able to digest cellulose), body covering, how they take care of their young.

MOVEMENT

Movement is such an important part of life. Everything we do—walking, touching, talking, eating—involves movement. Even when we are not moving, we are consciously or unconsciously controlling or inhibiting our movements. Children in the first plane are in a sensitive period for movement and are acquiring, refining, and learning to control movement. As they do this, they also develop their personality and will. It is through their will that they become able to control their movement and develop discipline and character. There is a correlation between movement and cognitive development. Our goal is to help our children develop coordinated movement connected to their mind.

Movement for the 3- to 6-year-old child	Dr. Montessori described the 3- to 6-year-old child as a conscious worker. They move in a conscious, coordinated way and have developed basic gross-motor skills (for movements that use big muscles, like walking, running, and throwing) and fine-motor skills (for movements that use small muscles in the hands, like writing, threading, and cutting). Now they are in the process of refining their movement—improving, fleshing out, adding details, perfecting—through their activities.
Gross-motor skills	Gross-motor skills include body awareness, bilateral integration, and the ability to cross the midline. These are usually developed in the first subplane and then refined from the ages of 3 to 6.
Body awareness	Body awareness is the understanding of one's body in relation to a space, thereby improving coordination and reducing accidents. We can provide our child with opportunities to crawl around the floor or through tunnels and obstacle courses; push vehicles or toys; roll and play on the floor; jump; carry heavy things like groceries, trash bags, library books, logs, or buckets of water; push and pull a wagon or wheelbarrow; or climb a jungle gym, ladder, or trees.
Bilateral integration and crossing the midline	Bilateral integration is the ability to use both sides of the body in a coordinated way and is a significant part of the refining of movement. Bilateral integration reflects communication between the left and right sides of the brain. It is required for walking, running, climbing, dressing, and many other gross-motor activities.
	Crossing the midline is any action that involves moving our eyes, hands, or feet from one side of the body to the other side, like crossing arms or reaching for something on the right side of one's body with the left hand.
	A lot of practical life activities encourage bilateral integration and crossing the midline. For example, kneading dough, pouring from a pitcher, carrying heavy objects like watering cans, sweeping and mopping, woodworking activities, threading activities, sewing, working with clay, cutting strips of paper with scissors, baking, and tying shoelaces. Additionally, gross-motor-skill activities like climbing stairs or play equipment, skipping, doing jumping jacks, jumping from log to log, hopping on one leg, using monkey bars, engaging in movement games with rhymes, playing with silk streamers, bouncing balls, and playing hand and clapping games all also support bilateral interactions and crossing the midline.
Refining movement	One of the ways that the child from 3 to 6 refines their movement is by perfecting their balance and control of their body. They not only want to walk, they want to walk on a straight or curved line, run, climb, slide, jump, hop, pedal, somersault, cartwheel, do a handstand, stand really still, carry things, stack things, and be able to complete movements that require a higher level of control. They want to gain mastery of their body and balance. We can support this by first providing space, freedom, and opportunities for both free play and purposeful movement in our indoor and outdoor environment.
Movement in the outdoors	We can prepare an outdoor environment with things like logs, blocks, or rocks to carry, roll, push, stack, climb, and jump on and from. We can also create opportunities for purposeful activities that require big movements like sweeping or raking leaves, packing them into a wheelbarrow, pushing them into a pile, and jumping on the pile. Indoors, they can use large cushions to build forts, stacking them, arranging them in different ways, and jumping from them.
	Our child wants to be able to control and stop their bodies. Ledges, fallen trees, and balance beams are invitations to balance. Stumps are invitations to jump, lift, roll, carry, stack, climb, or squat by to observe the little ecosystems hidden in the dirt around them.
	If we have a garden, the child can run after butterflies, bend to pick flowers, harvest some produce, pull out weeds, or carry a heavy watering can or hose to water the plants. We can have a soft grass lawn, a soft rug, or padded foam surface for cartwheels and somersaults. If we don't have these at home, we can make visiting a park or playground a part of our daily or at least weekly routine.

Movement in daily life	Our children can pick up the mail, wash cars, or ride their bicycles to run errands with us. All of Junnifa's children learned how to ride their bikes by 3 years old. They started with balance bikes at 18 months or 2 years old and transitioned very easily to regular bikes around 3 years old without needing training wheels. Older children can also start with balance bikes, which can make it easier for them to learn to ride a regular bike.
Other movement activities	The followng invite control and refinement of gross-motor movements and also really interest and engage the child at this stage of development.

- Walking with a bell without having it chime; walking with an egg or a ball on a spoon without dropping it; walking with a cup full of water without spilling it; or walking with a beanbag, book, or other item balanced on their head without dropping it. We can invite them to walk slowly at first and then attempt to go faster while still maintaining this control.

- Walking in a specific way, such as heel to toe while on a line or balance beam.

- Walking on lines indoors or outdoors—a straight line, a curved line, a zigzag line, a line that goes through tight corners—or on shapes made with chalk, tape, or even paint.

- Music activities that invite moving in different ways: walking, running, galloping, skipping.

- Rhythmic activities in which different movements are assigned to different songs. (We can use the CD *Walking on the Line & Rhythmic Activities on the Line* with music by Sanford Jones or make a playlist with songs of different tempos.)

- Reciting rhymes and singing songs that involve accompanying movements, like "If You're Happy and You Know It," "The Ants Go Marching," the "Hokey Pokey," "Head, Shoulders, Knees, and Toes," "Ten Little Monkeys," "The Goldfish (Let's Go Swimming)" by Laurie Berkner, etc. We usually do these with younger children, but older children would benefit from them, too.

- Command games like Simon says; move, freeze; duck, duck, goose; and hide-and-seek.

- Action-card activities where the child can choose a card and do the action.

- Moving like different animals—galloping like a horse, jumping like a frog, spinning like a spider, flapping their arms like a bird or butterfly flaps its wings.

- Moving around our home quietly or without bumping into furniture. We can set up obstacle courses to make this interesting. And they could practice:

  ○ Walking, standing up from a chair, and sitting down without making a sound

  ○ Lifting, moving, and putting down an object or piece of furniture without making a sound

  ○ Closing doors, jars, boxes, and lids without making a sound

- Playing ball—catch, throw, throw into a container/box, kick, etc.

- Pushing the shopping cart in the grocery store and having to turn at corners and navigate past other customers

Gross-Motor Skills Starter Kit	*Find this online at workman.com/montessori*

Movement for the 6- to 12-year-old child	All of the activities for the 3- to 6-year-old child can be enjoyed by older children, too, and will also help improve any gross-motor challenges. The 6- to 12-year-old child is very strong. They have a lot of energy, and they know it. They want to exert themselves and push themselves to see how far they can go. They are also very social and enjoy working in groups. This is a key period for social and moral development, so this is a great time to introduce group sports and activities. They will enjoy: races (individual and relay), tennis, soccer, swimming, basketball, baseball, cricket, hockey, badminton, gymnastics, jumping rope, scouting (usually involves hiking/other physical activities). In competitive sports situations, we can support them in developing the right attitude toward winning and losing. We can encourage them to focus on doing their best and improving as they can. We can choose groups with positive approaches to competition where collaboration and support are encouraged. We can observe to see what our child is interested in and has talent for and then provide opportunities for them to build skills in this area. If they are not sure, we can expose them to different opportunities and see which one they become interested in.
Fine-motor development	Dr. Montessori said that the hands are the instruments of intelligence. The work and creations of our hands tell the stories of culture and time. They are what we use to manipulate, work on, and improve our environment. Most occupations, from chef to teacher, artist to doctor, coder to tailor, involve the use of our hands. It is our hands that have helped create and preserve history and therefore helped each generation learn from the last. Dr. Montessori believed that cognitive development can be limited if it is not supported by the hands. Fine-motor-skill development includes hand-eye coordination, hand strength, manual dexterity, and the pincer grip.
Practical life activities	All of the practical life activities discussed earlier support the development of fine-motor skills. Buttoning, unbuttoning, tying, lacing, zipping, and unzipping strengthen hand-eye coordination, the pincer grip, and manual dexterity. Opening and closing different containers, mixing, peeling, and chopping support hand strength and manual dexterity. Peeling eggs, plucking stalks or leaves, and sorting seeds promote the development of the pincer grip.
Open and close activities	We can also set up a specific open and close activity by gathering six to eight small containers with different kinds of closures. There can be boxes, containers with flip caps, bottles with screw caps, snap purses, coin purses, and drawstring purses. We can show the child how to line up the lid on the top and then how to close it, to lift and open and operate the latch or closure, etc. It is also fun to put a bead, button, or other small object to find in each of the containers, and the child can extend the activity by taking out the objects and matching them to their containers. They can also be responsible for opening and closing windows, cupboards, and doors.
Locks and keys	Turning keys in locks. We can start with one key and one padlock. Putting the key into the lock requires hand-eye coordination; twisting and unlocking uses manual dexterity; and locking builds hand strength. We can then add one or two locks and keys to distinguish which key goes with which lock. We can also add a variety of locks, e.g., a twist lock, one with number codes, etc.
Screwing and unscrewing nuts and bolts	They can start with large nuts and bolts and then progress to smaller ones and then to using tools.
Pouring, spooning, and cutting to support manual dexterity	We can set up specific transferring activities with two containers holding things to pour or transfer. This could be beads, pom-poms, seeds, sand, or colored water. For pouring, it is better to start with dry objects like beans that are easy to pick or clean up and then progress to sand and then to liquids. We can contain the activity in a deep tray, encourage the child to work somewhere that we don't mind spills, and put out only as much as we are okay with potentially spilling all over the floor.

Using a hole/ shape punch or perforator	Strengthens the hand and improves manual dexterity. The punched-out shapes can be glued onto another piece of paper to make art. Picking up the shape and using a brush to apply the glue both support the development of the pincer grip.
Using scissors	Scissors can be used to cut paper, blades of grass, fabric, ribbons, yarn, play dough, or paper straws. The paper, fabric, and yarn can be used for mixed-media art. The straws can be threaded onto yarn or ribbons to make bracelets or necklaces. This supports hand strength, manual dexterity, hand-eye coordination, and threading. Our child can progress through cutting skills; they can start by cutting narrow strips (around 1/2 inch/1 cm wide and 4 inches/10 cm long) that require just snips, then they can cut along lines on a thicker cutting strip (around 3/4 inch/2 cm wide and 4 inches/10 cm long)—straight, curved, zigzag—and proceed to cutting out shapes, spirals, symmetrical designs, drawings, and then intricate designs.
Poking/prick pen	The children can trace the outline of a shape (or we can prepare shapes); and they can poke them out using an awl, toothpick, or skewer, following the line. It is easier to use thicker paper and place it on felt to poke. They can learn shapes, continents, animals, and vehicles. The poked-out shape can be glued to another piece of paper and assembled to make a book, chart, or map that can be used to review the vocabulary.
Folding	Supports the pincer grip, dexterity, and hand strength. Children can fold cloth or paper. Napkins are a great place to start. They can fold the squares into smaller squares or triangles. They can also fold socks and proceed to tucking socks in to make a ball. They can proceed to folding paper, which requires more accuracy and refinement. A piece of square paper can be folded just like a napkin into smaller squares or triangles. The children can proceed to folding different kinds of clothes and then to simple origami and more complicated folds.
Doing puzzles	Knobbed puzzles support the pincer grip, but jigsaw and layered puzzles are also good for hand-eye coordination and spatial awareness.
Tracing	In the classroom, we use various metal shapes from a circle to more complicated polygons for children to trace around. At home, we can find objects with different shapes, such as a plate or box, for children to trace around with their finger first and then with a pencil. They learn how to follow a contour and use a firm touch. It prepares their hand to apply sufficient pressure when using a writing instrument.
Threading	Supports hand-eye coordination, manual dexterity, and the pincer grip. The child can start with large flat beads with big holes; then proceed to large solid-shaped beads—cylinders, spheres, cubes—then tiny beads. Pipe cleaners and dowels are great to start with because they are stiff, and then we can progress to rope or yarn. The rope or yarn being used to thread should be stiff at the starting point. Purchased activities usually have addressed this, but if we're setting up the activity at home, we can use tape to stiffen the thread. The knot on the end should be big enough to not let the bead pass through, or use one bead in making the knot. As the child gets better at threading, they can also learn to thread needles.
Using clothespins	Uses the pincer grip and builds their hand strength. They can use a clothespin to hang up clothes after washing, or we can put clothespins in a container and the child can affix them around the rim of the container or to a piece of cardboard or plastic. We can also have a line that they can affix things to, e.g., their art or cut-out felt cloth. The clothespins can be big to start with and gradually get smaller and smaller. A fun DIY is to use paint chips from a hardware store with a matching colored clothespin.
Stickers	Working with stickers, peeling them and sticking them, first anywhere on the paper and then on specifically designated spots, supports the development of the pincer grip, hand-eye coordination, and manual dexterity.
Arts and crafts activities and handwork	Scribbling, drawing, painting, collage, and modeling with play dough and different kinds of clay all support the development of fine-motor skills. Children can also trace stencils of shapes, letters, and patterns. (See page 258 for examples.) Handwork is also wonderful for fine-motor development including sewing, woodworking, modeling, knitting, and crocheting. (See page 259 for lots of handwork ideas.)

Other fine-motor-skill activities	• Latch board; busy board, box, or van.
	• Dressing frame—practicing zippers, buttons, buckles, etc.
	• Lacing model (we can also just use a shoe that is not being worn).
	• Tying bows—on doll clothes, with shoelaces or fabric belts.
	• Braiding rag doll, using three laces or ribbons attached to a surface.

LANGUAGE

Language is the basis of the human tendency for communication. It is how we convey information, express our feelings, ask for help, and listen to others. It is how we can keep safe, learn, share what we learn, and build relationships and culture. An environment rich in language will help our child develop their vocabulary and ability to express themselves.

LANGUAGE HELPS OUR CHILD:

• Order, classify, and categorize the world around them.

• Express themselves with exactness and precision when they have the vocabulary.

• Orient themselves by knowing the names of things and places.

• Abstract and share what they know, express what they imagine, and paint vivid pictures out loud—Dr. Montessori called language the "abstraction of intelligence."

• Give and receive directions and enhance the lessons and demonstrations we share with them.

• Comprehend the vastness of the universe in a story and explore big ideas in books; find information in encyclopedias; and explore people, places, and cultures far away.

The child from ages 0 to 6 years old is in the sensitive period for language. After the acquisition of language (between 0 and 3 years old), the 3- to 6-year-old is ready to refine their language. They do this by building their vocabulary. There is unlimited potential for the amount of vocabulary the child can acquire at this stage. They also refine their articulation, pronunciation, syntax, and grammar and become able to communicate not only through speech but also through written language.

From around 4 to 5 years old, they begin to really understand the power of language and the effect of their words on others. This is a good time to consciously begin to help them develop empathy.

The 6- to 12-year-old child uses language to express themselves with more precise and specific vocabulary; to debate or argue their view; to write down their ideas and document their experiences; and to use language in artistic ways such as through story (written and oral) and poetry.

Spoken language	**We can help our child build the ability to express themselves clearly, logically, and articulately. The ability to express themselves will build self-confidence, which will stay with them. Spoken language is also the foundation for written language.**
Conversations with us	Conversations are a great way to connect with our children, learn about their interests and experiences, and build strong bonds while also supporting their development. We can tell them about our day and what is going on in the world; have discussions about our thoughts and their thoughts and encounters; and answer their questions. They can learn to introduce themselves and members of their family to others and talk about their ideas and identity and those of others. We can listen and ask probing questions that require thought and expression and take the conversation further. Objects, books, art, pictures, magazines, and things seen from the window or in stores can be great initiators of conversations in which they can describe, introduce, and explain.
Conversations with others	These could include weekly phone or Zoom calls with grandparents or family friends. Resist the temptation to answer for children when they are asked questions.

Question games	Question games are used in a Montessori classroom to help the children organize their thoughts and add details to their stories. They can also be used at home. When our child tells us about an event or occurrence, we can help them add details and develop the story by asking What? Who? Where? When? Why? With whom? We then end by summarizing the information they have provided. We don't have to ask all the questions. We can observe when the child is still sharing excitedly and notice when they are losing interest; then we can summarize and move on.
Use rich language	When conversing, we can use rich and specific language. Don't be afraid to use big words as long as they are being used correctly and in context. Instead of saying "Do you need me right now?" we can say, "Do you need me urgently?''; instead of saying "Show me how you did it," we can say "Show me your technique"; instead of "hungry," try "famished"; instead of "thirsty," we could say "parched," and so on.
Sharing stories	Children love hearing our stories. These stories can provide opportunities for connection and new vocabulary. Bedtime, car rides, and long waits in the doctor's office are all opportunities to share stories. We can tell stories about ourselves or people in our lives, places we have visited, or world events or share fond memories or funny experiences. We can practice telling these stories with expression and interest. They do not have to be too long. We can start with shorter stories for younger children and keep the story within 10 minutes even for older children. We can be very descriptive and speak slowly so that our child can paint a mental picture as we tell the story. When we are done, our child might ask questions or express their thoughts. Or they may not, and that is fine, too. These stories are simply for them to digest and enjoy. PERSONAL STORIES WE CAN TELL OUR CHILD: • The day they were born • Our favorite birthday gifts as a child • The first time we went on a trip Our child will learn that they can tell their own stories both from their experience and their imagination. Simone enjoyed writing these down for her children, and they still enjoy looking at them together, years later.
Reading books	Reading to our children also supports the development of language, especially when we choose books with relatable stories and also those that expand our child's horizons. The books can be fiction, but especially for children under 6, we can choose books that are realistic. That way, our child gets to hear familiar-sounding dialogue and descriptions of things they may have experienced or might one day experience. They hear and gain new vocabulary, and they see how stories can be shared with words and pictures. As the reader, we can use different voices, tones, pitches, and expressions to reflect the emotions and characters. We can start with short stories for younger children and move on to longer stories for older children. Folktales, fairy tales, and fantasy can be introduced when the child is old enough to distinguish between reality and fantasy, usually when they're over 5 years old. When we read, we can introduce the names of the author and illustrator. We can also model how to handle the book with care. If the child wants some time to observe the illustrations and notice details, give them time to do so.
Reading and reciting poetry	Like books, poetry introduces our child to another form that language can take, a form that they would not usually hear in everyday conversation. It also introduces them to new vocabulary, styles, and syntax. Many poems include rhymes and are fun to read as well as compose. Listening to poetry can also inspire the child to create their own poetry. When choosing poetry to introduce to children, we can choose a variety of lengths, styles, and content. The excitement with which we present poetry to our children will rub off on them. Some examples: • *A Family of Poems* by Caroline Kennedy • *Joyful Noise: Poems for Two Voices* by Paul Fleischman • *Malaika: A Poetry Collection for Children and Those Who Love Them* by Dike-Ogu Chukwumerije

Grammar and syntax	With time, children become more aware of grammar and syntax, but they might initially make mistakes with things like tenses and plurals. Rather than correcting them, we can model using the words correctly in our reply and, with older children, share any applicable rules at a later time. For example, "We use *an* when a word starts with a vowel: an owl, an orange." These errors usually resolve over time. If our child always answers questions with a single word, we can practice with them to incorporate the question or subject into their response. For example, to the question, "Where did you go?" instead of saying, "Outside," they can say, "I went outside."
Introducing nomenclature/ vocabulary	We can support the development of spoken language also by introducing nomenclature: the names of people, things, places, specific shapes, parts of an object. We can do this using the three-period lesson (see below). We can give names of real objects, replicas, and also things shown in pictures.
The three-period lesson to introduce nomenclature/ vocabulary	This is a technique used to introduce nomenclature (vocabulary) to children. It usually begins with a sensory experience. It could be the child looking at, touching, tasting, smelling, or listening to an object. When they have gained sensory knowledge, we give them language to attach to it. There are three stages to the three-period lesson.
	1. *Association.* This is the connecting of sensory perception with the name. In this part of the lesson, we give the noun (the name of the object) with no article attached. For instance, "turmeric." The word is pronounced distinctly.
	2. *Recognition.* This is when the child is given the opportunity to practice recognizing the object and connecting it with its name. It can be done by asking a question or making a request. For instance, "Please get me the turmeric," "Can you show me the turmeric?" "Please put the turmeric in the basket," or "Point to the turmeric." This stage reinforces the name and is where we spend the most time. We can see which words the child has mastered and which they are still learning.
	3. *Remembrance or recollection.* This is when the child is required to remember the name of the object. This is done by asking "What is this?" and pointing. We do this when we have observed that they know the name in the second period above.
Command games	Giving the precise names of actions and playing command games where we give the child commands and they act on them can provide a lot of fun and laughter. We can start with one-word commands (e.g., blink, clap, jump, glide) and then give one-step sentence commands (e.g., touch your nose, reach up high) and then progress to more descriptive and elaborate commands, adding adjectives, adverbs, and multiple steps to the command (e.g., stand on your toes and reach high for the sun—now jump quickly!).
Rhyming and other games	We can play rhyming games where we choose a word and each person takes a turn calling out rhyming words. With older children, we can also play games where we choose a category and they take turns coming up with words that fall into that category. It can be animals, vehicles, places, or things found in a kitchen or a garden. We can add a challenge by having each person find a word that starts with the next letter of the alphabet or the last letter of the previous person's word. For children who have been introduced to parts of speech, we can do this with adjectives, prepositions, or adverbs.
Spoken language— skills for our older child	The older child can be supported to further develop their spoken language. We can practice with them and also model for them how to present an idea, argue a point, defend a stance, debate respectfully, or get information by formulating the correct questions.

| Writing | In the Montessori classroom, we introduce writing before reading as it is easier to sound out words to write them than to sound them out and then to synthesize them to read them. Our child will learn to read and write at school, but there are activities we can do at home to support them. Remember, we follow the child. Every child will develop on their own timeline. We do these activities with our child because they show an interest and enjoy them, not because we want to teach them to read early. Observe your child. If they begin to recognize their name; spot letters on signs, in books, and on labels; or ask what certain letters spell, they are ready for these activities. |

In Montessori, the primary purpose of writing is to document and communicate one's thoughts. It's quite exciting for a child to learn that if they write it down, someone else can read and understand their idea. To prepare our child for writing, we can:

- Prepare their minds by helping them develop their thoughts, vocabulary, and expression through spoken language (page 243).

- Prepare their hands for writing, which comes with practicing their fine-motor skills (page 241).

- Introduce them to the mechanics of words and writing.

| Introducing the alphabet | When introducing the alphabet in Montessori, we start with the sounds of the letter, e.g., "cuh," rather than the names, e.g., the letter "c." This gives the child the ability to sound out many words they come across. |

| The sound game | To introduce letters, we can start with the sound game (with children from around 2.5 years). This is similar to playing "I spy," except we ask them to look for something starting with a sound; for example, "buh." This is one activity that we encourage playing at home to give the child lots of practice listening for the sounds they will need for writing and reading. |

This is a game that helps the child realize that words are made up of individual sounds and also helps them learn to isolate the sounds in a word, which will be important when they start to write words.

According to *Montessori Read & Write* by Lynne Lawrence, there are six stages of the sound game.

1. (around 2.5 years) Take one object that the child already knows the name of, like a cup, and isolate it on a table or in our hands. "I can see something on this table that begins with 'cuh,'" or "I spy with my little eye something that begins with 'cuh'"; because there is only one object and the child knows the name "cup," they will make the connection. We can play this game over and over with many different objects until we can tell that they have grasped the idea. It can be made more difficult once they master single letters to add phonograms like "tr" for "tree" or "traffic light."

2. (around 2.5 to 3 years) Play the sound game with two or more objects with distinct first sounds like a cup and a pen. The game now involves the child discriminating to make a choice between the options. It might help to keep track of the sounds that our child identifies easily.

3. We can expand the child's area of exploration to a section of the room, the whole room, in the car, or outdoors. We can invite the child to find objects that start with a specific sound. When they find several examples with the same sound, like cup, can, and corn if playing in a kitchen, we can repeat the game with another sound.

4. (between 3.5 and 4.5 years old) The child identifies objects that begin with a specific sound and end with a specific sound. "I spy something that begins with 'cuh' and ends with 'tuh.'" We can play this first at level two, where we isolate some objects that they can choose from, and then at level three, where the span of exploration is increased.

5. Invite the child to identify all the sounds in the words they have previously analyzed. They can identify the first, middle, and last sounds. They can do it without necessarily seeing or finding the objects.

6. We invite the child to think of words that begin with a specific sound, contain a specific sound, and end with a specific sound. We can also go beyond the limits of the room or environment. We can also invite them to think of words within a specific category. "Can you think of an animal that starts with the sound 'sss'?" "Can you think of any of your friends whose name starts with the sound 'sss'?" It might help to include an example in our question: "I'm thinking of a name that starts with the sound 'sss,' like Sophie. Can you think of any other names that start with the sound 'sss'?"

The activities for spoken expression can be enhanced with some emphasis on sounds. We can choose poetry that highlights a specific sound or play rhyming games that focus on a specific sound.

Letters	When the child can recognize the sounds of letters, we can then introduce the written alphabet. Ideally, we've already created an environment that is text rich: framed quotes around our home, the child's name over their door, time spent reading the signs in our neighborhood, and reading books at home.

Ideally, we introduce the lowercase letters first, using the three-period lesson (see page 245).

We can give our child a lot of experience with the letters to reinforce their ability to identify the letter symbols. They can color in an outline of the letter, do seed collages of the letter, do letter hunts in the house. We can write the letter on Post-it Notes or cards and place them around the house for the child to find, or they can look on labels, pictures, and signs around the house. They can check in books or old magazines—they can circle or underline the letter—and point it out on signs around our neighborhood.

Activities to support letter recognition

- *Alphabet books.* We can provide alphabet stamps and a blank booklet in which the child can stamp the letter and draw, stamp, or paste pictures of an object that start with that sound.

- *Alphabet collection books.* We can provide a blank booklet for each letter and have the child fill each booklet with items that begin with each letter.

- *Sandpaper letters/letter rubbings.* Sandpaper letters are often used in Montessori classrooms and can be purchased or cut out of sandpaper found at a hardware store. The child can trace the letters with their fingers to get a sense of their shape. They can also create rubbings by laying a plain piece of paper over the sandpaper letter and rubbing the side of a crayon over it.

- *Knock-knock game.* We can play this game once our child can recognize letters. We can write three to five letters or sounds on individual cards. We can turn the cards face down. Then our child knocks, picks a card, and thinks of a word that begins with the sound. For example: "Knock knock." "Who's there?" "T!" "T who?" "T turtle!"

Building words

Once we observe that our child knows several sounds, including some vowels, they can begin to build words. (Junnifa usually introduces *s, m, a, t, v, b, e, c,* and *f* first.)

It is ideal to have a movable alphabet for word building: individual letters that can be placed to make words. This enables our child to write before they have complete control over their pencil. We can purchase simple plastic letters or letter magnets, or make our own letters on little cards. Our child can start building words within a category (like *pets*) and ideally, words that can be spelled phonetically. The child can increase the complexity of the words as they progress. If our child wants to build long, nonphonetic words before they seem ready, that's okay; the spelling will probably be wrong, but we don't need to correct them. The focus is on the sounds and allowing our child to express their thoughts.

When our child has mastered the basic sounds, we can then introduce digraphs (or phonograms) in the same way. These are one sound made by more than one letter; for example, *ch, sh, th, ph, ae, ai, oi,* and *oy.*

Writing

Lots of fine-motor-skill work, including tracing, working with clay, and cutting with scissors, prepares our child's hand for writing. Our child will also have seen us write their descriptions under their artwork, make shopping lists, and make notes in our notebook or journal. When our child is ready, at around 3.5 to 5 years old, we can provide a variety of materials to support the development of writing. (See the online appendix for a writing Starter Kit.) Ideally, our child will begin by practicing drawing letters on a chalkboard, which is easy to erase and allows for lots of trial and error. (Sand trays, sticks in the sandbox, or mud outside are also great for this.) Our child can start with letters and sounds and then move on to words. When the child is ready, they can transition to writing on paper with a pencil.

We can collaborate with them as necessary. For example, when they are writing a thank-you note, they can dictate what they want to say while we write it out. They can then decorate it, sign their name, put a stamp on the envelope, or contribute as much as they can. Another idea: Our child can dictate a story to us that we can write out, then read back to them.

As the child starts to write in sentences, they will need to learn how to space their words. We can show them how to use a finger to leave a space after each word. We can also show them how to use a line guide or rule lines to keep their writing straight.

Activities to support writing for our younger child	**YOUNGER CHILDREN WILL ENJOY WRITING:** • Labels for items around the house • Lists—names of things, shopping lists, party plans • Thank-you notes • Directions • Short stories • Recipes • Names on maps • Answers to the question game introduced on page 244 • Commands for the command games on page 245 • Collaborative notes or sentences where we start a thought and they complete it **THEY'LL ALSO ENJOY MAKING DIFFERENT BOOKS:** • Alphabet books • Counting books • Collections of nouns by categories • Collections of verbs • Storybooks • Recipe books • Comic books • Magazines—they can make these around their interests, like a favorite animal or book series
Activities to support writing for our older child	For older children, writing is a way to share their ideas and document their experiences and discoveries. We can support their writing by encouraging them to be creative, curious, and playful with words and language outside of the work they do in school. We can: • Provide them with a thesaurus to use in finding synonyms or a dictionary to gain a deeper understanding of the meaning of words. • Provide them with examples of a range of writing styles, help them analyze the difference in styles, and encourage them to create their own writing styles. • Encourage them to write more elaborate and formal letters to friends, family, favorite authors, or even government officials. • Provide them with different styles of poetry and encourage them to write their own. • Provide them with a notebook and encourage them to keep a journal. They can start with the basics: the day of the week, the date, what time they woke up, meals they ate, the weather, some details about what they did and whom they saw, what time they went to bed. As they get older, they can add more details, ideas, and thoughts. They may also enjoy keeping a travel journal on vacations. • Encourage creative writing by asking them to come up with stories. We can prompt them to develop characters, settings, plots, problems to be resolved, and twists. • Introduce a word-collector book in which they write new and interesting words they encounter. • Offer blank comic strip paper to write and draw their own comic strip.

Writing skills for our older child	• Punctuation—we can introduce them to the different punctuation marks and their uses.

Writing skills for our older child

- Punctuation—we can introduce them to the different punctuation marks and their uses.

- Editing—we can guide them on how to edit their work and help them understand the importance of editing. It is helpful to have a simple editing checklist with which they can check their writing.

  ○ Check that all sentences start with a capital letter and end with a period.

  ○ Check that all the proper nouns—names and places-names—start with a capital letter.

  ○ Check that items in lists are separated by commas.

- Grammar—we can invite them to be descriptive in their writing by using adjectives, adverbs, and precise vocabulary to add details and interest.

- Poetry—they can try different forms such as a couplet, quatrain, haiku, limerick, or cinquain.

- Writing a biography—this is a fun exercise that can be done for people, animals, and even inanimate objects. The child can use the following pattern:

  ○ First name
  ○ Last name
  ○ Three adjectives
  ○ Child of . . .
  ○ Who loves . . .

  • Who fears . . .
  • Who needs . . .
  • Who gives . . .
  • Who would like to be . . .
  • Is a resident of . . .

- ABC—the child comes up with a word or line for each letter. They can challenge themselves to make each line rhyme or every two lines rhyme like a couplet.

- Researching—they can learn how to conduct research and write reports, how to summarize, quote, and how to cite references.

- Word studies—these will also expand the child's vocabulary and improve their writing. They can study and make games around affixes (prefixes and suffixes), homonyms, homophones, homographs, synonyms, and antonyms.

Writing Starter Kit   *Find this online at workman.com/montessori*

Reading

Reading opens up the world (even the universe!) to children. Through reading, our child can travel through time and space, visit faraway places, meet people of different cultures, and learn about diverse topics and experiences. We want to support our children so they not only learn to read but also come to love and enjoy it.

Reading together

We can start reading to our children when they are in the womb and continue to read to them even when they are able to read to themselves. They will absorb the pleasure we feel when we read to them and always reference that feeling when they read.

When we read to our children, we can:

- Point to the words as we read.

- Act out what we read.

- Use tone, emphasis, and inflection to add interest.

- Discuss the illustrations.

- Point out the page numbers and keep track as we read.

Reading together builds the child's vocabulary and familiarizes them with many words. This helps when they are starting to read for themselves and have to decode words; they will be able to decode faster or guess more accurately because they have heard a lot of words in context.

Create a reading environment	In addition to reading to our child, we can model a love for books by reading ourselves and also surrounding ourselves with books. We can also ensure that the child has access to rich, quality books. We want books that interest them, expand their experiences, stretch their imaginations, help them make sense of their lives, and encourage them to experience and understand the lives of other people whose circumstances may be different from their own. We can visit libraries and bookstores with our child and choose quality books. We can build reading into our lifestyle and family culture.
Path to independent reading	The journey to independent reading is the same as the journey to independence in other areas. It starts with dependence on the adult. We read to our child from birth until they are ready for the second stage. The second stage is collaborative, also known as guided reading. This is when they read with us. The youngest child can point to the pictures as we read. An older child might say the last word in each sentence or read the words that they recognize as we read the rest. Gradually, they read more, with us there providing support as needed. This stage requires patience and observation to know when to help and provide the word the child might be struggling with and when to wait patiently and let them try to figure it out. Some books might allow us to read one page and the child to read the next. When our child first starts trying to read, they might just recite from memory books that they have heard often. This is not a bad thing and is a normal part of the process. We should not discourage them. The third stage is independent reading, when the child is reading by themselves. The other two stages continue even when our child is able to read independently. We continue to read to them and read with them. They will go through different levels of books, tackling more challenging ones as they are able.
Reading simple words	When our child starts reading simple words (usually as they practice their writing), we can provide things for them to practice with, such as: • A small collection of items with phonetic names with labels to match to them. • Simple labels to read and use to label items around the house, on their bodies, or in a book (pen, fan, red, cup, sink, flag, shirt, socks, etc.). • Phonetic command labels to read and act out, like jump. These can increase in complexity as the child becomes more proficient. • Little notes for them to find and read. We want them to see writing and reading primarily as a way to communicate. • Phonetic flash cards that have pictures with sounds or those that have pictures with words to match.
Phonograms	When the child has mastered phonetic reading, we can start to introduce words that include phonograms (for example, "ch," "sh"), using similar activities.

Books to read	WHEN OFFERING BOOKS:

- We want to offer our child books that they can be successful with.
- We can choose books that have simple text with related illustrations that help the child predict or remember if they're struggling.
- The text should reflect their everyday, familiar vocabulary.
- Books with one or two sentences that have repetitive or predictive text on each page are ideal for this stage.
- The youngest reader can start with phonetic readers.
- They will enjoy books that they have heard many times.
- We can choose books based on their interests.
- Counting, alphabet, and song books are great options for a beginning reader.
- We can use the Goldilocks analogy. We want books that are not too easy and not too hard. We want them to be just right. A child will be able to read 95 percent of words on each page of a "just right" book.
- We can introduce guided reading. This is when we collaborate in reading. We sit beside them and help with the challenging words or read alternate pages.
- When trying new books, we can read to them first and then have them read to us. We can have them point to the words as they read and do the same when we read. The illustrations can clue them in when they are unsure.
- When we notice them guessing, we can encourage them to read each word, pointing to it as they go. Gradually, they will become more proficient and fluent. While building proficiency and fluency, they might enjoy reading to their siblings, dolls, or grandparents.

OLDER CHILDREN WHO KNOW HOW TO READ CAN EXTEND THEIR READING BY EXPLORING:

- Different genres
- Longer books
- Book series
- Historical books with different language structure
- Biographies

Puzzle words	As the child is practicing phonetic words, we can also start to introduce sight or puzzle words like *through* or *because*. These are words that do not sound how they look, and many of the ones we introduce to the child are used frequently and learned through repetition. Children who are frequently read to will see these often and will find them easier to remember.
Be patient	The process of reading is unique for each child. It requires us to be patient and enjoy the journey with our child. They will eventually learn to read. If we suspect any signs of a learning challenge, we can visit a specialist to have them assessed.

Teaching respect for books	When reading to children, we can consciously model treating the book with respect: lifting it up and putting it down carefully, flipping the pages consciously from the top or bottom corners instead of pushing the page or wrinkling it, putting the book back on the shelf when we're done with it instead of leaving it out or dropping it on the floor.

As the child gets older and starts to handle books independently, we can:

- Talk about the importance of books and treating them carefully.
- Teach them about the components of a book, including the dust jacket or cover, spine, and endpapers.
- Show them how to take it from the shelf and put it back with the spine showing so it is easy to locate.
- Show them how to use a bookmark to remember their page.
- Repeat any lesson when we see the need for it.

SENSORIAL DEVELOPMENT

Children need and seek out sensory experiences. We can provide them with these in purposeful ways. Many of the practical life activities we have discussed provide sensorial experiences.

We can help the child acquire ways to classify and categorize the sensorial impressions they receive. We allow them to explore specific sensorial qualities and then give them the specific language for these impressions, such as big, small, bigger, smaller, biggest, smallest. In the period from ages 3 to 6, the child refines their sensory perceptions. With practice, they become able to discriminate and distinguish; they observe and make judgments about similarities and differences. At first, they may grade the objects by trial and error. With practice, they'll be able to discriminate through careful use of their senses. There are specific materials for this in the Montessori classroom, but we do not need them at home; we can find opportunities for our child to refine their senses in our home environment.

Three-period lesson	They can learn the names of the sensorial impressions using the three-period lesson technique (see page 245) or from absorbing through use in daily life.

Sensorial experiences

VISUAL

- Size: height, width, length, thickness
- Shape
- Color: primary (red, blue, and yellow), secondary (orange, purple, green), tertiary colors, white, brown, black, gray, pink, and shades from lightest to darkest

AUDITORY

- Pitch
- Timbre (tone quality)
- Sound

OLFACTORY

- Scent (e.g., different spices or citrus smells)

GUSTATORY

- Sweet
- Bitter
- Salty
- Sour
- Umami

TACTILE

- Texture: rough, smooth
- Thermal: hot, warm, cold
- Barometric/Weight: heavy, light

Refining and classifying sensorial experiences	• Identifying objects by their characteristics:

• Identifying objects by their characteristics:

  ◦ Listening game: "I have three objects that make three different sounds." The objects might be, e.g., a piece of paper being crumpled or torn, a spoon being tapped on the table, and a hammer hitting a piece of wood. Then the child identifies the objects based on the sound. We also can do this for color (e.g., identifying fruits by their colors) or even taste (e.g., identifying citrus fruits by sweet, sour, bitter).

  ◦ Stereognostic game: This game involves the stereognostic sense, the sense of touch when we can identify an object without looking at it. Place several items that feel different in a bag; the child puts their hand in and tries to identify an object before pulling it out; they can also pull out an object requested by another child. Suggest variations where the objects are paired or arranged by a theme.

• Sorting items by their characteristics.

• Matching items with similar characteristics.

• Matching things that go together. This can be real objects, like lids to their containers, or pictures of items like a pen and paper or a paintbrush and paint.

• Grading items by their qualities, e.g., shortest to tallest or quietest to loudest.

• Matching at a distance; e.g., we show them a yellow tile, and they cross the room to find the matching yellow tile.

• Treasure hunts/finding items with similar qualities. We could say, "Go outside and find as many things as you can that are red or this long."

• Patterning: color, shapes, sounds, textures.

• Sequencing: pictures in a story, ingredients for cooking or baking.

• Finding comparatives (e.g., hotter and colder) and superlatives (e.g., hottest and coldest).

• We can add challenge by using a blindfold to do the previous activities.

• Labeling items by their qualities, including comparatives and superlatives.

• Measuring items and comparing, such as by:

  ◦ Measuring the length or height of furniture, people, or distances with a ruler or tape measure.

  ◦ Measuring weights—of food items, people, books—using a scale. The child can guess which items are closest to each other in weight and measure to check.

  ◦ Tracking the daily temperature.

• Older children can:

  ◦ Find the average, mean, mode, or median for a group of items (we might need to look these up ourselves!).

  ◦ Calculate the area of rooms.

  ◦ Collect data—favorites, ages, heights—and analyze or graph them.

Sorting, matching, and grading

• Some things that we can sort, match, and grade include beads, buttons, blocks, toys, grains, seeds, clothes, shoes, socks, utensils, fruits, vegetables, leaves, flowers, cutlery, paper, pictures, paper clips, hair accessories, rubber bands, nuts and bolts, and locks and keys. In Montessori classrooms, we don't use sensory bins because we find so many opportunities for exploring the senses with objects already around us.

Other sensorial experiences	<ul><li>Following the sound. Children close their eyes, we make a sound—maybe clap or ring a bell—and they have to point to the direction where the sound is coming from.</li><li>Taking a listening walk to try to identify what sounds they hear, like a bird cooing, a leaf rustling, or the wind blowing.</li><li>Going on a nature treasure hunt for objects, colors, or shapes.</li><li>Finding as many items of a certain color that they can in our home and grading them from lightest to darkest.</li><li>Playing "I spy" with colors, shapes, or sizes. This can also be done on the bus or in a car.</li><li>Going on treasure hunts in the home. We can challenge them to find all the squares they can, all the curved lines, all the cubes, any rough surfaces, any smooth surfaces.</li><li>Picking an item and having the child describe it with as many sensorial attributes as they can and as many descriptive adjectives as they can.</li><li>Teaching them the names of different materials, textures, smells, senses, tastes, colors, shapes, weights, and temperatures.</li><li>Identifying a song by listening to someone humming the tune.</li><li>Finding similar sounds, smells, and tastes. "This sound is similar to _____."</li><li>Exploring colors by doing some color-mixing activities with primary colors, secondary colors, and tertiary colors. The child can also do some tinting and shading to further explore grading of colors. Mixing colors of handmade play dough is also a beautiful way to discover that yellow and red make orange.</li><li>Nesting boxes or bowls to stack or nest in order. They can be hidden around the room, and the child finds the next size and brings it to us.</li><li>Searching for items while blindfolded.</li><li>Listening to music.</li><li>Learning to play instruments, which tunes the ears to different pitches and timbres.</li><li>Filling glasses with water up to different heights and tapping with a spoon to observe the different sounds.</li><li>Collecting an even number of spice containers or jars and filling up pairs with the same item (e.g., salt, sand, beans, rice, coins). The containers should not be transparent and can be wrapped if necessary. Then they are mixed up and the child tries to find each pair by shaking the jars.</li></ul>

We can find time to prepare some of these activities for our child, but many can happen during the normal course of practical life. For example, when we do laundry, we can ask our child to sort the clothes by color, fabric, texture, or type.

GEOGRAPHY, HISTORY, AND NATURAL SCIENCES

Our children love to learn about the world around them, past, present, and future. We can learn about our local area and follow any of our child's interests. If it's possible for our family, traveling is a great way to give our children the world. We can travel with them and also share our travel experiences with them through stories, souvenirs, and books.

These subject areas can be taken is so many directions but here are a few ideas to get started:

Earth and globe	• Learn about hemispheres.
	• Study compasses and learn the cardinal directions (north, south, east, west).
	• Explore Earth by studying and making maps. We can get map puzzles for the individual continents, especially our own continent.
	• Trace map pieces or stencils and cut or poke them out.
	• Draw the continents, countries, or states and label them with their names. Older children can add additional details, like the capital city.
	• Explore oceans, seas, lakes, and rivers.
	• Study flags, make a flag book, or make a map and color each country as its flag.
	• Research—people, food, landmarks, clothing, languages, architecture, animals, biomes, flora, fauna, art, music, and religions. Children, animals, and food are often good places to start.
	• Further the research by:
	◦ Cooking meals from the places
	◦ Making models of the places, people, and things
	◦ Sewing clothes or making paper dolls
Landforms	• Learn about the different kinds of landforms (islands, lakes, peninsulas, gulfs, isthmuses, straits, capes, bays).
	• Make models in a sandpit or by using clay, paint, sand, or paper.
	• Bake a cake or cookies in the shape of a landform. Color half of the batter or dough to represent water.
	• Make booklets or charts. Younger children can illustrate and label them with names, while older children can add a description or definition.
	• Find landforms on the globe and on the maps of different continents and countries.
	• Identify the biggest examples of each landform in our own city, state, and country, and on our continent and other continents.
Astronomy	• Solar system—read books, make and hang mobiles, do puzzles, make models.
	• Learn, identify in the night sky, and draw constellations.
	• Space—explore inventions and technologies developed for space exploration, such as spacesuits, rovers, telescopes, satellites, and the International Space Station; black holes; astronauts.
	• Rocks—research asteroids, meteoroids, meteorites, comets, moon rocks, impact craters.
	• Moon—moon phases, surface features, moon exploration, moon buggies.
Weather	• Seasons
	• Clouds
	• Rainbows

History	• Tell stories about the child's life.
	• Make a timeline of their life.
	• Make a family tree.
	• Help them research people and topics of interest.
	• Explore music, art, and dance around the world.
	• Study various beliefs around the world.
	• Discuss how people have met their fundamental needs (for nourishment, clothing, housing, transportation, defense) through time.
	• Explore interdependencies by coming up with a list of all the people who might have been involved in the production of their favorite piece of clothing or something they ate.
Botany and gardening	**We can engage our children in planting and growing seeds from fruits (e.g., it is fun to watch an avocado grow); plants from leaf cuttings; vegetables (potatoes, celery, carrots, yams) and alliums (onions, garlic) from scraps; herbs; bulbs. They will also love to build a terrarium. Below are other botany and gardening activities to explore with our child.**
Caring for plants	They will enjoy watering and misting; weeding; cleaning and washing leaves; cutting dead leaves and pruning; making and applying manure; crushing eggshells and adding to the compost; collecting scraps for the compost.
Observing and learning about parts and types of plants	• Look at plants and weeds to learn about their parts and their relationships: leaves, roots, stems, flowers, seeds.
	• Examine and learn the names of the parts of a leaf, root, stem, flower, and seed. Notice if all plants have all of the parts.
	• Draw plants in a nature journal or press samples in a leaf press.
	• Identify plants by leaves, flowers, bark.
	• Classify types of leaf by shape—such as cordate (heart-shaped) or flabellate (fan-shaped)—and arrangement. Can learn tree names and do a hunt to find examples.
	• Dissect a plant.
	• Make a chart or booklet of the plant parts.
	• Explore seed dispersal.
	• Dig up plants with similar leaves and see if they have similar roots.
Preserving plants	• Press flowers in a press.
	• Use petals to make scented water or perfume.
	• Sew petals or dry herbs into pouches to make sachets.
	• Create a nature table, jar or box.
Studying plant needs and characteristics	• Plant beans in different conditions—with and without water, light, soil, warmth.
	• Grow potatoes in the dark.
	• Explore plant experiment books.
	• Choose a plant to observe through the seasons. Write down observations about leaf color, shedding, flowering, fruiting, and animals feeding on it.

Researching plants	• Study specific plants or specimens—describe them, draw them, document changes to them over time, look up and write down interesting information about them.
	• Learn about seasonal plants.
	• Focus on regional plants by biome or geographic area.
Botany Starter Kit	*Find this online at workman.com/montessori*
Zoology	• Visiting an aquarium
	• Setting up a bird feeder
	• Finding tadpoles and frogs
	• Using a bug viewer
	• Going on insect/spider hunts (we can use an identification chart if we live somewhere with dangerous insects or spiders)
	• Raising chickens
	• Finding butterfly eggs and watching their life cycle
	• Building models of animals and insects
	• Using binoculars for bird-watching and on nature walks
	• Studying anatomical models and books
	• Exploring the differences and similarities between animal bodies and human bodies
	• Studying any animals of interest
Examples of some science experiments	• Sink and float experiments
	• Magnetic and nonmagnetic objects
	• Density of liquids—water, oil, and honey arranging themselves
	• Viscosity and fluidity—which liquid moves faster?
	• Different ways of combining—water and salt/sugar, water and sand/chalk, water and alkaseltzer, milk, and vinegar
	• Effect of heat on different materials—ice, wax, butter, etc.
	• Making crystals
	• Gravity—working out what will drop first: paper or a rock or another object
	• Condensation and evaporation—observing how condensation builds up when a lid is placed on a saucepan, or what happens when a container is left outside overnight
	• Making different weather instruments
Science Starter Kit	*Find this online at workman.com/montessori*

ART AND CREATIVITY

Open-ended art activities and projects are ideal for younger children, and we focus on the process over the product. We can be conscious of the way we give feedback about our child's art (refer to page 96 about giving feedback). We can model creating and enjoying art. Art can be a lovely way to spend time with our child. Think of how to display and store our child's creations—on the wall, strung on ropes with clothespins, in albums, portfolios, or photo books featuring pictures of each year's work.

Drawing	• Drawing, scribbling, open-ended drawing.
	• Drawing with different materials—oil or chalk pastels, charcoal, crayon, pencil.
	• Stencil tracing or drawing—shapes, animals, vehicles, nature; there are probably stencils for any subject that interests the child. We can also print out any outline onto sturdy paper and cut it out to make a stencil.
	• Guided drawing, using step-by-step drawing books. Some children enjoy these.
	• Drawing still lifes, self-portraits, and portraits of humans or animals. It can be helpful to draw from a picture of the person or thing at first, instead of using a mirror or live subject, as the subject is then stationary for them to draw.
	• Zentangling—making doodles, drawings, and patterns from dots, lines, and curves.
	• Symmetry drawing.
	• Shadow or silhouette drawing: We can put an object or person in front of a light source or window and outline the shadow or silhouette.
Painting	• Exploring colors—primary, secondary, tertiary.
	• Mixing colors, including tints and shades.
	• Painting by numbers or letters.
	• Painting on paper or canvas, at a table or easel.
	• Painting with different media—watercolors, tempera paint, and acrylic paints. These can be explored on different kinds and colors of papers.
	• Abstract painting.
	• Painting an object, scene, or person.
	• Marble painting; coffee filter–paper painting.
Collage	• Use paper, leaves, fabric, seeds, feathers, googly eyes, glitter, sequins, pom-poms.
	• Collect pictures and combine them to make Picasso-style collage art or mixed-media art.
	• Add letters cut out from the newspaper.
Beading	• Explore using paper beads or clay beads or make their own beads out of paper, clay, or felt.
	• Make different things with beads: bracelets and necklaces, earrings, bags, and bowls.
Printing	• Make prints with a leaf, a sponge, an onion, fruit, found items, or a shape carved into a potato.
	• Make fingerprint and hand art.
Rubbing	• Use a crayon to rub the imprint of a coin or leaf onto paper.
	• Make texture art by finding different textures around the house and rubbing them side by side on the same piece of paper. Can use the same or a different crayon color.
Mixed media	• Combine various media.
3D and other crafting	• Build models using papier-mâché or salt dough.
	• Make recycled art using toilet paper rolls, milk or juice boxes, plastic bottles, bottle caps, fabric scraps, food containers, lids, paper, and foil.
	• Make recycled paper.
	• Create nature art and mandalas using leaves, petals, flowers, rocks, and twigs.
Folding and cutting	• Do origami.
	• Try kirigami (a variation of origami in which the paper is cut as well as folded).

Art and artist appreciation	• Explore various artists' styles and try to replicate them. We can put up postcards of one artist's work weekly, biweekly, or monthly.
	• Collect examples of different styles from different artists; they can explore and try to create their own art in that style.
	• Visit local markets and galleries to see the work of local artisans.
	• Collect art for our home to appreciate and support Indigenous artists, emerging artists, and local artists.
	• Explore the intersection of art with history, geography, math.
	• Go to art galleries with a sketchbook; do a treasure hunt.
Performance art	We can offer various opportunities for performance art: puppet theaters using sock puppets, finger puppets, shadow puppets, and origami puppets; plays; debates; dances; poetry and spoken word performances; and comedy.
Art Starter Kit	*Find this online at workman.com/montessori*
Handwork	**Finger knitting, crochet, knitting, beading, needlework, sewing, embroidery, woodworking, sculpting with wire, weaving, soap carving, papier-mâché, and so on. Ideally, we can start with those that we enjoy ourselves or maybe learn alongside our children. Handwork is wonderful for their fine-motor-skill development, concentration, and creativity. It can also be very relaxing; they may choose to make something for a cause, like knitting squares for charity, and it can be a social activity when done in a group.**
Sewing	Sewing is a great activity for children from ages 3 to 12 years old. It supports the development of concentration and independence. It also supports the development of all the facets of fine-motor skills and is a practical skill that will serve the child throughout life. Sewing skills can be introduced gradually and scaffolded as the child acquires each skill. Here are some suggestions for developing sewing skills:
	• Threading a shoelace through perforated holes. The perforated holes can be on a piece of cardboard. Choose a shoelace with a narrow tip to fit through the holes or look for sewing cards.
	• A tapestry needle can be used to sew lines on cardboard. Holes can be poked or perforated or marks made so the child knows where the needle goes. We can start with a diagonal line, then a shape, and then the child might enjoy making simple paper purses. We can introduce running stitches and whipstitches.
	• We can show them how to sew on a button. This can be done on a strip of felt and made into a bracelet with a button closure (also great for buttoning and unbuttoning practice). They can also sew buttons onto any fabric. They can start with two-holed buttons, then move on to four-holed buttons and other kinds of buttons. When they have mastered sewing on buttons, they can sew buttons on a bag or cloth to decorate it.
	• The child can go on to improve their running stitches and whipstitches and learn other kinds of stitches.
	• Felt is an ideal fabric for beginning projects. Children can make wallets, softies, finger puppets, bookmarks, key chains, and many other items.
	• As their skills improve, they can start to sew with cotton and other fabrics. They can make pillows, bags, stuffed animals, doll clothes and accessories, and beanbags. Buttons can be used to make eyes or as decoration.
	• An older child may be interested in learning to use a sewing machine.

Knitting and crochet	Knitting and crochet support hand-eye coordination, manual dexterity, the development of the pincer grip, and creativity. Finger knitting can be introduced to 3- to 4-year-olds. They can use their fingers or a knitting fork, also called a lucet. Knitting with two needles can be introduced at around 4.5 to 6 years old. We prefer to introduce knitting before crochet to allow children to persevere to first master the challenge of knitting. Crochet can then be introduced to make dishcloths, doilies, necklaces, and then more complicated projects like amigurumi (small, stuffed yarn creatures).
Weaving	Weaving is great for hand-eye coordination and building concentration because it usually involves a repeating pattern, and to follow and repeat specific processes requires some alertness and focus while also being relaxing. There are so many different kinds of weaving that can be introduced to children at different stages: PAPER WEAVING • They can make simple squares or rectangles that can become place mats. • An older child can make baskets. YARN WEAVING • They can use straws to make a basket. • They can learn about and use sticks to weave an ojo de dios, a weaving on two crossed sticks. A younger child can start with two sticks and increase the number of sticks and patterns with proficiency. LOOM WEAVING • There are many different kinds of looms—vertical, horizontal, rectangular, circular. • We can purchase a loom, or an older child can make their own with cardboard, pieces of wood and some nails, or even an old picture frame. • They can learn how to weave different items. • It might be interesting to research weaving and looms around the world or through time.
Woodworking	Woodworking builds hand-eye coordination, strengthens hands, and builds manual dexterity and the pincer grip. Here are some woodworking ideas: • A young child can start with hammering nails. • They can also use tools like screwdrivers and wrenches. • Sanding wood also strengthens the hands. • The child can work on simple projects and then progress to more complicated ones like building miniature furniture or designing their own houses. • They can make yarn or rubber-band art, which involves hammering nails in a specific shape and then using yarn or bands to connect them. • A lot of geometry concepts—shapes, angles, diagonals, vertices—can be further explored through woodworking.
Woodworking Starter Kit	*Find this online at workman.com/montessori*
Modeling	There are many different modeling media, including play dough, clay, plasticine, modeling clay, beeswax, papier-mâché, and wire. All of these build hand strength, manual dexterity, and other aspects of fine-motor skills. Children will enjoy making their own play dough. (Find our favorite recipe in the online appendix.) Start with using their hands, then explore using different tools. First engage in open-ended exploration and then try to make or replicate specific models. Do wet and needle felting.

Handwork ideas for 6- to 12-year-olds	Older children can work on specific projects and can use handwork to express or explore what they know about topics of interest. They can build models of civilizations they have studied, make drawings or knitted items to reflect geometric concepts, or explore the art and handicrafts of different people around the world. They can also try higher levels of the handwork described earlier, like cross-stitch, embroidery, and other needlework as an extension of sewing; candle making and sculpting as an extension of modeling; and building furniture and other items as an extension of woodworking.

MEMORY

The memory supports every area of learning, and we can offer our child activities to build their memory by:

- Giving them multistep directions to act on

- Creating distance games to extend matching by attributes (e.g., the matching games mentioned in the sensorial section on page 252)

- Telling them a story and having them retell the story to us

- Asking them to memorize rhymes, poems, songs, passages, or religious scriptures (if applicable)

- Arranging some things on the table for the child to look at and then going to another room or closing their eyes and trying to list as many as they can remember

- Observing a picture together, like an illustration in a picture book, then closing the book or turning the picture face down and trying to remember as many things as we can from the picture

- Arranging some items on the table, asking the child to close their eyes, taking away one item, then asking them to open their eyes and see if they tell us which one was removed

- Playing memory games

- Doing spot-the-difference activities

MUSIC

Music is a form of expression and another language. We can expose our children to different kinds of music and give them opportunities to build skills around music.

Music appreciation	- Have a music player and a collection of different genres of music, including classical, that they can explore.
	- Have an old record player and records to listen to.
	- Make playlists for the family.
	- Attend concerts and other events where we can enjoy music.
	- Introduce any special music related to our family's culture.

Researching and studying music	- Read books about composers.
	- Study composers.
	- Introduce our child to the rich art of music. Attend concerts, listen to music at bedtime or on Sunday mornings while having breakfast, or play records on Sunday evenings.
	- Learn to read music or practice solfège, i.e., do, re, mi, fa, so, la, ti, do.
	- Explore instruments: of the orchestra, from around the world, and from musical categories.

Playing music	• Learn to play an instrument.
	• Use percussion instruments to explore rhythms.
	• Learn about different tempos and volume.
Dance and movement	• Free movement and expression
	• Ballet, modern dance, break dancing, etc.
Singing	• Traditional children's songs
	• Songs from our culture/religion/other
	• Songs that we hear on the radio
	• Songs with actions for younger children

MATH AND NUMERACY

	Dr. Montessori believed that humans, including children, have a mathematical mind that notices differences and relationships between things. It pays attention to details and notices patterns and sequences. It is how we are able to plan our day, anticipate our bill at the grocery store, and know how far to reach when we want to pick up something. This mind is the foundation for mathematics, which is an abstraction of these relationships. To support our child's development with math, we can first support the use and development of the mathematical mind and can also help our child understand and build proficiency with math concepts.
Provide opportunities to observe	This might include watching the sun rise, watching birds build a nest, tracking a plant's growth over time, or watching shadows change shape throughout the day. Our children might spontaneously wonder about the process and ask questions, or we can seed their curiosity by wondering aloud and inviting them to think and wonder along. "I wonder what happens to the sun when we can't see it." "I wonder how long the shadow will be in an hour."
	These opportunities to wonder invite the child to use their mathematical mind, to think logically, to try to figure it out. The goal is not necessarily to find the answer but to inspire curiosity. If the child is interested, we can guide them in researching and gathering more information about the questions.
Provide opportunities to estimate and make judgments	• All through food preparation, the child is estimating: Do I have enough water to fill my measuring cup? How much flour do I need to scoop to fill up the remaining space in the cup?
	• When playing, they will also estimate, for example, to figure out how far away to stand when they throw a ball into a basket, how much force to apply, and in what direction to throw.
	• Working with puzzles, as they figure out which piece fits in which space, they are estimating area and perimeter.
	• When preparing and serving a snack or lunch for multiple people, they might estimate how many pieces are needed in total and how much to give to each person.
	• When watering plants, they estimate how much water each plant needs, depending on the size of the pot or the plant.
	• In daily life, there are also opportunities for estimating, like how many cookies, erasers, or buttons it would take to fill up a certain container.

Patterning and sequencing	• Stringing beads
	• Pattern blocks
	• Playing clapping games
	• Sequencing pictures from a story
	• Finding differences between two similar pictures
Sorting, matching, and grading	• See activities for this in the sensorial area on page 252. All the sensorial work is a preparation for math.
Problem-solving	• Taking apart an object, such as a pen, a flashlight, or an old electronic item, to figure out how it works
	• Finding solutions to simple problems: wedging unstable furniture, finding something the right height to climb to reach something they need
	• Figuring out what size of paper they need for a project or for making a book
Counting and number sense	• Counting
	◦ While climbing stairs, how many cars drive past us, while skipping, etc.
	◦ Rote counting forward and backward. Note that knowing their numbers is different from counting. A child may be able to rattle off 1, 2, 3 . . . [know how to rote count] but not know how many things are in front of them [understand quantity]. By practicing counting, they will consolidate both skills, too.
	◦ Count the number of Legos or blocks used to build something—they can see how it gets taller as they add a piece.
	• Command activities including numbers
	◦ For example, clap ten times, blink five times, gather four erasers, find six flowers.
	◦ Pick a certain number of items from the shelves when shopping.
	◦ See how many of a given object they can find in our home—pillows, scissors, blue boxes, etc.
Number identification	• Hang number charts.
	• Identify numbers in books, on signs and mailboxes, in house addresses, in pictures.
	• Do number treasure hunts.
	• Memorize our address and phone number.
	• Order numbers.
	• Lay out number flash cards and put them in order.
	• Answer questions like what number comes after 4 and before 6. We don't do this to test them but to have fun. If they don't know or they get it wrong, we can make a mental note to practice counting from 1 to 10 at another time.
Counting and making associations with symbols	• Number cards with items to count and match them to items like toothpicks, matchsticks, rocks, buttons, and beads.
	• Differentiate odd from even numbers.
	• Invite an older child to count the money and pay in the grocery store.
	• Recite and sing counting rhymes and songs; read counting books; count items in illustrations.
	• Use a calendar to encourage counting. Each day the child can count up from the first day of the month to the day's date.

Writing numbers	• Young children around 3.5 to 4 years old can practice writing the numbers 1 through 9. They can learn this before learning to write the alphabet or concurrently.
	• They can write on chalkboards or in sand trays, with a stick in the dirt, with paint, with a pencil on paper.
	• When they master writing these numbers, they can combine them to form teens and other numbers.
	• Making calendars is a good way to practice writing numbers purposefully. Children can make a calendar each month and cross off the days as they pass; older children can write something interesting about each day. This is also a nice way to track improvements in their writing skills.
	• They can make counting books and illustrate them with drawings or stickers.
	• 4.5- to 5-year-olds can work on 1 through 100.
	• 5- to 6-year-olds can work on 1 through 1,000.
	• A number roll is fun to make. This is a series of strips of paper around 1 inch (3 cm) wide and 12 inches (30 cm) long on which the child writes numbers vertically, beginning at 1 and working on it a few strips a day, then attaching the strips together. The strip grows longer and longer until they reach their final number, usually 100.
Working with the decimal system (around 4.5 to 5.5 years old)	• Naturally introduce the idea of zero. Point out when something is empty. Talk about how there are zero cookies left in the box or zero words left to read of the book.
	• Play the zero game: Tell the child to do something a number of times and then eventually zero times. "Jump two times. Jump five times. Jump zero times." We might have to model a few times before they get it.
	• Read books about zero, like *Zero the Hero* or *Zero Is the Leaves on the Tree*.
	• Introduce the numbers 1, 10, 100, and 1,000. Point out how many zeros each has. In a Montessori classroom, golden beads are used for these lessons, but there are also other commercial materials available for exploring this concept.

	• Introduce all the members of the units, tens, hundreds, and thousands. Each of them has only nine members or possibilities:
	  ◦ 1, 2, 3, 4, 5, 6, 7, 8, 9 (units)
	  ◦ 10, 20, 30, 40, 50, 60, 70, 80, 90 (tens)
	  ◦ 100, 200, 300, 400, 500, 600, 700, 800, 900 (hundreds)
	  ◦ 1,000, 2,000, 3,000, 4,000, 5,000, 6,000, 7,000, 8,000, 9,000 (thousands)

	• Play "bring me" games where we request a number and the child brings it to us:
	  ◦ We can start with requesting from only one category: "Give me five units."
	  ◦ We can increase the challenge by asking for two categories and then three categories.
	  ◦ We can show how to combine categories and name them; for example, 6 tens and 4 units makes 64.
	  ◦ When the child has mastered this and also how to write, we can dictate numbers to them and then they can write the numbers.

	• Write a number and have them read it out to us.

Introduce operations (around 5 to 6 years old)	• Addition is putting together.
	• Subtraction is taking away.
	• Multiplication is putting the same quantity together several times.
	• Division is sharing equally.
	• It is best to introduce these concepts in concrete ways:
	◦ If I gave you two cookies and Biendu gave you three more, how many cookies would you have all together?
	◦ If you had seven balloons and you gave Metu one, how many would you have left?
	◦ If five of us each put three marbles in a jar, how many marbles would we have put in all together?
	◦ There are twelve chocolates in a box and there are four of us; how many chocolates would each of us get?
	• Snack preparation provides a lot of opportunities to explore operations.
Math facts	• We can provide opportunities to pratice memorizing basic facts like times tables. Children can use Legos, rocks, or buttons initially and then recite the times table from memory. Play games to reinforce math facts. Lay cards face down. Two people pick cards and then try to say the sum, difference, product, or quotient.
	• Ideas for memorizing math facts:
	◦ Color by facts—the child does a sum to work out what color to make that area of the picture.
	◦ Chains of knowledge—these are paper chains that we or our child can make. On each link of paper, there is a math fact based on one number, such as $2 \times 2 = 4$. Each subsequent paper link has a math fact related to 4.
	• Multiples paper—circling all the multiples of 9, etc.
Fractions	• Sharing—an egg, a pizza, a piece of fruit, a cake, a cookie, a pack of juice.
	• Folding—napkins, paper.
	• Baking provides a lot of opportunities to explore fractions. The child can use measuring cups and spoons to explore the relationship between whole numbers and fractions. They can halve, quarter, or double a recipe.
Geometry	• Learn the names of various shapes—2D and solids. We can start with *triangle* and get more specific—*scalene triangle, isosceles triangle*—as the child gets older.
	• Make a model with straws and yarn, cardboard, or toothpicks.
	• Make a chart or book of shapes.
	• Hunt for the shapes in your home—a can or cup in the kitchen for a cylinder, a plate for a circle, a ruler for a rectangle. An older child can write a list or make a book. They can also use this for data to graph/analyze. Compare how many examples they found for each shape.
	• Use stencils of various shapes to trace and make patterns.
	• Draw or paint shapes.
	• Explore shapes and their relationships with Magformers, Magna-Tiles, blocks, etc.
	• Play with tangram sets.
	• Draw by using shapes.

Telling time	

- Introduce the parts of an analog clock.

- Show how the clock is laid out: twelve numbers with the 12 point also being the 0 or o'clock point.

- Help the child draw a clock or make a clock with moving parts of paper or straws or sticks.

- Introduce the hour or o'*clock*. We can explain that whenever the long hand is on 12, it is o'*clock*. We look to see what number the short hand is pointing to and call it first and add o'clock.

- Introduce *half past*, which is when the long hand is pointing to 6. We look at what number the short hand is pointing to, then say "half past" before that number.

- Introduce *quarter to* and *quarter past*.

- Read books about telling the time.

- Make a timeline of the child's day.

- Make a book about the child's day, indicating what they do at different times.

- Discuss concepts of time, like yesterday, tomorrow, and next week. These can be introduced at any age. For a while, children will use words like *yesterday* for any time in the past and *tomorrow* for any time in the future. We don't need to correct them, but we can respond with the correct usage for them to absorb: "Yes, we saw them at the park 2 weeks ago." We can use it correctly, and over time it will correct itself.

CONNECTING WITH AND FEEDING EARTH

Montessori children are connecting to the world and universe around them through exploration with their hands and minds. Through cosmic education, they learn that all living things have a purpose and deserve respect. They are appreciating and caring for nature (including the flora and fauna) and their community. They are becoming social citizens of the world. They are learning to think globally and act locally. And they are coming to realize that we and the world around us are all interconnected.

We may get to witness moments when, for example, they carefully collect eggs from a chicken, carry a worm on the road to safety, make a habitat for insects, write a letter to the local government about starting a neighborhood vegetable garden, or make a sign for a rally for the climate.

We can introduce our family to ideas like regeneration. This is how we look for ways to leave the Earth and our community better than we found it. It's looking beyond green alternatives, which still consume resources, and even beyond climate-neutral solutions for which there is a net effect of zero on the planet. It includes but goes further than reusing (repurposing items, from cardboard to clothing), reducing (learning to use less resources), and recycling (allowing resources to be made into a new item). It's about working to benefit Earth and heal the damage to natural systems.

We could explore permaculture in our home or community; collect rainwater; use a compost bin or worm farm; preserve, protect, and restore our local habitats; grow pollinating gardens to encourage bee communities; join a community garden; bake our own bread, make our own jam, and preserve fruits and vegetables; be involved in a beach cleanup; improve the soil quality in our schoolyards; help our school become a zero-waste school; campaign to stop the use of plastics in the community; or join people in our community or global community who are making a difference.

Bigger projects in the family could involve producing our own energy and improving our home design to need less heating and cooling. We might also work with our school community to connect with schools in other parts of the world to share experiences, ideas, and solutions.

Rather than making these efforts top-down, we can solicit ideas from our children. What are they interested in? Can they be involved in the research? Then we can make a plan together to effect change.

THE GREAT LESSONS

The Great Lessons are fables developed by Dr. Montessori to spark the 6- to 12-year-old child's imagination about the universe and to connect the different aspects of the cosmos.

There are 5 great stories

- the beginnings/creation of the universe (Geography and Science)
- the coming of life to earth (Botany and Zoology)
- the coming of man (History)
- the history of language
- the history of math

These stories give context to the child's learn and stoke an appreciation for man's conquests and creations through time.

Refer to the online appendix "Introduction to the Great Lessons" for more.

OPEN-ENDED CREATIVE PLAY

Children enjoy open-ended play that allows them to explore reality in different ways. We can support this interest. Various materials can be available to allow these creative explorations like building, counting, and making up their own stories. Some examples would be:

- Farm and animals
- Dollhouse
- Kitchen
- Airport or garage and vehicles
- Train tracks
- Blocks—unit blocks, Keva or Kapla planks, logs, architectural blocks
- Marble runs
- Building sets with connectors and rods.
- Lego
- Magna-Tiles

BOARD AND CARD GAMES

We can also build a selection of games for our family to use. Here are some of our favorites:

CLASSIC BOARD GAMES

- Chutes and Ladders
- Chess
- Scrabble
- Monopoly
- Candy Land

COOPERATIVE GAMES

- Max (the Cat)
- A Walk in the Woods
- Orchard

LITERACY GAMES

- Shopping List
- Match and Spell
- Alphabet Lotto
- Bananagrams

MATH GAMES

- Yahtzee
- Ligretto
- Rummikub

LETTER TO PARENTS, CAREGIVERS, AND LOVED ONES

FROM YOUR CHILD

To my lovely parents, grandparents, caregivers, and loved ones:

I appreciate your love. I see you always doing your best to love and raise me, and so I want to share some ideas from my perspective.

Please accept me for who I am. I know that you have dreams you'd like me to fulfill and that that you may feel the pressures from what other people might think, but it's safe to let go of these worries. You don't need to keep asking me what I'm going to do when I grow up. All I need is for you to support me to be and become the best version of myself.

Trust that I am developing on my own timeline, with my own interests, and learning in my unique way. Be patient with me and try not to nag me, scold me, or get frustrated with me. You can collaborate with me as I figure things out. I need your love and understanding.

I am really not trying to give you a hard time, so please don't take my misbehaviors personally. I am doing the best I can in this moment. I am probably trying to tell you what I need, but I don't know how. Help me to regulate myself, and once I'm calm, I can make a repair if needed.

As much as possible, please do not interrupt me when I'm concentrating. You can tell I am concentrating when I show intense interest in something. My face might be focused, my breathing might be smooth, and I might even have my mouth open or my tongue sticking out. It may not be what you would choose me to be interested in, but please let me finish. I'd be happy to tell you why I enjoy it.

Make time to connect with me each day. I may not want to answer all your questions as soon as I walk through the door. But if you wait, there will be time to talk, maybe while we are in the car, washing the dishes together, folding laundry, eating a meal, or throwing a ball. Or come listen to some music I'm playing for 5 minutes; or talk about animé; or this week's football results. You can also tell me about your day.

Allow me the space to rest and have quiet, too. I'm not being lazy. I need to decompress from all the input around me.

It is so much easier for me to learn from what you do than from what you say. So be aware I'm always watching you. Use your phone mindfully and put it away during meals, look into my eyes and listen with your whole body, and apologize when you get it wrong and do better next time.

I love you as you are. Be yourself when my friends are around. You don't need to act cool. If there are snacks, we'll be sure to hang out at the kitchen table. Then give us space to also hang out by ourselves.

I'll say it again, do not nag me. If something is bothering you, let's discuss it and make a plan together at a neutral time. We can make agreements, and I'll do my best to stick to them. We can review them regularly and see which ones might need adjusting.

If I push back on something, I'm usually trying to work out who I am or my thoughts on it. Give me space to explore this. You don't need to worry.

I don't need you to do my homework. I don't need you to solve my problems. I might complain about them. Just listen. Maybe ask if I need any help with planning. Otherwise, let me feel the consequences myself.

Focus on my strengths instead of what is not going right. I need to feel loved, accepted, and seen.

Allow me to make mistakes. But step in when I am doing something that hurts me, someone else, or the environment. It's nice to know you'll keep me safe, even if I don't seem happy about it at the time.

Keep me close and give me space. I want you to be interested in me, but you don't need to know everything in my mind.

Observe and seek to understand me. Assume the best in me (not the worst in me). Look for joy and moments when I'm engaged and can be myself.

I'm going to be happy. I'm going to be sad. Love me through it all, and let's journey on this road of life together.

I love you right back. xoxo

THE DECALOGUE OF MONTESSORI

1. Never touch the child unless invited by [them] (in some form or the other).

2. Never speak ill of [them] in [their] presence or in [their] absence.

3. Concentrate on developing and strengthening what is good in [them]. Take meticulous and constant care of the environment. Teach proper use of things and show the place where they are kept.

4. The adult is to be active when helping the child to establish relation with the environment, and remain outwardly passive but inwardly active when this relation has been established.

5. The adult must always be ready to answer the call of the child who stands in need of [them] and always listen and respond to the child who appeals to [them].

6. The adult must respect the child who makes a mistake without correcting directly. But [they] must stop any misuses of the environment and any action which endangers the child or the other members of the community.

7. The adult must respect the child who takes rest and watches others working and not disturb [them], neither call or force [them] to other forms of activity.

8. The adult must help those who are in search of activity without finding it.

9. The adult must, therefore, be untiring in repeating presentations to the child who refused them earlier, in teaching the child who has not yet learned, in helping the child who needs it to overcome the imperfections in animating the environment, with [their] care, with [their] purposeful silence, with [their] mild words, and [their] loving presence. [They] must make [their] presence felt to the child who searches and hide from the child who has found.

10. The adult must always treat the child with the best of good manners and, in general, offer [them] the best [they have] in [themselves] and at [their] disposal.

GRATITUDE AND APPRECIATION FROM JUNNIFA

Grateful to my savior, Jesus Christ, for the grace to do all that I have been called to do.

My dear husband, for your patience and support. Writing and my passion for Montessori often leaves you with so little of me, but you are always there, steadfast and supportive. I love and appreciate you. To my children, Solu, Metu, Biendu, and Nalu, for being my biggest inspirations and teachers. My lab specimens and big pieces of my heart. Thank you for giving me purpose and for sharing me so graciously with work. I love you more than words could ever express.

My dad, my first love, who was looking forward to this book and always asking for updates. Daddy, your pride in my work spurred me on. I'm so sad you won't be here to touch and bless this book. I hope you are resting peacefully. My mum, my strong and consistent support. Helping me with every aspect of my life from the first day until now. I wouldn't be the woman I am without your help, and I wouldn't have been able to come so far on this Montessori journey or to write this book without you. Thank you, Mummy.

Manma, for supporting in all the ways you know and can. I love you and hope that you fly far, knowing that you'll always have a base to come back to. My brother, Udo, whose home was my writing retreat. Thank you so much for sharing your beautiful home with or without notice. Mandela and Fortune, who inspired me with their dedication to WheelZup, and Genti and Jamie and Debbie.

Sophie Ohuabunwa, my very able partner in work. Thank you for being my sounding board. For reading through this book and especially for all the times you had to be away from your family to work on this book with me. You have been such a gift to me, and I hope you know how much I appreciate you. Bidemi Adetutu and Pamela Chukwu for holding the fort in my elementary class as I worked on the book. The entire staff of Fruitful Orchard Montessori: Thank you for supporting me over the last two years as I worked on this book and also for partnering with me to build the dream. Fruitful Orchard parents and children, thank you for trusting me and for walking this journey with me. I don't take it for granted, and I feel so grateful for what we are creating together . . . now and for the future!

Mrs. Bola Kalejaiye, you are a key piece of my Montessori journey. God brought you into my life to keep me on this path. Thank you for inspiring me with your understanding and dedication to Montessori and the child. My trainers, Patty Wallner, Sylvia Dorantes, and Carol Hicks, who gave me keys to deeper knowledge of the child. Thank you! All my Montessori inspirations: There are too many of them to list, but I'll say Zoe Paul; Jennifer Turney McLaughlin and Pilar Bewley; and Regina Sokolowski to represent each level. Thank you!

Pastor Deborah Life Alegbemi, thank you for the constant and consistent prayers and spiritual support. I appreciate you. My friends Ijeoma Okoli, Lucy Agwunobi, Lilian Ibeh, and Paulette Ibeka, who inspired and encouraged me. Thank you for bearing with me and supporting me in spite of my unavailability.

To our publishers Workman and our amazing editor, Maisie Tivnan. Thank you, Maisie, for your grace, patience, and dedication. For having tough conversations with so much kindness that they don't feel tough. For believing in us and midwifing us through the birth of another book. Thank you, Analucia, for all your work on different aspects of the book. Thank you, Ilana, Cindy, Rebecca, Moira, and Chloe, for all your work promoting and selling the book. Thank you, Allison, for all your work in spreading the book around the world. And to everyone else at Workman/Hachette who works in big and small ways, maybe behind the scenes, to make our work successful. We are so grateful!

Thank you to Galen for laying out our book so beautifully and just knowing intuitively what we want. It has been such a delight to work with you on both books. Thank you to Naomi Wilkinson, our illustrator, for your beautiful drawings that perfectly illuminate our words. Thank you to Hiyoko Imai for the original book design. Your simple, timeless, and beautiful design has become a signature that has helped make these books all they are, and we are so grateful!

To my dear friend Sveta, thank you for living Montessori with your amazing family and for sharing your story with us. Thank you to Yuliya: You have been generous to me in many ways on this journey; I am grateful. Thank you to Jasmine, Nusaibah, and Joshuaa for sharing your stories and contributing to the book.

Finally, I want to thank my amazing partner in birthing these books, Simone. It has truly been a joy to go on this journey with you. You are a gift to me, to Montessori, and to the world. I'm not sure I could have done this with anyone else, and I am so grateful. Thank you, Simone, for being you: for your patience, flexibility, thoroughness, humor, experience, and most especially for your heart. You, Emma, and Oliver have inspired me in so many ways. Thank you!

I hope this book helps everyone who reads it enjoy the gifts they have been given!

"Children are a gift from God"—Psalms 127:3

GRATITUDE AND APPRECIATION FROM SIMONE

THE WORKMAN PUBLISHING TEAM—Maisie, you are a wonder. This book has become the book it is thanks to your keen eye, your patience and understanding, your kindness, and let's not forget your ruthless editing skills. Cindy, Ilana, Rebecca, Moira, and Chloe, thank you for being such fun and always so helpful. We could not have asked for a sweeter marketing, PR, and publicity team. Analucia, we appreciate your support whenever it was needed. To dear Allison, thank you for helping this book find its way into many more countries. And to the rest of the team: You have all helped spread Montessori into so many more homes than we ever possibly imagined. Thank you so much!

OUR DESIGNERS—To our ultra-talented illustrator, Naomi Wilkinson, thank you for bringing life to our words. We appreciate the care you have taken, and the beautiful illustrations add so much to the book. Galen, we love your design work and the fact that that you know even better than us how we want each page to look. And a big thank you to Hiyoko Imai for the gorgeous book design. It makes the book so beautiful and easy to read. We love it so much.

OUR CONTRIBUTORS—To Joshuaa, Nusaibah, Jasmine, Sveta, and Yuliya, who opened up their doors and shared their stories in the book; we appreciate you so much. As well as Mira and Angela, for contributing your expertise on the Montessori research.

EXTRA HELPERS—Terry Millie, Andy Lulka, Regina Lulka, and Tammy Oesting, thank you for guiding us as you read chapters for us. And to Kathy Porto Chang, Ksenya Kolpaktchi, Sophie Chamberlin, and Ruben Dahm for your helpful feedback to help make the book the best it could be.

MY FAMILY AND FRIENDS—To Mum, Dad, Jackie, Tania, Oliver, Emma, Luke, Blue, and all the family, thank you for all your love and support. To Debbie, Rachel, Agnes, Frans, Birgit, Monika, Floris, Carly, and Rich, I appreciate all the fun we've had together to fuel the writing and the endless times you had to hear about this book.

MONTESSORI MENTORS—To Ferne van Zyl for lighting the spark; to Judi Orion for sharing her love of the child; to Heidi Phillipart-Alcock who welcomed the whole family to Amsterdam; to An Morisson and Annabel Needs for being the best guides to my children and showing the way; and most recently to Vikki Taylor, Alison Awes, and Jenny Marie Höglund for giving me a deep dive into the 3- to 6-year-old child, 6- to 12-year-old child, and adolescent. I have also learned so much from my Montessori Everywhere friends—Dr. Ayize Sabater, Seemi Abdullah, Andy Lulka, Tammy Oesting, Barbara Isaacs, Wendelien Bellinger, Sue Pritzker, D. Ann Williams, Ochuko Prudence Daniels, and Gabriel Salomão—and so many others, like Kim Anh Nguyễn Anderson, Pamela Green, Jeanne-Marie Paynel, Britt Hawthorne, and Trisha Moquino.

FAMILIES AT JACARANDA TREE MONTESSORI—I am humbled to have been working with so many families here in Amsterdam since 2008. I learn from you all every day. Together we are growing, developing, and deepening our practice. Thank you for being such a special community.

YOU, DEAR READER—Thank you for picking up this book, putting our words into action, and bringing Montessori into your home. We love changing the world one family at a time and hope you find the same joy that we have in adopting the Montessori principles in your family.

Last but not least, **MY DEAR JUNNIFA**—Thank you so much for being on this journey with me. You and your family inspire me and fill me with hope, and I love seeing you shine so brightly. This book has been such a pleasure to birth together.

"Acknowledging the good that you already have in your life is the foundation for all abundance."

—Eckhart Tolle

INDEX

BRING THE MAGIC OF MONTESSORI HOME

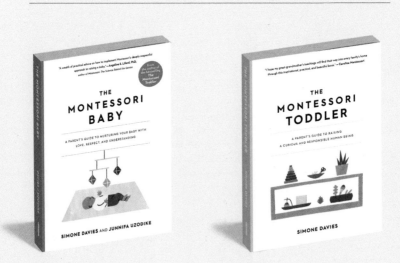